Poster's
RADIO & TELEVISION
PRICE GUIDE
1920–1990

Poster's RADIO & TELEVISION

SECOND EDITION

PRICE GUIDE

1920–1990

HARRY POSTER

Wallace-Homestead Book Company
Radnor, Pennsylvania

Copyright © 1991, 1994 by Harry Poster
Second Edition   All Rights Reserved

Published in Radnor, Pennsylvania 19089, by Wallace-Homestead,
a division of Chilton Book Company

No part of this book may be reproduced, transmitted or stored
in any form or by any means, electronic or mechanical,
without prior written permission from the publisher

Designed by Anthony Jacobson
Manufactured in the United States of America

Library of Congress Cataloging in Publication Data

Poster, Harry.
    [Radio and television price guide, 1920–1990]
    Poster's radio and television price guide, 1920–1990 / Harry
Poster. — 2nd ed.
        p. cm
    Rev. ed. of: Illustrated price guide to vintage televisions and
deco radios. 1991.
    Includes index.
    ISBN 0-87069-687-4
    1. Television—Receivers and reception—Collectors and collecting.
2. Radio—Receivers and reception—Collectors and collecting.
I. Poster, Harry. Illustrated price guide to vintage televisions
and deco radios. II. Title.
TK6653.P675   1994
621.384′18′075—dc20
                                                    93-30047
                                                      CIP

1 2 3 4 5 6 7 8 9 0   3 2 1 0 9 8 7 6 5 4

To Anna,
who convinced me to buy my first Catalin;
helped me buy, and carry, my first television;
and helped me decide on my first transistor radio

Contents

Acknowledgments

First, I would like to thank Harry Rinker. Although we don't agree on many subjects, he prevailed, after two years, in convincing me that this comprehensive price guide needed updating.

To all the collectors and fellow dealers who have called to support my previous books, articles and endeavors, I do appreciate your help. To those who have bought from me and sold to me, the experiences have helped determine the real market value and trends that are reflected in this price guide.

In particular, I'd like to thank:

John Sakas, P.O. Box 4124, South Hackensack, NJ 07606, who helped with information and pricing and gave me access to his Catalin and Deco radio collection. He collects and deals in Catalin and Plaskon radios, plus mirror, unusual, and Deco sets; Chris Cuff, 2674 Route 42, Forestburgh, NY 12777, a transistor radio collector, dealer, and restorer, who helped price some of the early transistor sets and helped me enlarge my own collection; Jim McKinnon, 605 North Bridge St., Bridgewater, NJ 08807, a dedicated collector who knows the value of many, if not all, of the early battery and AC table radios, and who has shared his knowledge and collection; Doug Heimstead, 1349 Hillcrest Dr., Fridley, MN 55432, a collector with particular interests in unusual and mirror radios from both well-known and obscure manufacturers.

Doug has probably seen, if not owned, most of the varieties of mirrored sets produced, and is always on the lookout for more; Bruce Mager, 32 East 13th St., New York, NY 10003, a collector-dealer who helped price Zenith and RCA radios, plus many other console and tabletop sets from the 1930s and 1940s.

In addition, collectors and dealers will find countless photos, plus historical information in the following highly recommended books:

Radios of the Baby Boom Era by Sam's Photofacts, Prompt Publications, Indianapolis, Indiana, 1991. This company produced the original series of service manuals, starting in 1946, and has just released this six-book set which includes thousands of photos gleaned from their original folders.

Radio Manufacturers of the 1920's, Alan Douglas, Vestal Press, Vestal, New York, 1988, 1989, 1991. This three-volume work covers most of the 1920s sets, with lots of information about the companies that produced them.

And, last but not least, I would like to thank all of the local clubs and groups for providing newsletters, updates, and other information about collectors and collections throughout the United States. Consult the appendix and consider joining the radio club nearest you.

Poster's
RADIO & TELEVISION
PRICE GUIDE
1920–1990

INTRODUCTION

Radio collectors actively search for the earliest vestiges of telecommunication. Just after the turn of the twentieth century, crystal radios were used to listen to wireless communications. Twenty-five years later, portable, tabletop, and console radios were used to listen to regularly scheduled programs. Many radios from both of these periods are collectible, as are those from the middle of this century, when circuits containing tiny hearing aid tubes, and then transistors, were produced to allow mobility while listening to radio programs.

Televisions were the experimental realm of many radio listeners by the end of the first quarter of this century. By the time of the great World's Fairs in the late 1930s, television was being introduced to a limited, wealthy segment of the United States, albeit only in four or five metropolitan areas. As World War II wound down, television research and production geared up once more. Many families could now afford a television. There were huge combination sets for the wealthy who wanted a television to match a specific furniture grouping, and small, cheap portables for those with less grandiose tastes and budgets. Certainly, television collecting sprung up soon after.

Nearly as soon as radios became transistorized, "carry along" televisions were sold. Even color could be captured on the television, in relatively faithful rendition, fifteen years after World War II. During the 1950s manufacturers introduced unique styling to both tabletop radios and television sets. Some of the strangest looking sets were manufactured in the late 1950s and early 1960s. Although a few radios and televisions became milestones during the last quarter of the twentieth century, the move has been toward square plastic boxes and away from truly innovative styling. This price guide provides a single reference of facts, dates, and values for collectible radios and televisions. Prices are given for items which are externally and internally clean and not necessarily in working order. Where "rare" appears in the place of a price, this indicates that only one or two examples of the item exist and you will have to pay whatever the asking price is to obtain it.

By studying the history, styling, and price of the many types of radios and televisions, hobbyists can establish a collection in whatever area interests them most. This completely illustrated price guide will also aid dealers and historians in their search for important and resalable radios and televisions.

Chapter One
TUBE RADIOS

History

Since the early use of vacuum tubes in radio circuitry, tube radios have been produced in a variety of different chassis and cabinet styles. Many of the radios are collectible, but many more of these radios are not collectible! An informed buyer or seller, must recognize which sets are which. (Model numbers can generally be found on the bottom or on the inside of the back of the radio.)

Crystal radios, those sets with no tubes, are usually distinguishable by looking first at the case and then at the insides. A crystal set will usually have a "cat's whisker" attached to an adjustable metal rod at one end and touching a small block of metal at the other end. Nearly all factory-built crystal radios will be of some value. Often, even the crudest home-brewed crystal set will be of value for the parts, if not for the set itself.

Although crystal sets were re-introduced in the 1940s, these later sets were often small plastic boxes made in Japan, with modern markings and modern wiring, and were more of a novelty than a way to listen to radio. These new crystal sets are often traded among transistor radio collectors; many were marketed as "transistor" radios although most contain a small glass diode (to replace the cat's whisker crystal) instead of transistors.

Soon, one or two tubes were added to the crystal sets, making a hybrid of sorts which is quite collectible. One-, two-, and three-tube radios quickly followed. Often "building blocks" were stacked or attached to each other, forming composite radios. Detectors, tuners, amplifiers, and other blocks could be added to form a complete radio. Manufacturers soon realized that more money was to be made by introducing a better marketed complete set, or line of sets.

The radios of the 1920s were produced by dozens of companies, often with a similar chassis, but in very different cabinets. Some manufacturers' radios are collectible in all styles and cabinets; some companies produced sets which are only desirable in certain tube complements or cabinet styles.

First the age and then the style of the radio offers some estimate of its desirability. Tubes often can give an approximation of the age of the set. After all, each and every "tube radio" will have tubes in it, or at least the set will have sockets to accept tubes.

The earliest sets have one or two tubes, usually with twist-in bases and a point at the top. Some early tubes were also shaped like old light bulbs ("balloon" style with a glass point on top), and many of these tubes have value themselves, either in or out of an early radio. Sets from the 1930s often sported tubes with a Bakelite bottom and four to seven pins, which were used to plug the tube into the base. Some 1940s sets contain smaller glass octals (a tube with eight pins), or metal octals, which were a pre World War II innovation.

By the late 1940s and 1950s, the tubes had become "peanut" sized, with all-glass envelopes and the tiny leads coming directly out of the bottom. No longer was there a need to use a Bakelite base. By the late 1950s and 1960s, printed circuit boards were used to hold the tubes in place.

"Sub-miniature" tubes, about the size of the end of a pencil, were developed after World War II and were used in the production of some radios until the late 1950s when the transistor took over. Sometimes these sub-miniatures were combined with peanut tubes; sometimes they were added to transistor circuits. These special hybrid radios made an appearance for a short time after the introduction of the transistor, but before most manufacturers began selling all-transistor radios.

Style

The next most important feature of a radio is style. Primitive 1920s sets were offered in wooden boxes, or in partial boxes which nested beside other partial boxes. "Breadboard" style radios (those that have the tubes and controls on an open wooden board), a type offered by Atwater Kent and a few others, have again become popular. Elongated metal or wooden cabinets were some of the earliest tabletop models. Wooden boxes have a hinged, or partially hinged, lid at the top for access to change tubes. The metal boxes must be flipped over to see the internal parts. Both styles are common and usually undesirable.

Manufacturers, many of whom had ties to the furniture trade, were quick to produce large floor models with openings at the back to allow a breadboard or long set to be slipped into the console. Lowboys (short-legged) and highboy (tall-legged) consoles were introduced, as were floor models (non-legged) consoles and tables which accepted radios inside. The controls were accessible from the front or top; often doors or panels were opened or shifted for access.

Many of the four- and six-legged floor models are not desired by the majority of radio collectors, although floor models with intricate carvings or wood appliqués are popular. Also, most floor models with ten or more tubes are more desirable than the less expensive five-, six-, or seven-tube sets. The weight of the console often indicates its quality; a very light set is probably a cheaper cabinet with a skimpier chassis, or a less desirable battery-powered set.

By the 1930s, small table sets were again becoming popular with consumers. Although a large console was great for the living room or parlor, many people did not have the money or the space to accommodate large radios. "Farm Sets" were also manufactured at this time for use in parts of the country which did not yet have access to alternating current (AC). These sets were lightweight, inexpensive, and are not very popular with collectors today. Several manufacturers produced a six-tube chassis, and then put it into a wooden tabletop model, a lowboy, or possibly even an elaborate console.

In the early 1930s, Bakelite, a pourable plastic-type material, was becoming more popular for stylish accessories, and tabletop radios of the period were no exception. Art Deco and Bakelite were the combination by which Air King, FADA, Emerson, and many others sold poor quality tabletops. These once-inexpensive tabletop wood substitutes are very popular with collectors today. Unfortunately, most early plastic materials are very brittle and subject to minor and major damage. Many radio collectors will pass up all but the most outlandish Bakelite tabletops unless they are in perfect condition. Generally, the sets need not work, but the cabinets should be examined to ascertain that the case has no chips or breaks, and that the trim and knobs are original.

Composition

Catalin radios are among the most expensive and collectible radios today. This celluloid-type material is hard to describe, but there are a few clues which will help you discover whether the material in question is Catalin, Bakelite, or Plaskon.

First look at the thickness of the radio; Catalin is usually as thick as the wooden sets. Next check the radio bottom; nearly always, the bottom of a Catalin set will be lighter and brighter than the sides and top. Also, check the following listings, nearly every Catalin set is carefully noted.

Bakelite is quite opaque; a flashlight will only barely shine through even the thinnest Bakelite radios. And, Bakelite often has ripples which were produced when it was poured, compared to most Catalin sets which were carefully cast and then machined and polished to a mirror finish. A bit of polishing at the edge of a Catalin radio will often brighten or even change the color; Bakelite is one color throughout.

Plaskon, and other thick, colored Bakelite materials, have become increasingly popular as Catalin prices have escalated unbelievably. If your set is white, brown, or black, and resembles Bakelite, it probably is. Look for Plaskon in light pinks, blues, greens, and yellows; often made into cases as thick as Catalin, but as opaque and rippled as Bakelite.

Although most wooden sets can be restored or repaired, Bakelites and Catalins cannot. Usually collectors expect to pay one-quarter to one-half less for a Catalin radio with even the slightest "hair-line" fracture or minor chip. Often, common Catalins will not sell at all if damaged. Reproduction trim (lately, even radio bodies have been poorly reproduced) or missing or broken trim can detract from all but the rarest of these sets.

By the late 1940s and 1950s, many companies realized the benefits of plastic (easily molded and fast and inexpensive to produce). Catalin and Plaskon were all but gone by the late 1940s. Unless a radio is quite unusual, either in design or use of special tubes, most modern plastic radios can be purchased for the cost of a Catalin radio knob.

In 1951 Philco released a list of "modern" plastics used in their current radios. The list included polystyrene for the portable case and clear dial, cellulose acetate butyrate for the knobs, polyvinyl-butyral for formed windows, and occasionally methyl-methacrylate! Trade names for the early 1950s plastics include Bakelite, Tenite, Plexiglas, Lucite, and Vinylite, to name only a few. These new plastics were often colorful and marbled, so 1950s sets are occasionally described as Catalins. To tell the difference:

- Check the thickness—most of these new plastics are very thin and will bend easily under the pressure of your thumb.

- Check the transparency—most 1950s plastics will be nearly opaque.

- Check the bottom—most plastic radios will be the same color on the sides and bottom.

- Check the chassis—Catalins were not made with printed circuit boards.

You may like the styling of a 1950s or 1960s plastic tabletop or console radio, but it will be worth little and probably will not sell to a radio collector. There are collectors of the 1950s "retro" styling, but generally radio collectors do not qualify 1950s and later tube-type radios as "must haves" on their purchasing lists.

Ace (See Crosley)

A.C. Dayton

R-12, long wooden case, 3 large and 4 small dials, 4-tube set, 1924, **$150**

XL-5, 5-tube set with 3 large and 4 small dials, Bakelite front, lid lifts to expose tubes, **$75**

XL-10, 5-tube set with 3 large and 2 small knobs on Bakelite front, **$75**

XL-20, XL-25, 5-tube tabletops with Bakelite front panel, **$85**

XL-30, 6-tube tabletop or console, Bakelite front panel with meter at top, center, **$100**

Adams-Morgan/Paragon

III, IIIA, wooden radio about 1 cubic foot, 1924, top lifts, front doors open to expose Bakelite panel, **$750**

Four, 3- or 4-tube set, 1924, long wooden case with lift-up top, jacks to accept speaker at right front, **$150**

A-2, 2-tube amplifier, 1922, small wooden set with 3 large knobs on Bakelite front panel, **$500**

DA-2, 3-tube amplifier in small wooden box, 1922, Bakelite panel and knobs in front, **$600**

Adams-Morgan/Paragon RA-10, $750.

Adams-Morgan/Paragon VT Control, $150.

RA-10, small wooden box, 1920, 3 large dials, tuner with not tubes, **$750**

RD-5, 1-tube radio, 1922, 3 large dials on front Bakelite panel, **$650**

Type Two, small 2-tube radio with 3 knobs on front, **$150**

Type Three, wooden tabletop, 1924, 1 large dial in center, 2 small knobs at left, jacks to accept speaker at right, **$125**

VT Control, small Bakelite board with 1 tube, 1 knob, screw posts at both sides, **$150**

Addison

2A, small Catalin radio, 1939, ridges around body and left grill wrap over top in contrasting color, green or maroon body, **$700**

2A, yellow Catalin body and knobs, burgundy trim, **$1,500;** red trim, **$2,000**

2A, maroon, white, or brown Bakelite body, **$400;** red or black body, **$700;** bright blue or bright green body, **$1,000**

5, large, 1939, Catalin set, dial at top edge in protrusion, 5 grill bars and 3 knobs in contrasting color, yellow, green or red, **$1,000**

Admiral

4-A-1, 1946, wooden tabletop with circles cut to form grill, dark wrap around panel at bottom with dial, **$50**

Addison model 2A Catalin radio, $700.

6

4-A-15, very square-lined AM/FM console, 1948, top door opens to expose radio and controls, front door exposes pull out phono, **under $25**

4-A-27, small Bakelite tabletop, 1947, elongated dial on small sloping area at bottom front, **$35**

4-A-37, *4-A-42*, traditional AM/FM consoles, 1947, dial and push-button tuning at top front, center door pulls down to expose phono, **$35**

4-A-60, similar to model *4-A-15*, double doors on front reveal radio and phono, **$15**

4-A-61, similar to model *4-A-27*, **$35**

4E21, streamlined portable, late 1950s, large "V" on front, knobs on sides, **$35**

4V18, portable, 1952, semicircular dial and oversized pointer at top, grey, maroon or green with gold trim, **$35**

4X11, plastic portable, circa 1954, large grill on front, round tuning dial under fold-down top handle, black, maroon, grey or green, **$45**

4Y12, similar to model *4X11*, metal flip-up handle on top, maroon, grey or green, **$45**

5A32, clock radio, 1952, circular clock face and dial on plain front panel, brown or white, **$25**

5F11, plastic portable, late 1940s, front flips up to expose radio controls, **$15**

5M21, 5-tube, 1950, large Bakelite radio-phono with lid at top, **$15**

5R11, very square-lined Bakelite tabletop, circa 1948, **$15**

5R32, 5-tube typical plastic tabletop, mid-1950s, **$15**

5S21, plastic tabletop, 1952, concentric grill circles and oversized cross at left, semicircular dial at right, brown, black or white, **$15**

5T12, large clam shell 5-tube Bakelite tabletop, circa 1949, radio controls on front, lid covers phono, **$15**

5X12, *5X13*, plastic tabletops, 1949, large circular dial, **$25**

5X21, modern styled plastic clock radio with trapezoidal clock face on front, 1952, white, brown or black, **$45**

5Y22, large Bakelite radio-phono, 1952, similar to model *5M21*, **$15**

5Z22, plastic tabletop, 1952, round top corners, oversized dial covers front sides and front top, **$35**

6A22, Bakelite tabletop, 1949, large grill across front, AM band only, **$15**

6C11, similar to model *5F11*, 5-tube chassis, **$15**

6C22, *6C233*, Bakelite tabletops, 1952, oversized dial across front sides and front top, **$25**

6C62, Deco console, 1946, 3-band dial at top edge, small double doors open to allow phono to be pulled out, **$45**

6J21, similar to model *5M21*, 6-tube chassis, **$15**

6N26, simple square wooden cabinet, circa 1952, pull out radio-phono behind double doors, **$25**

6P32, alligatored leatherette portable, mid-1940s, double handle at top, front drops, palm trees on grill, **$40**

6Q12, similar to model *6A22*, AM/FM bands, **$25**

6R11, similar to model *6V12*, AM-FM radio, **$15**

6RT42, *6RT43*, square wooden tabletops, 1946, elongated dials on front, lid covers phono, **$15**

6RT44, similar to model *6RT42*, 7-tube radio, **$15**

6S12, similar to model *5M21*, 6-tube chassis, **$15**

6T01, *6T02*, rectangular Bakelite tabletops with molded grill louvers across front, 1946, white or brown, **$25**

6T04, *6T05*, similar to model *6T01*, wooden cabinet, **$25**

6T06, Deco version of model *6T04*, contrasting panels and 3 circles forming grill, **$40**

6V12, similar to model *5T12*, 6-tube chassis, **$15**

Admiral 6T02, $25.

Admiral 34-F5, $15.

7C60, simple square-lined console, 1947, front has record storage and large speaker, cloth, lid exposes radio and phono, **$25**

7C65, 1947 square-lined traditional console, double doors reveal pull out phono and radio controls, walnut, mahogany or blonde, **$15**

7C73, 9-tube, 1947, AM-FM console with very square-lined, double doors open to expose pull out phono and pull-down radio, **$25**

7P33, briefcase-style portable, 5 tubes, 1946, front drops to expose radio and controls, **$25**

7T10, typical late 1940s Bakelite tabletop, brown or white, **$25**

8D15, similar to model *9E15*, AM only, **$25**

9B14, similar to model *7C73*, **$25**

9E15, similar to model *7C73*, **$25**

10A1, Deco console, 1946, dial at top edge, pull out phono in middle, **$25**

33-F5, 5-tube portable economy radio with simple dial and cloth covering, 1940, **$15**

34-F5, similar to model *33-F5*, plastic trim around grill and dial, **$15**

35-G6, similar to model *34-F5*, detachable front lid, **$15**

37-G6, similar to model *34-F5*, wooden front and cloth-covered sides, **$25**

51E5, 1941 "farm" tabletop radio, 4-tube rounded top brown Bakelite, grill wraps around left side, **$35**

69-M6, square wooden tabletop, 1941, simple radio on front, lid lifts to expose phono, **$15**

70-N6, Deco version of model *69-M5*, radio and phono under lid, **$45**

71-M6, Deco console, 1941, 6-tube set with simple exposed radio and pull out phono, behind center door, **$35**

76-P5, brown Bakelite portable, 1941, 5 tubes, rounded corners with grill and dial molded, into front, **$15**

77-P5, similar to model *76-P5*, leatherette-covered case, **$15**

78-P6, 79-P6, similar to model *77-P5*, front lid conceals radio controls, **$15**

202, portable, late 1950s, large grill and dial on front, back snaps open to change tubes, **$25**

292, rectangular plastic tabletop, 1958, offset clock at left with elongated dial beneath, **$15**

302, rounded Deco Bakelite radio with exposed record player on top, 1940, brown or white, **$50**

303, square-lined tabletop, 1960, large cloth grill and dial insert, AM/FM, **$15**

361, typical 1939 Bakelite tabletop with small rectangular dial, **$25**

392-7C, wide Deco console, 1939, lid lifts to expose radio and phono, **$65**

521, Deco 5-tube tabletop radio-phono, late 1930s, contrasting veneers, **$50**

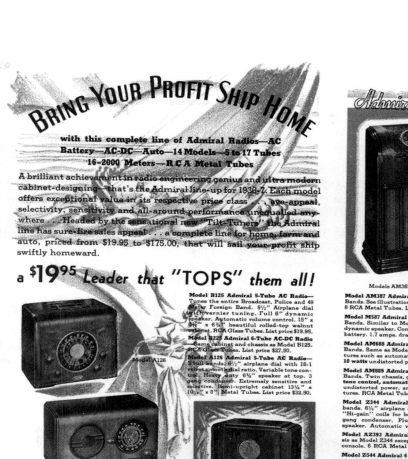

Admiral radios for 1936.

802, square cloth-covered portable, 1940, simple dial, **$15**

935, 940, Deco 11-tube consoles, 1938, tilted and elongated dial at top, **$75**

945, Deco wooden 8-tube console, late 1930s, large circular dial, **$75**

AM387, 8-tube console with unusual wide oval area with circular dial and 2 tuning eyes at top edge, 1936, **$225**

AM488, 12-tube Deco console with unusual sloping top, circa 1936, large oval dial and tuning eye at top edge, **$275**

AM688, 10-tube version of model *AM387,* **$250**

AM786, Deco console with large oval dial and tuning eye at top front, 11 tubes and 3 bands, 1936, **$150**

AZ393, 6-tube, 3-band Deco console, 1936, large circular dial and 4 knobs below, **$45**

AZ593, 6-volt "farm set" version of model *AZ-393,* **$35**

B125, wooden tabletop, 1936, nearly square face with large circular dial and 4 knobs, **$45**

B225, 6-volt farm radio version of model *B125,* **$25**

Y833, similar to model *292,* circular radio dial beside circular clock face, **$15**

Y1149, Colonial-style buffet, 1960, center door opens to expose AM/FM stereo radio above pull out phono, **$15**

Z344, 6-tube wide wooden tabletop, 1936, large circular 3-band dial with 4 knobs below, **$35**

Z544, 6-volt "farm radio" version of model *Z344,* **$25**

Air Castle (Spiegel, Inc.)

102B, plastic portable, late 1940s, back snaps open, **$15**

153, square-lined console, circa 1951, double doors expose radio over phono, **$15**

211, plastic tabletop, late 1940s, oversized tuning knob, **$25**

350, similar to model *153,* **$15**

568, metal tabletop, mid-1940s, circular perforated grill, dial and knobs within oval areas, **$50**

651, typical Bakelite tabletop, 1947, long grill ribs beneath elongated dial, **$25**

652.5X5, square wooden tabletop, mid-1950s, radio and controls on right side, lid lifts to expose phono, **$15**

659.511, rounded plastic AM radio, 1952, circular clock face at left, **$15**

659.520, model *659.511,* added lamp, **$75**

935, typical Bakelite tabletop, late 1940s, round clock face at left, circular tuning knob at right, **$35**

2271, small Bakelite tabletop, 1949, bottom lip continues to the right side, **$35**

5001, Bakelite tabletop, mid-1940s, large grill cloth at left, square dial at right, **$25**

5003, typical late 1940s Bakelite tabletop, dial at top edge, knobs at front of top surface, **$25**

5008, wooden tabletop, 1948, dial above large rectangular grill cloth, knobs below, **$15**

5111, similar to model *5008,* AM/short wave bands, **$25**

5020, tall, simple cloth-covered portable, grill, dial, knobs on front, **$15**

5022, leatherette-covered portable, 1951, front plastic forms grill and dial opening, **$25**

5025, 5027, cloth-covered portable, large inserted grill and knobs on front, dial on top near handle, **$15**

6541, 6547, wooden table radios, 1947, dial at sloping top edge, lid lifts to reveal phono, **$15**

7553, typical Bakelite radio, late 1940s, dial across top edge, **$25**

9008, small Bakelite tabletop, 1949, vertical ribs form speaker grill, **$35**

9009, Bakelite tabletop, late 1940s, rounded left side, **$50**

9012, similar to model *2271,* **$35**

9151, similar to model *935,* plastic case, **$15**

10003, similar to model *9009,* **$50**

10005, Bakelite tabletop, late 1940s, AM/FM dial across top edge, 4 knobs at bottom, **$35**

108014, similar to model *10005*, AM-only radio, **$35**

121104, square-lined console, 1949, double doors reveal pull out phono and tilt-down radio, **$15**

131504, similar to model *10005*, **$35**

138124, similar to model *121104*, **$15**

G-516, G-518, similar to model *6541*, **$15**

Air Chief (Firestone Tire and Rubber Co.)

4-A-2, Bakelite tabletop with rounded corners, large grill across front, long dial above, 2 knobs below, 1947, **$25**

4-A-20, large wooden tabletop, mid-1940s, dial at top edge, **$25**

4-A-23, multiband wooden tabletop with dial at top edge, 1946, **$35**

4-A-24, similar to model *4-A-20*, AM/FM, **$15**

4-A-25, Bakelite tabletop, mid-1940s, rounded corners, large elongated dial and 2 knobs at top front, **$25**

4-A-26, similar to model *4-A-2*, **$25**

Airite

Desk set, elaborate Bakelite radio with pen set on one end, clock on the other, **$250**

Air King

52, skyscraper-style Plaskon tabletop designed by Harold Van Doren in 1933, cut out at top with Egyptian motif insert, uncracked white, **$1,750**; black or brown, **$2,500**; green, yellow or lavender, **$5,000**; blue or red, **$7,000**

66, similar to model *52*, cut out with clock or double globe insert, uncracked white, **$1,500**; black or brown, **$2,000**; green, yellow or lavender, **$4,000**; blue or red, **$6,000**

222, small Bakelite tabletop late 1930s, **$50**

771, similar to model *52*, tuning eye and cut out grill with speaker cloth, uncracked white, **$1,000**; other colors, **$2,000**

800, 8-tube square console radio, 1949, double doors open to expose pull out phono and pull-down AM/FM radio, **$15**

911, wooden tabletop with push-button tuning, mid-1930s, **$25**

4603, wooden tabletop, 1946, sloping dial at front top, **$25**

4604, "Baron," rectangular AM/short wave tabletop, circa 1947, dial at top edge, 4 knobs below metal grill, **$25**

4607, 4608, small Bakelite tabletops with inserted metal grill, mid-1940s, white or brown, **$50**

4700, large, square 1950s style radio-phono combination with wire recorder, **$75**

4704, wooden tabletop with radio and controls at top left, phono beneath door at top right, late 1940s, **$15**

4705, Bakelite tabletopo, slanted front, **$15**

5000, portable, with leather handle, 1940, front drops to expose simple radio dial and controls, **$15**

A-400, "Minstrel," small Bakelite tabletop, 1947, rounded top, large tuning pointer at right front, white, black or brown, **$25**

A-403, small wooden tabletop with radio at front and exposed phono on top, **$25**

A-410, small alligator-covered portable, 1947, flip-down at top conceals inexpensive *828* camera, **$75**

A-510, "Royal Troubador," cloth-covered portable, 1947, Bakelite grill and radio dial, **$35**

A-511, "Prince," simple brown Bakelite tabletop, 1948, **$25**

A-512, similar to model *A-511*, white finish, **$25**

A-520, plastic 4-tube portable with round dial and knob at front right, handle at top, 1948, maroon or white plastic, **$35**

A-600, "Duchess," Catalin tabletop with case and knobs in one color, contrasting surround with dial, 1947, yellow and maroon, **$600**; green and yellow, **$800**

A-625, large two-tone Bakelite radio, 1948, large grill inserted above elongated plastic dial, **$25**

A-650, model *A-625*, AM/FM radio, **$35**

A-800, console with double doors expose pull-down AM/FM radio and pull out phono, 1949, **$15**

X-3950, alligatored leatherette-covered 5-tube portable, 1941, hinged front panel conceals radio, **$15**

Airline (Montgomery Ward)

05-GCB, "Lone Ranger," plastic tabletop, child's radio with crude illustration of the Lone Ranger on Silver, **$350**

05-GHM-1061, 4-tube, leatherette-covered portable, 1951, **$15**

05-WG

Line of wooden tabletop radios with AM/FM band and 4 knobs below the dial, 1950, **$15**

Line of very square consoles, double doors expose radio and pullout phono, 1950, **$25**

15-GAA-995, cloth-covered portable radio, lid lifts to expose phono, **$15**

15-GHM-934, portable radio-phono, 1952, controls hidden inside suitcase-style case, **$15**

15-GHM-1070, suitcase-style portable with controls on front, 1951, **$15**

15-GSL-1564, plastic tabletop with large tuning knob on front, early 1950s, **$15**

25-BR-1549, typical square alarm clock radio, early 1950s, square clock at left, square dial at right, **$15**

25-GHM-1073, similar to model *15-GHM-1070*, **$15**

25-GSE-1555, 5-tube Bakelite tabletop, circa 1952, large circular dial on front, **$15**

25-GSL-1814, wooden tabletop, 1952, large circular dial across front, **$15**

25-WG-1573, "Global" multiband tabletop Bakelite, 1953, **$35**

35-GHM-1074, metal-bodied portable, 1954, large circular dial and knobs on front, handle on top, **$15**

35-WG-1573, "Global," similar to model *25-WG-1573*, **$35**

54-BR-1501, *54-BR-1502*, rounded Bakelite tabletops, mid 1940s, grill ribs at front top, **$50**

54-BR-1505, *54-BR-1506*, Bakelite tabletops with large rectangular dial on front, push-button tuning, 1946, **$50**

54-WG, console radio with pull-down phono, mid-1940s, **$15**

62-290, large Deco tabletop, square-lined with push-button tuning and tuning eye, late 1930s, **$125**

62-606, wooden tabletop, 1940, telephone-dial type station control, **$65**

64-BR

line of rectangular wooden tabletop radios, 1946, **$25**

line of typical Bakelite tabletop radios, mid-1940s, **$25**

65-BR-1051, cloth-covered portable, metal grill and elongated dial on front, **$15**

64-WG

line of wooden tabletop radios, mid-1940s, large rectangular grill cloth in center above elongated dial, **$25**

line of Bakelite and painted Bakelite radios, **$25**

line of tabletop wooden radio-phono, circa 1946, **$15**

line of portable AM radios, 1946, front door reveals radio dial and controls, **$25**

74-BR-2001, rounded Bakelite tabletop with exposed phono on top, **$50**

74-WG

line of simple console radios and radio-phonos, late 1940s, **$25**

line of Bakelite and painted Bakelite radios, typical rectangular cases with rounded corners, 1947, **$35**

line of wooden tabletop radio-phonos, **$15**

line of economy portable AM radios, **$25**

84-GAA, radio with built-in recorder/player, **$35**

84-GCB, plastic portable, late 1940s, flip-up front exposes clear plastic front and controls, **$25**

84-WG-1060, plastic portable with flip-up front, 1948, **$15**

94-BR-1533, large Bakelite tabletop, 4 knobs under AM/FM dial, circa 1948, **$25**

94-BR-2740, square-lined AM/FM radio and pull out phono behind double doors, 1950, **$25**

94-HA-1529, similar to model *94-BR-1533,* **$25**

94-WG-1059, portable in box-type cloth-covered case, lid opens, late 1940s, **$15**

94-WG-2748, similar to model *94-BR-2740,* **$25**

345, wooden tabletop with telephone-dial tuner, **$65**

GAA-1003, cloth-covered radio-phono, late 1950s, controls on side, lid lifts to expose phono, **$15**

GEN-1090, -1103, 4-tube portables, 1957, small leatherette-covered with handle on top, **$25**

GSE-1620, thin plastic tabletop, 1956, large dial on front right, **$15**

GSE-1625, Bakelite table radio, 1955, very square-lined, large dial at front right, **$15**

GSL-1650, square tabletop clock radio, 1957, large rectangular dial on front left, **$15**

GTM-1639, rectangular plastic table radio, late 1950s, long dial with knobs on either side at bottom, **$15**

GTM-1666, similar to model *GTM-1639,* AM/FM bands, **$25**

WG-2673, -2683, square-lined sets, late 1950s, small double-door exposes radio, top opens to expose phono, **$15**

All-American Mohawk

44, wide wooden tabletop, 1937, large metal dial on front with 2 knobs, lid lifts, **$75**

60, wooden tabletop, 1928, long style with 2 knobs and switch below dial, lid lifts to expose 6 tubes, **$75**

100, large wooden tabletop, 1925, 1 large and 3 small dials, lid lifts to expose 5 tubes, **$75**

105, 6-tube portable, 1925, leatherette-covered, lid lifts to expose controls, **$125**

110, 115, console version of model *100,* large protruding speaker on top, **$125**

Cherokee, square wooden tabletop, 1926, large metal dial on front, lid lifts to expose six tubes, **$75**

Duet, 6-tube wooden tabletop, 1926, 5 knobs on Bakelite front panel, top lifts to expose tubes, **$75**

Forte, 7-tube wooden tabletop with drop-down front, Bakelite panel with 2 knobs and small dial, lid lifts, 1926, **$75**

Model R, wooden cabinet with 2 large dials on front panel, **$75**

Model R Highboy, tall wooden 4-legged console with drop-down front, **$75**

Navajo, 1927 version of "Cherokee," **$75**

Winona, wide tabletop, 1926, large metal front dial with 3 knobs, lid lifts, **$75**

AMC

126, Catalin radio, 1939, 3 superimposed rings form grill, yellow body and yellow trim, **$1,200;** yellow body and maroon trim, **$2,500;** red body and yellow trim, **$6,000**

American Bosch

16, "Amberola," 6-tube tabletop, with wide metal dial on front, 1925, **$75**

28, simple wooden tabletop with 3 knobs on wide metal dial, lift-up top, 1928, **$75**

35, "Cruiser," 5-tube simple wooden tabletop, 1926, 3 knobs and dial on front, **$75**

46, "Little Six," 6-tube wooden tabletop, 2 knobs at lower front, metal dial and logo at top corners, **$75**

66, 6-tube tabletop, simple front with 3 small knobs and metal dial, lid lifts, **$75**

66AC, model *66,* original Bosch metal battery eliminator and cables, **$125**

116, 6-tube tabletop for AC power, 1927, 3 knobs and metal dial at front, **$100**

126, wide 6-tube wooden tabletop with metal dial and logo, 2 small knobs below, for AC power, **$75**

Amrad (American Radio and Research Corp.)

2331, square wooden crystal receiver with 1 large dial and screw posts on front, 1920, **$550**

2575, square wooden box type crystal radio with 1 large dial and crystal on front, **$500**

2596 plus *2634,* "double decker," 2 wide wooden boxes, each with 3 large dials, stacked together to form radio, **$750**

Amrad 2575, $500.

Amrad 2596 plus 2634, $750.

Amrad 7-tube Neutrodyne (similar to 5-tube Neutrodyne), $150.

3366, small wooden box with 2 large dials and crystal on front, 1 tube inside, 1922, **$550**

3475 plus *2634,* pair of wooden boxes with 3 large dials each, stacked to form radio, circa 1923, **$800**

3730 plus *2634,* 2 wide boxes stacked to form radio, **$800**

AC-5, radio with 4 knobs and 4 dials on front, 1926, various cabinets, **$125**

AC-5-C, 4-legged console with model *AC-5* behind drop-down door, **$125**

Inductrole, large wooden tabletop, 1924, 2 large dials on upper Bakelite panel, doors at bottom conceal batteries, **$350**

Neutrodyne, wide wooden radio with 2 large and 1 small knob on front, top lifts to expose 5 tubes, 1924, **$150**

S-522-C, battery version of model *AC-5-C,* **$125**

S-733, 7-tube console similar to model *S-522-C,* **$125**

Andrea

6H44, wooden wide tabletop, 1941, 3 bands, 7 tubes, walnut and black-painted cabinet, **$45**

CO-U15, wooden radio, late 1940s, top opens to expose phono, **$15**

P-163, cloth-covered multiband portable, late 1940s, front exposes dial and controls, **$15**

T-16, Deco wooden multiband tabletop, radio with semicircular grill cloth on front, 1946, **$65**

T-U16, similar to model *T-16,* AC/DC operation, **$65**

Apex (may also be marked: Case)

5, simple tabletop with 3 knobs, switch and dial on front Bakelite panel, 1926, **$75**

6, wooden tabletop, 1926, front drops to expose dial and several small knobs, **$75**

60A, 60B, 6-tube wide wooden set with 2 large knobs on front, **$65**

61A, simple wooden tabletop with large metal dial plate and knob, **$75**

62B, wide wooden tabletop, 1927, top exposes 6 Kellogg tubes and battery eliminator, **$150**

66A, wooden tabletop with 6 tubes, metal dial plate with 2 knobs, 1928, **$70**

70

    wide metal case, 1929, 2 knobs and dial, lid lifts to expose 9 tubes, **$65**

    4-legged console with speaker below radio, **$75**

89, similar to metal tabletop model *70,* deluxe two-tone finish, **$75**

90, 9-tube wide wooden tabletop with large metal dial plate and knob in center of front, 1927, **$75**

90C, console version of model *90* with drop-down door at front exposes radio, doors at bottom conceal batteries, **$125**

500, wide wooden cabinet with 3 large dials on front panel, lid lifts to expose 5 tubes, 1926, **$75**

503, similar to model *500,* 3 large pointers, 6 tubes, **$75**

701, console version of model *503* with drop-down front, area behind lower doors to hold batteries, **$75**

Super Five, wide wooden tabletop, 1925, 3 large dials and 2 small knobs, **$75**

Arvin

140-P, suitcase-style cloth-covered portable, 1947, large handle on top, grey metal trim, **$15**

150-TC, wooden tabletop radio-phono, 1947, dial at top edge with large lid exposing phono, **$25**

152-T, Bakelite tabletop with semicircular dial at left, 1948, brown, **$25**

153-T, similar to model *152-T,* white Bakelite, **$25**

160-T, brown Bakelite tabletop, 1948, large grill cloth in front, dial at top edge, **$25**

161-T, similar to model *160-T,* white Bakelite, **$25**

182T, AM/FM wooden tabletop, 1948, elongated dial wraps around top edge, **$15**

242T, 4-tube white-painted Bakelite tabletop, 1948, **$35**; red, yellow or green, **$55**

250P, AC/DC portable, 1948, lunch-box style, green plastic with metal top, bottom and grill, **$35**

253T, black Bakelite tabletop, 1948, similar to model *242T,* **$35**

254T, similar to model *253T,* brown Bakelite, **$35**

255T, similar to model *253T,* white Bakelite, **$35**

302, brown Bakelite radio-phono, exposed turntable and arm, grill and radio controls on rounded front edge, **$50**

Arvin 302A, $50.

LOOKS! PERFORMANCE! VALUE!

ARVIN *Top Flight* **RADIOS**

242T   253T   152T   160T

Four Arvin triple-threats for All-American profit honors!

242T

253T

152T

160T

ARVIN MODEL 242-T $**14**⁹⁵ *
Red, Yellow, Green, Ivory

Choice of smart colors! Top-of-the-minute styling! Non-breakable cabinet! Amazing sensitivity and selectivity! There's an array of sales-scoring features your customers can't resist! Put this sensational Arvin on display and watch it roll up the profit total! Yes—and it's Underwriters' listed, too!

ARVIN MODEL 253-T $**16**⁹⁵ *
254-T, Walnut, $17.95*   Ebony
255-T, Ivory $19.95*

Here's a ground-gainer that's way out in front for sheer value—a truly terrific triumph for Arvin dealers. Sharp modern styling puts the plastic cabinet in a class by itself! Built-in antenna. Four tubes plus rectifier. Easy to trade up from ebony to ivory and increase your profit percentage!

ARVIN MODEL 152-T $**22**⁹⁵ *
153-T, Ivory $24.95*   Walnut

Thousands are cheering the outstanding performance of this keen, competent superhet. Reception to top anything else in its price class! Styled for eye-appeal. Engineered for ear-appeal. Built-in antenna. Lighted dial. Underwriters' listed. Pace your pre-holiday sales with this profit package!

ARVIN MODEL 160-T $**34**⁹⁵ *
161-T, Ivory, $36.95*   Walnut

Here's the champion in the 5-tube-plus-rectifier class! Stack it up against any of the other leaders in the field, and you'll find the Arvin comes out ahead on all counts! Smart style. Real distance-getting reception. 3-gang condenser, one stage of tuned radio frequency! Tone control. Underwriters' listed!

Noblitt-Sparks Industries, Inc.
Columbus, Indiana

NATIONALLY ADVERTISED in
LIFE, SATURDAY EVENING POST, COUNTRY GENTLEMEN

Slightly higher in zone 2.

Arvin 1948 radios.

16

302A, similar to model *302*, white, **$50**

341T, small tabletop, 1949, similar to model *442*, **$45**

350P, plastic portable with concentric circles forming grill and dial, 1950, green, blue, brown or maroon, **$25**

358, 359, tabletop similar to model *152-T*, 1949, tan or green, **$25**

402, brown Bakelite tabletop, 1941, large metal dial behind tuning knob at right, **$45**

417, "Rhythm Baby" wooden tombstone tabletop with 4 tubes, circular dial, oval grills, 1936, **$125**

420A, similar to model *420*, white, **$45**

441-T, "Hopalong Cassidy," child's radio, 1951, metal cabinet, foil front with cowboy and horse, antenna-lasso on back, black or red, **$200**

442, small plastic 4-tube set, 1941, louvers wrap around left side, small knob over dial at right front, white or brown, **$45**

444, small metal tabletop, 1946, similar to plastic model *442*, rectangular dial at top right, **$45**

446P, pocket-book-shaped plastic portable, 1951, maroon, tan or red with contrasting trim, **$35**

450T, tabletop with large circular dial molded into plastic cabinet center, 1951, brown or white, **$25**

451T, similar to model *450T*, Lucite dial on white, green, brown or black cabinet, **$35**

460T, rectangular plastic tabletop, 1951, clear dial at right with 3 knobs below, white, green or tan, **$25**

462CM, AM-only version of model *482CFM*, **$25**

467, "Belle," 4-tube wooden tabletop, 1936, **$135**

480TFM, wide Bakelite tabletop, 1950, large AM/FM dial at right, brown or white case with gold-tone trim, **$30**

482CFM, wooden console, 1951, exposed AM/FM radio above pull out phono, **$25**

517, "Junior," similar to model *417*, 5 tubes, **$150**

522, brown Bakelite tabletop, 1941, rounded top, small square dial and 2 knobs at right, **$45**

522A, similar to model *522*, white, **$45**

527, "Senior," Deco console, 1936, 5 tubes, circular dial above large oval grill, **$200**

532, Catalin radio with inserted grill and matching knobs, 1937, yellow with tortoise or maroon with yellow trim, **$1,000**

540T, "Rainbow," metal tabletop, 1953, semicircular grill across front, yellow or orange, **$55**; green, tan or white, **$40**

544, rounded Bakelite tabletop, 1946, rectangular dial at left, brown or white, **$45**

547, Bakelite tabletop with rectangular dial at left, vertical grill bars wrap over top, 1947, **$35**

551T, "Stadivara," square-lined wooden tabletop, 1951, large dial and pointer in front of grill cloth, **$15**

552, rounded Bakelite tabletop, 1946, vertical bars form grill, brown or white, **$25**

553T, "Serenade," similar to model *551T*, dial molded into plastic case, **$25**

554CCB, blonde console, 1951, similar to model *462CM*, **$25**

554CCM, mahogany version of model *554CCB*, **$25**

555, similar to model *552*, push buttons, **$25**

557T, clock radio in plastic case, 1952, tuning knob on right side, **$15**

Arvin 441-T, Hopalong Cassidy, $200.

THEY'VE GOT
Sales Rhythm!

Rhythm Master Model 627—A genuine masterpiece of styling and performance. Six octal base "G" type tubes, all-wave dial, Traveling Spotlight Station Finder.
List: $74.50

Rhythm Queen Model 927—A "blue blood" of radio royalty, with rhythmic performance that amazes everyone. Nine octal base "G" type tubes, all-wave dial, "Electric Eye".
List: $99.50

Rhythm Junior Model 517—A smartly styled big table model. Five tubes, standard and foreign short wave bands, Traveling Spotlight Station Finder.
List: $34.95

Look at 'em! There's sales rhythm in every detail of the new 1937 Arvin Radios! The two consoles pictured here typify the rhythmic beauty of every model and indicate the "family resemblance" of design that unifies the *complete* Arvin line. Fourteen models in all, designed to anticipate every customer desire. Consoles from $54.95 to $150.00. Four splendid battery models—two consoles and two table sets—for unwired farm homes and summer cottages—a rich market! Snappy little bedroom models, beautiful big table models. Sleek little AC-DC portables. All beautifully styled with big, handsome, reverse-lighted dials, and perfectly engineered with Traveling Spotlight Station Finder and many other new developments. You'll profit with Arvin sales rhythm. Get complete details early from your jobber or write us.

NOBLITT-SPARKS INDUSTRIES, Inc., Columbus, Ind.
Also Makers of Arvin "Tailor-Fit" Car Radios
(Prices slightly higher west of Denver)

ARVIN RADIOS

Arvin 1936 radios.

558, square wooden tabletop, 1946, dial and controls on front, lid lifts to expose phono, **$15**

580TFM, similar to model *460T,* FM band added, white, green, tan or brown, **$35**

582CFB, blonde radio-phono similar to model *554CCB,* **$25**

582CFM, mahogany version of model *582CFB,* **$25**

617, "Maid," similar to model *417,* 6 tubes, **$175**

622, very rounded brown Bakelite tabletop, 1941, rectangular dial at right, **$55**

622A, similar to model *622,* white Bakelite, **$55**

627, "Master," Deco console similar to model *527,* 6 tubes, **$250**

650P, "Vacationeer," plastic and leatherette portable with large handle at top, 1952, very large circular dial and concentric grill on front, **$35**

651T, "Cosmopolitan," rounded plastic tabletop, 1952, dial numbers on oversized speaker cloth, white or green, **$35**

655SWT, "International," AM/shortwave plastic tabletop with dial and 3 knobs at right, 1952, **$25**

657-T, "Sleeptimer," clock radio with square clock face at left, open slot dial at right, 1952, white, tan or green, **$25**

664, Bakelite tabletop with vertical grill bars at left, square dial at right, handle on top, 1946, white or brown, **$15**

665, square-lined console, 1947, false drawers on front, lid lifts to expose phono and radio, **$35**

722, square brown Bakelite tabletop, 1941, square dial with 3 knobs, handle on top, **$30**

722A, similar to model *722,* white, **$30**

732, similar to model *722,* wooden cabinet, no handle on top, **$25**

746P, plastic portable, 1953, metal grill front with logo, folding metal handle and 2 knobs on top, **$25**

753T, painted Bakelite tabletop, 1953, speaker grill with oversized circular plastic dial at right, **$35**

840T, redesign of "Rainbow" model *540T,* 1955, painted metal tabletop, **$55**

850T, redesign of model *753T,* 1955, **$34**

851T, plastic tabletop with diamond pattern molded into front, large circular speaker and dial, 1954, **$25**

927, "Queen," very Deco console similar to model *527,* 9 tubes, veneer panels and stepped top, **$300**

1127, "King," 11-tube deluxe version of model *927,* **$350**

1581, plastic tabletop, late 1950s, grill with molded slots and logo on front, radio knobs on sides, **$15**

2564, rectangular tabletop, 1957, irregularly shaped knobs at left, **$25**

2581, redesign of model *1581,* contrasting trim, **$15**

3582, metal tabletop with large protruding speaker on top of flat radio, 1960, **$30**

3586, AM/FM version of model *3586,* **$35**

Atwater Kent

19, wooden tabletop, 1924, Bakelite front panel with controls and metal logo, lid opens, **$400**

20, "Big 20," wide wooden tabletop, 1924, lid opens to expose tubes, **$80**

20C, wide wooden tabletop, similar to model *20,* **$70**

Arvin 622A, $55.

Atwater Kent 41 (similar to model 42), $50.

32, 33, simple wide wooden tabletops, 1926, 2 controls on front, **$70**

35, wide metal tabletop, 1926, 2 controls on front, **$60**

37, metal tabletop, 1927, lid lifts to expose tubes, **$50**

38, wide metal tabletop with 2 controls in 1 row, **$50**

42, similar to model *37,* **$50**

46, similar to model *37,* black and green, **$65**

48, similar to model *30,* 1928 version, **$70**

49, 1928 version of Model 33, **$70**

50, wooden tabletop, 1927, lid lifts to expose metal areas with 7 tubes, **$850**

52, 53, 56, 57, metal consoles, 1928, large circular metal grill, controls above, **$50**

188, 4-legged console, 1932, arc-shaped dial with 4 knobs, **$100**

228, 8-tube cathedral, 1932, semicircular dial with 3 knobs, **$250**

567, 7-tube version of model *228,* **$200**

810, 10-tube Deco console, 1935, arc-shaped dial with 5 knobs below, **$200**

976, simple Deco console with 6 tubes, 3-band circular dial, 4 knobs, 1935, **$150**

3925, breadboard radio with 2 tubes on "island," 2 large controls to left, 1923, **$1,000**

3945, similar to model *3925,* 3-tube island, **$850**

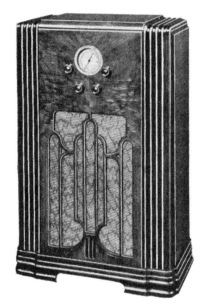

Atwater Kent 976, $150.

Atwater Kent 57, $50.

Atwater Kent 3945, $850.

3955, breadboard radio with 2 controls on left, 1 tube in center, 2-tube island at right, 1923, **$1,000**

3975, similar to model *3955,* dial and 2 switches on front, of left-most control, **$1,000**

4052, breadboard, tube switch and coil between 1 control at left and 3-tube island at right, **$900**

4205, similar to component layout of model *4052,* additional tube and coil, **$900**

4333, "Model 5," small 1923 breadboard with 1 control at left, 5-tube island at right, original (not reproduction), **$3,500**

4340, "Model 10," wide breadboard with 3 controls and 5 tubes, finished in green, **$850;** finished in black, **$800**

4375, "Model 12," breadboard with 2 2-tube islands plus 2 other tubes, 3 controls, **$1,100**

4445, "Model 9," controls at left and center with tube between, 3-tube island at right, **$850**

4550, 4560, model "10A," 3 large controls and 5 tubes on breadboard, brown or black, **$750**

4600, "Model 10," similar to model *4340,* brown, **$800**

4660, "Model 9C," breadboard with 2 large controls and 1-tube plus 3-tube island, 1924, **$1,000**

4700, similar to model *4550,* **$750**

4910, "Model 12," long breadboard 2 2-tube islands, 2 single tubes and 3 controls, 1924, **$1,000**

Kiel, table model, 6 legs, lid lifts, Atwater Kent radio inside, **$150**

Automatic

62M, 7-tube, 3-band console, late 1930s, **$50**

612X, rectangular wooden tabletop with inserted grill at left, semi-spherical dial at right, 1946, **$50**

614X, Bakelite version of model *612X,* **$65**

640, tabletop radio-phono, phono under lid, **$15**

660, 2-band wooden tabletop, 1946, 6 tubes, dial on sloping lid, **$35**

670, radio-phono, 1946, wooden tabletop, lid lifts to expose controls and phono, **$15**

720, wooden tabletop, 1946, metal mesh grill at left, square dial and 2 knobs at right, **$25**

933, "Deco Tom Thumb," small tabletop with rounded left corner, intricate grill cut with circle and squares, 1938, metal cabinet with crystalline lacquer color, **$200;** yellow Catalin case and knobs, **$1,500;** Catalin case and knobs, red, green, grey or orchid, **$3,500**

ATTP, tall portable, 1948, 4-tube, alligatored finish, front door opens to expose radio, **$15**

Bike Radio, small metal portable, 1948, antenna on left side, elongated dial at left front, hammertone finish, **$50**

C-60, two-tone portable with square dial at right, 3 knobs below, 1946, **$15**

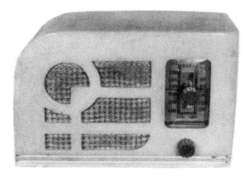

Automatic "Deco Tom Thumb" Catalin radio, $200–$3,500.

Atwater Kent breadboard 4700, $750.

Automatic "Tom Thumb" Catalin radio, $3,500.

C-65, wide portable, 1948, alligatored leatherette, rechargeable battery, similar to model *C-60,* **$15**

Camera Radio, tall cloth-covered inexpensive portable with 4-tube radio in back, front holds plastic 127-film camera, 1948, **$70**

P-57, cloth-covered portable with large dial in front center, handle on top, 1957, **$25**

Tom Boy, wide portable 4-tube radio, 1947, small version of model *C-60,* **$30**

Tom Thumb

   Thin coat-pocket plastic portable, 1960, folding handle on top, oversized dial at right, **$35**

   Small Catalin tabletop, oval dial at right front, 3 cut out areas form grill, yellow or black, **$750**

   Catalin tabletop with red or blue cabinet, **$2,000**

Belmont

4B17, wooden tabletop, 1946, intercom-style radio with small elongated dial at bottom, **$25**

5D128, Deco Bakelite tabletop, 1940, rounded left side, small dial at left with push buttons, tuning knob on right side, **$65**

5P113, "Boulevard," very thin metal shirt-pocket portable with 5 sub-miniature tubes, built-in earphone, 2 knobs and dial at one end, **$200**

Belmont C-640 (similar to 6D111), $65.

6D111, unusually styled Bakelite, similar to model *5D128,* flattened left side, **$65**

6D111 Series, Bakelite with rounded left side, semicircular dial and push buttons at right, tuner on right side, 1941, **$100**

6D120, similar to model *5D128,* horizontal grill wraps around left side, **$75**

151, rounded Deco tabletop, late 1930s, 5-tube Bakelite set with push-button tuning, **$125**

526, Deco tabletop, late 1930s, thin cut out for grill, push-button tuning, white, black or brown, **$75**

602, Deco Bakelite tabletop, 1937, thin cut outs in body with grill cloth behind, **$75**

686, wide wooden tabletop, 1936, oval dial and 4 knobs below, **$40**

770, deluxe Deco console with 7 tubes, elaborate oval dial, 4 knobs below, 1935, **$150**

778-A, wide wooden tabletop version of model *770,* **$45**

1170, Deco console with large circular dial, late 1930s, **$50**

Bendix

55P2, 1948 redesign of model *110,* less streamlined, **$15**

69B8, square-lined AM/FM radio, double-doors conceal controls and phono, blonde, **$35**

69M8, mahogany version of model *69B8,* dual speed phono, **$35**

69M9, similar to model *69M8,* single-speed phono, **$35**

Bendix 110, $35.

79M7, similar to model *69M8*, buffet-style cabinet, **$35**

110, rounded Bakelite tabletop, 1946, dial at top edge, vertical grill bars and 2 knobs below, **$35**

300W, white Bakelite tabletop, 1948, handle slot molded into top, 3 knobs below speaker slots, long dial above, **$25**

0526A, brown Bakelite tabletop, 1946, elongated dial at top, **$50**

0526B, similar to model *0526A*, white-painted Bakelite, **$50**

0526C (also marked *526*), tabletop, 1946, green Catalin body and large black plastic grill attached in front, **$550**; tan and brown plastic or cream and burgundy plastic, **$150**

0525E, wooden tabletop, 1946, slanted dial at top edge, **$25**

636-A, brown Bakelite tabletop, 1946, long AM dial glass across top edge, **$25**

646, 646-A, drop-leaf Sheraton-style cabinets, 1946, hidden phantom dial behind fake top drawer with veneer appliqué, **$65**

656-A, wooden tabletop, 1946, long lid lifts to expose phono on left, radio on right, **$25**

676-C, small square-lined consolette, 1946, 5-tube set with shortwave, in mahogany, walnut or pine, **$25**

687-A, leatherette and plastic 5-tube portable, 1946, front drops down to reveal radio, **$15**

697-A, end-table style radio, 1946, similar to model *646-A* large area of table concealing phono, **$35**

736-B, Deco radio-phono console with large lift-up lid, 1946, **$45**

747-A, AM/FM blonde wooden table radio, 1947, dial set within speaker cloth on front, **$35**

753, square wooden clock radio, 1953, very small radio dial at bottom of face, 2 knobs on front glass, **$35**

951, traditional console with double-doors concealing slide-out radio on left, storage space and AM/FM radio on right, 1951, **$15**

1117-B, traditional mahogany double-door set, 1946, 10-tube radio with phono, **$25**

1117-C, similar to model *1117-B*, oval cutouts on doors, blonde or mahogany, **$25**

1417-A, similar to model *1117-B*, 13 tubes, **$25**

1533, square blonde console with radio and phono, 1948, **$15**

Bond

Bond's radio, silver mirror-covered wide wooden tabletop, lyre cutout and etched grill on left front, 3 Plexiglas knobs under small rectangular dial, **$1,000**

Capehart

1P55, plastic portable with fold-down handle, large circular dial in front center, 1955, **$35**

2T55, plastic tabletop, 1953, large oval grill cloth, oversized dial at right, **$25**

15, plastic portable, 1952, round dial turns under lip at top, handle folds down, **$15**

115N2, square-lined radio-phono, 1948, double doors reveal radio controls and phono, **$25**

501PR, deluxe version of model *504PR*, **$45**

504PR, square wooden console, 1949, AM/FM radio plus phono and room for optional TV, **$45**

T-30, plastic AM tabletop, 1951, rectangular raised grill in center, 2 knobs, dark green, **$15**

T-522, plastic tabletop, 1953, modern design with tuner numbers across front sides and front top, **$45**

TC-20, clock radio, circa 1952, oversized clock dial extending to left, radio controls on right side, **$15**

TC-62, "Deluxe 6," similar to model *TC-20,* 1953, various colors, **$25**

TC-100, typical square clock radio, 1952, plastic cabinet, brown or white, **$15**

Case (See Apex)

Clapp-Eastham (Radak)

Baby Emerson, "Loud Speaker Set" with large tuning dial and 2 small knobs, 1927, without tube, **$500;** with original tube, **$700**

C3, C23, wooden tabletops, 1923, controls plus holes to view 3 tubes on front Bakelite panel, lid lifts, **$350**

DD, wide wooden tabletop with 2 large dials at left and 2 small knobs at right, lid lifts, **$150**

HR, small, tall wooden box with Bakelite panel and controls on front, 1921, lid lifts to expose model information and tube access, **$175**

HZ, amplifier often found with model *HR,* amplifier alone, **$225**

Clapp-Eastham HR, $175.

R3 plus *A3,* 1-tube tuner and 2-tube amplifier in 2 small wooden boxes connected to form a complete set, **$400**

R4, 1-tube radio, 1923, 2 large dials and 1 small knob on Bakelite front panel, **$175**

RHM, sold by R.H. Macy in 1924, small tabletop with Bakelite front panel, lid lifts, **$350**

RZ, wooden tabletop with controls, screw posts and jacks on Bakelite front panel, lid lifts, **$350**

Unico Special, small set similar to model *R4,* 1923, **$250**

Colonial Radio Corp.

16, 5-tube, wide wooden tabletop with 3 large and 1 small dial on front with meter, 1924, **$75**

17, wide 4-tube tabletop with 2 large and 1 small knob on front with meter, **$75**

New World Globe, novelty Bakelite globe on 6-sided Bakelite base, 1930s, brown, white, or black, **$600**

Continental

44, plastic tabletop, 1955, grill wraps around left side, large circular dial and knob at right, brown, black or white, **$25**

1600, similar to model *44,* circular clock face at right, **$15**

Clapp-Eastham Baby Emerson, $500–$700.

Colonial New World Globe, $600.

Cord

Five-Sided Model, large wooden tabletop, painted white, blue-mirrored front, oval dial and 3 knobs, etched fish design, **$1,500**

Oval Model, elongated wooden tabletop, inserted Catalin front has two knobs and round dial, **$600**; blue etched mirror front and off-white painted wooden case, large round dial and 2 knobs, **$800**; peach or green mirror front, **$1,250**

Crosley (early sets also marked Ace)

3B, wide wooden set, 1923, 1 large dial with 5 small knobs, **$125**

Cord Oval Model with Catalin front, $600.

4, "Model IV," amplifier in wooden box, 2 large knobs and screw posts on front panel, **$200**

4-29, 4-tube wooden radio, 1926, 2 large dials and 2 small knobs on sloping front, top lifts, **$125**

5-38, 5-50, 5-tube wooden tabletop with controls on wooden front panel, lid lifts, 1926, **$65**

6, wooden tabletop, 1922, Bakelite front, lid lifts to expose 2 tubes, **$200**

6-60, 6-85, faces similar to model *5-50,* 3 protruding wheels, tabletop or console, **$65**

9-101, 5-tube Bakelite tabletop, 1948, dial over unusual arc-shaped grill bars, brown or black, **$35**

9-102, 6-tube version of model *9-101,* **$35**

9-104W, white-painted Bakelite tabletop, large metal grill, dial and 3 knobs below, **$35**

9-113, brown plastic tabletop, 1949, elongated dial under oversized speaker cloth, **$15**

9-118W, white-painted version of model *9-102,* **$40**

9-119, brown Bakelite with rounded corners, large circular dial with 2 knobs below, 1948, **$15**

9-120W, similar to model *1-119,* white, **$15**

9-121, 9-122W, Bakelite tabletop similar to model *56-TH,* 1948, **$40**

Crosley 9-101, $35.

Crosley 1937 radios.

Crosley 9-121, $40.

9-204, 9-205M, traditional consoles with 9 tubes, 1948, 2 large doors at top open to expose drop-down phono and AM/FM radio, doors at bottom conceal storage space, **$35**

9-212M, 6-tube square-lined wooden console with pull out phono behind left door, AM radio behind right door, 1948, **$35**

9-214M, 9-214ML, 12-tube AM/FM consoles similar to model *9-205M*, 1949, **$35**

10-127, brown Baskelite tabletop, 1950, slotted grill center, upper right corner forms unusual dial, **$35**

10-135, white-painted Bakelite radio with large circular chrome dial in center, chrome and white knobs at left and right, 1950, **$65**

10-304, "Playtime," plastic portable with plastic handle on top and circular dial and concentric grill on front, 1950, **$15**

28AZ, "Recordola," wide Deco console with radio and recording phono under lid, 1941, **$100**

33-BG, Deco table radio, 1940, tall area at top, lid lifts to reveal phono, **$50**

50

small square wooden tabletop, Bakelite front panel with 4 knobs and screw posts, lid lifts, **$125**

portable, 1924, wooden radio, front drops to expose controls, tube access under top, **$250**

50A, wooden 2-tube amplifier with 1 knob on front with screw terminals, 1924, **$200**

51, small 2-tube wooden box with Bakelite front, 5 knobs and screw terminals on front, **$75**

51A, 1-tube amplifier with 1 knob and screw terminals on Bakelite front, **$200**

52, wide wooden tabletop with 1 large dial and 4 small knobs, 1924, lid lifts to expose 3 tubes, **$100**

56TA, 5-tube, 2-band Bakelite radio with square dial and circular pointer at right with 3 knobs below, 1945, **$35**

56TC, 5-tube, 2-band wooden tabletop, 1945, wrap around wooden grill at left, circular pointer within square dial at right, **$35**

Crosley 9-204, $35.

Crosley 50, $125.

Crosley 66TCS, $45.

Crosley 56TD "Rondo," $85.

56TD, "Rondo" (also called "Duette"), rocket-ship styled tall Bakelite case, 1947, grill wraps under bottom, dial over top, brown, tan and blue, **$85**

56TH, Bakelite tabletop, 1946, wrap around ribs from grill, dial tilted on top ledge, **$40**

56TU, similar to model 56TH, Plexiglas handle on top, **$25**

56TW, similar to model 56TA, white, **$40**

58TK, similar to model 9-119, **$15**

66TA, 66TW, Bakelite radios similar to model 66TC, molded grill ribs on each side, **$45**

66TC, wide wooden tabletop with oversized square 2-band dial in center, speaker cloth on both sides, 1946, **$45**

68CP, wide 6-tube, 3-band radio-phono, 1948, controls under lid, **$25**

68CR, Deco console version of model 68CP, 1948, pull out phono in center, **$25**

88CR, traditional 8-tube, 3-band, 1948, AM/FM radio with phono behind double doors, **$25**

Crosley 88CR, $25.

88TA, similar to model 9-102, white or brown, **$35**

117, simple Deco console, 1936, 9 tubes, 3 bands, **$50**

137, 10-tube version of model 117, **$65**

167, 13-tube version of model 117, **$95**

250, tall wooden tabletop with 5 tubes, 2 bands, circular dial, 1936, **$35**

251, similar to *Fiver*, wide radio and dial, **$35**

295, similar to model 251, wide Deco cabinet, **$35**

299, nearly square wooden tabletop, 1936, 2 knobs, circular dial in center, **$35**

349, similar to model 250, more elaborate case and grill, **$55**

395, similar to model 299, more elaborate Deco cabinet, **$65**

401, 401A, "Bandbox, Jr.," metal, radio with 3 knobs and dial plate on front, late 1920s, **$50**

Crosley 58TK, $15.

449, tall wooden cabinet, 1936, 6-tube 3-band set, round dial, **$65**

495, Deco tabletop, circa 1936, intricate grill and circular dial, contrasting wooden panels, **$75**

499, 5-tube console, radio similar to model *250,* **$45**

525, 1937 version of model *250,* **$35**

529, 1937 version of model *295,* **$35**

537, 1937 version of console model *499,* **$45**

601, "Bandbox," wide metal radio with dial and 3 knobs on front, 1927, **$50**

608, "Gembox," similar to metal 601, 1929, **$50**

609, "Gemchest," Deco metal console with flamingo cutout on front grill, 4 metal legs, 1929, black with silver trim, complete, **$325**; green with rose trim, complete, **$400**; red with gold trim, complete, **$400**; simple metal radio with 4 metal legs, no speaker or grill, **$65**

629, 6-tube version of Crosley *Fiver,* circa 1937, **$35**

634, tall wooden tabletop, 1936, 6 tubes, large round dial, **$35**

644, 649, 1937 versions of model *699,* **$55**

699, Deco console similar to model *449,* **$55**

704, 704B, "Jewelbox," metal set, late 1920s, similar to model *601,* **$50**

705, 706, "Showbox," metal tabletop, late 1920s, lid removes to access tubes, **$50**

744, nearly square 7-tube wooden tabletop, 1937, circular dial, speaker on top, **$35**

759, 7-tube version of model *644,* **$55**

769, 7-tube version of model *117,* 1937, **$50**

804, "Jewelbox," metal tabletop, 1929, 3 knobs on front, lid removes to access tubes, **$50**

989, 1937 version of model *117,* **$50**

1199, 11-tube version of model *769,* **$60**

1211, 12-tube version of model *769,* **$65**

1313, 13-tube version of model *769,* **$65**

1465 (by Moffats, Ltd., Ontario), Catalin table radio with grill inserted behind 2 cutout areas at left, yellow, maroon or green body, **$800**

1516, 15-tube deluxe version of model *769,* **$100**

B-439, square-lined cloth-covered portable, 1936, **$15**

B-549, similar to model *B-439,* taller case, **$15**

B-5549, similar to model *B-439,* wind up phono under lid, **$50**

B-5579, 4-tube Deco console, early 1940s, battery operated, **$50**

B-5589, similar to model *B-5579,* 2-band battery console, **$50**

D-25, Bakelite tabletop with rounded top, circular clock face at left, circular dial at right, various colors, **$65**

E-10, "Dynamic," painted tabletop, 1952, large pointer in center, dial along front top and edges, white or maroon, **$45**; blue or chartreuse, **$65**

E-15, "Coloradio," 1953, large metal grill and dial across front of Bakelite case, **$55**

E-20, similar to model *E-15,* very square-lined case, **$25**

E-30, AM/FM Bakelite radio with circular grill at left, clear radio dial in upper right corner, 1953, maroon, tan, green or blue, **$45**

E-75, rectangular clock radio, 1953, square clock face at left within perforated metal grill, controls on right, **$35**

E-85, similar to model *E-75,* **$35**

E-90, similar to model *E-75,* bright chartreuse, red, grey, black or white, **$35**

E-100, plastic portable, 1953, circular clock face at left, circular radio dial at right, red, blue, green and black, **$30**

E-110, similar to model *E-100,* no clock, **$35**

Fiver, 5-tube, 2-band tall wooden tabletop with tall rectangular dial, 1936, **$35**

F-5

"Graduate," simple tabletop with controls on right side, 1953, **$30**

"Musical Chef," simple plastic radio with radio controls on right side, mechanical timer on left side, **$30**

F-25, "V.I.P.," square plastic alarm clock radio, 1953, green, maroon, blue or black, **$30**

Crosley F-5 "Musical Chef," $30.

F-120, leatherette-covered case with square clock in front grill, radio dials at right, lid lifts for phono, 1953, **$25**

Harko, Sr., small wooden tabletop, 1922, 1-tube set with Bakelite front panel, **$450**

Pup, small metal box, 1925, knobs on front and both sides, 1 tube on top, **$300**

RFL-60, RFL-75, wide wooden 5-tube tabletops, 1926, controls and gold stenciled scene on front panel, **$150**

Trirdyne, wide wooden tabletop with 3 tubes, Bakelite front, lid lifts, 1925, **$90**

VC, small wooden tabletop, 1923, lid lifts, Bakelite front panel, **$175**

VD, similar to model *VC,* **$250**

Crosley "Pup," $300.

X, wider version of model *6,* 2 large dials at left, 4 small dials at right, **$150**

XJ, similar to model *X,* slightly different knobs on front, **$150**

Cutting & Washington

11, wooden radio with 3 tubes, knobs and binding posts on front panel, 1922, **$500**

11A, wide wooden tabletop with 3 tubes, controls on front Bakelite panel, 1923, **$350**

11B, similar to model *11A,* **$350**

12, simple flat wooden radio, controls and posts at top, 1 protruding tube, **$450**

12A, tall wooden set with 4 dials on front, **$350**

Teledyne, 4-tube wide tabletop, 1924, 3 large and 4 small dials, **$200**

Cyarts

DeLuxe, 1947, modern orange or yellow Plexon design, rounded left side with circular grill, 3 clear Lucite knobs and dial, **$600;** red Plexon with clear Lucite, **$900**

Day-Fan

OEM7, OEM12, wide wooden tabletop, 1925, 3 large knobs on front panel, top exposes 3 or 4 tubes, **$75**

De Forest

D-7, D-7A, wooden tabletops with 2 small and 2 large knobs on front, 3 tubes, large antenna on top, complete, **$750**

D-10, leather or wood portable with large antenna, doors open to expose controls, complete, **$500**

D-12, square wooden tabletop, 1924, controls above speaker, large antenna on top, complete, **$400;** leatherette-covered, **$275**

DT-600, crystal set in wooden box, 1922, front opens to expose controls, crystal and instructions, **$275**

DT-400, 1-tube radio in box similar to model *DT-600,* **$475**

F-5-M, mahogany radio, 1925, similar to model *D-12,* **$150**

F-5-L, leatherette version of model *F-5-M,* **$100**

Detrola

274, Bakelite table radio with grill inserted behind 2 cut out areas at left, 1939, white, brown or black, **$150**; brightly colored Bakelite, **$400**

281, similar to model *274,* light green Catalin body with blue trim, **$3,000**

383, leatherette portable with handle on top, small square dial at right, 1941, **$15**

Pee Wee, very small one-piece cabinet design with ribs across front, solid white, brown or black, **$300**; white speckled cabinet, **$400**; red or blue cabinet, **$500**

Detrola "Pee Wee," $300–$500.

Detrola "Super Pee Wee," $300–$500.

Super Pee Wee, small Bakelire tabletop, contrasting grill and radio front wrap around left side, solid white, brown or black, **$300**; white-speckled case, **$400**; red or blue body with white trim, **$500**

DeWald

500-A, tabletop, 1946, rounded sides, elongated dial at top, brown or white-painted Bakelite, **$35**

501-A (also marked *A-501*), lyre-shaped Catalin radio, 1939, large dial across front, may have clock, yellow or brown, **$400**; red cabinet and knobs, **$600**

502-A (also marked *A-502*), "Jewel," Catalin tabletop with stepped shoulders at top, square cutout in front may have clock, yellow or brown, **$400**; red cabinet and yellow trim, **$600**

503, square-lined Bakelite tabletop with long ribs forming grill, dial at top edge, 1946, **$15**

538-L, rectangular Bakelite tabletop with wrap around grill, brown or white, 1939, **$25**

548, Bakelite tabletop, 1940, tall case with oversized grill bars, AM and police bands, push-button tuning, brown or white, **$65**

549, 3-band version of model *548,* **$65**

555, non-push button version of model *548,* **$65**

DeWald 548, $65.

556, "Moderne," wooden tabletop, 1941, large speaker cloth over rectangular dial, 2 bands, **$25**

558, 3-band version of model *556,* **$25**

561, 562, square yellow Catalin tabletops with large yellow applied grill on front, **$400;** maroon with yellow trim or yellow with dark red trim, **$600;** yellow cabinet and bright red or blue trim, **$1,000**

615, oval-shaped 6-tube wooden tabletop, 1936, round dial beneath square grill cloth, **$75**

663, 664, wooden radios with dial and knobs on front, slanted lid lifts to expose phono, 1940, **$35**

704, wooden tabletop, 1939, 2 bands, long dial with push-button tuning and 4 knobs below, **$35**

908, square wooden tabletop, circa 1940, lid lifts to expose phono and recorder, **$25**

A-507, "Hit Parade," suitcase-type portable, front detaches to expose radio, **$15**

B-400, square-lined portable, 1947, 4 tubes, two-tone leatherette case with handle, **$15**

B-504, plastic portable with handle at top, matching grill and back, 1948, **$45**

B-612, "Wireless FM Tuner," 1948, wooden radio-shaped tabletop, FM converter plays through standard radio, **$35**

C-500, wooden tabletop, circa 1939, small rectangular dial with push-button tuning, **$25**

DeWald 561/562 Catalin radio, $400–$1,000.

C-800, Bakelite tabletop with AM/FM bands, 1949, **$35**

F-404, 4-tube Bakelite tabletop, 1952, AM and police band, large circular tuning dial at right front, brown or white, **$40;** other colors, **$100**

G-408, flat plastic portable, 1953, folding handle on top, circular dial in front center, **$35**

Dictograph

Silent Radio, Deco wooden tabletop radio, 1937, rounded edges, front door slides open to reveal controls, cork top, miniature speaker, **$65**

DuMont

RA-346, 5-tube tabletop, 1955, white-painted simple pressed-wood grill and front, **$85;** red and gold painted scene on front, **$100**

RA-354, small leather-covered portable, 1957, strap on top, large dial at right front, **$25**

Eagle

A, 1923, wide wooden tabletop with 3 large dials on front panel, lid lifts to expose tubes and instructions, **$135**

B, 1924, wide tabletop with 3 large and 3 small dials on front panel, **$100**

D, 1925, wide 3-knob wooden tabletop, **$75**

Eaglet, 1925, 3-tube radio, sloping front panel with knobs and protruding tubes, **$175**

F, similar to model *D,* **$75**

H, 1926, wide 5-tube tabletop, 3 large knobs in front, top lifts, **$75**

Echophone (See Radio Shop)

Eiseman Magneto Corp.

6-D, 1924, wide wooden tabletop with 3 large dials across front, lid lifts to access components, **$75**

Emerson

17, small square 4-tube black Bakelite case with chrome trim, circa 1935, Deco lines on front, **$75**

19, similar to model *17,* brown Bakelite, **$45**

28, wooden tombstone-style tabletop, circa 1935, 5-tube AM/shortwave set, **$50**

32, 38, small wooden tabletops, mid 1930s, rounded top, **$50**

69, wooden Deco console with slightly stepped top and rectangular grill opening, veneer panels, mid-1930s, **$75**

71, tombstone-shaped wooden tabletop with slightly rounded top, 7 tubes, 1934, **$100**

77, Deco console, mid-1930s, 7-tube set with veneer inlays, simple dial and 3 knobs on front, **$75**

100, simple Deco console, 1935, 3-band, 6-tube set with slightly stepped top, **$50**

102, 105, Deco consoles with veneer panels, slightly stepped top, 1935, **$65**

106, wooden tabletop with 6 tubes and 2 bands, oval shape, very small dial near bottom above 3 knobs, 1935, **$100**

107, 5-tube, 3-band, wooden tabletop, mid-1930s, rounded hump at top center, **$75**

111, 3-band, 6-tube set, similar to model *107,* slightly more rounded top, **$75**

118, small wooden 5-tube AC/DC tabletop, circa 1936, molded-wood front with small circular dial, **$55**

180, advertised as model *180,* labeled *U-5A,* white or brown, **$150**

336, Bakelite tabletop, 1940, rounded corners, tall rectangular dial on right, **$15**

343, small Bakelite tabletop, 1941, grill bars run up center and over top, **$15**

352, wooden tabletop, 1940, square dial on right, curved wooden baffle over speaker, **$50**

365, Deco tabletop, 1941, unusual 20-Watt output, high-fidelity AM radio with tuning eye, **$65**

368, simple Deco console, 1940, elongated dial with push buttons below, **$50**

370, large Deco console, 1941, rectangular dial in center with tuning eye and push buttons, lid conceals phono, **$75**

375, 6-tube small wooden tabletop with ornate speaker grill, mid-1930s, **$50**

375, "5 + 1," small Catalin tabletop without handle, 1940, 5 grill bars at left, 1 bar at right, yellow body, **$600;** green body, **$800;** dark red body, **$1,500;** blue body, **$2,500;** handle on top, yellow or green body, **$800;** handle, red body, **$2,500;** handle, blue body, **$3,500**

380, square Bakelite portable with 2 knobs and radio dial beneath leather strap, 1940, **$50**

382, 384, cloth-covered portable radio-phonos, 1940, lid reveals simple dial and turntable, **$15**

383, 385, wooden versions of model *382,* curved wooden speaker baffle, rounded corners, and lid, **$60**

400

    "Aristocrat," table radio, designed by Norman Bel Geddes, 1940, 7 grill bars on left and round dial at right, yellow, green or brown body, **$400;** black body, **$500**

    "Patriot," similar to Aristocrat, patriotic red, white and blue, white body, **$750;** red body, **$1,000;** blue body, **$1,500**

410, "Micky Mouse," black-painted wooden radio, with metal Mickey cutout over grill, other Disney characters on metal corners, **$1,500**

Emerson 375 "5 + 1" Catalin radio, $600–$3,500.

Emerson Radio

"RE-CREATES THE ARTIST IN YOUR HOME"

19 Models — $17.95 to $129.95 — With METAL TUBES

Every model is a "4-Star" hit—every model is a DEMAND item—every one is a crowd-stopping feature in windows and in stores—and every Emerson has the merchandising qualities which favor volume and substantial profits. These facts, plus Emerson co-operative promotion, explain why Emerson distributors and dealers are enjoying unprecedented prosperity.

NOTE: Arrangements have been made between Emerson Radio and the C.I.T. whereby dealers may now discount their paper with that finance corporation — branches in all principal cities.

"Duo-Tone" Model 106....$39.95
*2-Band, 6-Tube AC-DC with Metal Tubes
Identical Grille Front and Back*

High Fidelity Model 105...$129.95
*11-Tube Superheterodyne—16 to 555 Meters.
12-inch, Auditorium Dynamic Speaker*

"Duo-Tone" Model 107..$49.95
*3-Band, 6-Tube AC-DC with Metal Tubes
Identical Grille Front and Back*

Emerson Compact Model 109.$17.95
*AC-DC Superheterodyne. Illuminated
Aeroplane Dial.   Bakelite cabinet*

Emerson Model 101....$59.95
*3-Band 6-Tube AC Superheterodyne
Incorporating Metal Tubes*

Send for Distributor and Dealer Proposition

Emerson Model 108....$24.95
2-Band, 5-Tube AC-DC Superheterodyne. Aeroplane Dial. Bakelite Cabinet

Emerson Compact Model 111.....$44.95
3-Band, 6-Tube AC-DC with Metal Tubes

Prices Slightly Higher in South and West Coast

Emerson Radio and Television

EMERSON RADIO & PHONOGRAPH CORPORATION, 111 Eighth Avenue, New York, N. Y.
The EMERSON Line Also Comprises Models for Every Foreign Market   Cable Address: EMPHONOCO, N. Y.

Emerson 1935 radios.

Emerson 400 "Aristocrat," $400–$1,500.

411, "Mickey Mouse," pressed composition radio with Mickey over speaker grill and other Disney characters with musical instruments on sides, 1934, original (not reproduction), **$1,500**

414, small pressed composition tabletop, mid-1930s, **$75**

423, wooden tabletop AM radio dial, 3 knobs on front, lid lifts to expose phono, 1941, **$15**

427, 6-tube portable, 1941, cloth-covered, similar to model *400,* brown handle and knobs, **$50;** tan or black handle and knobs, **$15**

428, similar to model *427,* front drops to expose controls, brown knobs and handle, **$50;** tan or black knobs and handle, **$15**

503, wooden tabletop, 1946, large circular dial at right set into perforated metal front, **$25**

506, wooden table radio, 1947, lid lifts to expose phono and radio, **$15**

508, plastic portable, sold throughout late 1940s, lid lifts to expose metal panel with radio controls, **$50**

511, white Bakelite tabletop, 1947, clear plastic dial in front of perforated gold-tone metal grill, **$35**

512, wooden tabletop, 1946, tall design with perforated metal grill, dial at top edge, **$15**

517, similar to model *511,* black body and maroon trim, **$55**

520, Catalin tabletop with large white grill across front and 2 white knobs, round cutout for dial at right, 1946, brown case, **$125;** green body, **$175**

523, cloth-covered portable with large round dial and grill cloth on front, 1946, **$15**

525, very square-lined radio with round dial on front, lid conceals phono, 1947, **$15**

536, cloth-covered portable with perforated metal grill, 1947, **$15**

540, small tabletop with square grill cutouts and tall dial at right, 1947, brown or white, **$35;** red or green, **$65**

541, similar to model *511* square wooden cabinet, **$15**

543, plastic tabletop, 1947, large perforated metal grill across front, white or black, **$15**

Emerson 427, $50.

Emerson 540, $35–$65.

547, Bakelite tabletop, 1947, large grill slots above thin, elongated dial, **$25**

558, portable, 1947, plastic case, lid lifts to expose radio controls, **$30**

559, 567, aligatored leatherette-covered portables, 1947, large plastic speaker grill with dial on front, **$25**

564, small Catalin radio with 15 grill slots cut into front, tall dial at right, 1939, black body and knobs, **$300;** green body and clear maroon knobs, **$650;** red body and knobs, **$900**

568, large 1948 portable, smooth finish, semicircular area at top, front with logo, dial, and recessed knobs, **$15**

570, "Memento," black Catalin portable with gold trim, looks like small black box, radio under lid, inside top holds photo, 1948, **$75**

574, "Memento," similar to model *570,* latch on side, red or black morocco leather, **$50**

580, "Memento," burled walnut jewelry-box look, lid lifts to expose plastic radio and picture holder, cabinet by Ingraham, **$45**

584, deluxe version of model *640,* perforated metal lid, white, green or black, **$65**

602, "Conqueror," FM-only plastic tabletop, 1948, dial forms cylinder at bottom front edge, **$50**

604, simple console with exposed AM radio and pull-down phono, 1949, **$25**

Emerson 610, $35.

610, similar to model *602,* AM radio, maroon with gold trim, **$35**

640, coat-pocket size portable, 1950, lid lifts to expose plastic panel with radio controls, white, green, tan or maroon, **$65**

641B, Bakelite tabletop with square lines, concentric squares form grill at left, long dial and 3 knobs, 1953, brown or black, **$25;** red body with red and gold knobs, **$55**

645, simple plastic portable with large round dial, 1947, maroon, tan or beige, **$15**

646, plastic portable, 1950, handle at top, similar to model *652,* maroon, green, tan or white, **$25**

652, Bakelite tabletop with circular grill at left, elongated dial across center, brown or white, 1950, **$35**

653, Bakelite tabletop, 1950, large grill area above elongated dial, brown or white, **$15**

656, portable, 1950, semicircular grill with dial on front, maroon or tan plastic, **$35**

657, similar to model *656,* brown alligatored leatherette, **$45**

659, rectangular plastic AM/FM radio, 1951, concentric squares form grill, white or brown, **$25**

671, radio alarm clock with circular clock face at right, elongated dial at left, 1950, **$15**

704, 705, plastic portables, 1952, thin coat-pocket style with handle at top, large circular tuning dial in front center, **$35**

Emerson 559, $25.

706, 707, small tombstone-shaped tabletops, 1952, oversized pointer at front bottom, **$50**

729A, rectangular plastic tabletop, 1953, checkerboard-style grill at left, large pointer at right, **$35**

729B, wooden version of model *729A,* **$15**

744, plastic tabletops, 1954, semicircular dial on front, 2 knobs at top edge, uncracked, **$35**

747, coat-pocket portable, 1953, 4 sub-miniature tubes, large tuning dial at right, "EMERSON 7" across front, complete and unbroken, **$75**

756B, similar to model *641B,* **$25**

778B, tabletop with concentric circles form grill, round dial in center with oversized pointer, 1953, black or white, **$25**; red or green with gold-tone trim, **$35**

Emerson 747, $75.

801, two-tone plastic portable, 1954, coat-pocket style with large circular dial above slot grill on front, handle folds, **$35**

805B, small plastic tabletop, 1954, oversized pointer and molded dial at left, brown or white, **$25**

808B, small square plastic tabletop, 1954, concentric circles in center form grill with concentric dial, maroon, white, black or grey, **$25**; red, green or orange, **$35**

811, square plastic tabletop, 1954, semicircular dial covers much of front, oversized plastic pointer, black, white or colors, **$25**

825B, rectangular clock radio with square clock face in center, knobs on right side, 1955, **$15**

826B, similar to model *825B,* oversized circular clock face in center, **$25**

830, similar to model *801,* AC/DC and battery, **$35**

AM-169, tabletop, late 1930s, protruding grill at left, **$35**

AU-190, tombstone-style Catalin tabletop, 1938, cloth-covered speaker, round Catalin knobs, yellow or yellow-brown, **$900**; green or dark brown, **$1,100**; blue case and trim, **$5,000**; red case and trim, **$7,000**

AX-211, "Little Miracle," Bakelite tabletop, circa 1938, rectangular cabinet with square corners, **$35**

Emerson 778B, $25.

Emerson 808B, $25.

Emerson AU-190 Catalin "Tombstone," $900–$7,000.

AX-212, unusual wooden tabletop, late 1930s, rounded left side with concentric circles forming grill, **$100**

AX-219, 5-tube square wooden tabletop with phono at top, **$25**

AX-235, "Little Miracle," small Catalin tabletop with rounded top, square inserted grill on left, 1938, yellow body, **$700;** green or dark red body, **$1,500;** very bright red body, **$2,000;** black body, **$3,000;** blue body, **$4,000**

B-131, wooden tabletop, 1930s, 3 chrome bands across grill, **$50**

Emerson AX-235 "Little Miracle" Catalin radio, $700–$4,000.

BD-197, "Mae West," tabletop with 2 large conical protrusions on radio front, late 1930s, **$500**

BM-258, "Big Miracle," Catalin tabletop with large inserted grill on left front, 1936, yellow or yellow-brown body, **$400;** green or dark red body, **$1,000;** dark blue body, **$2,000**

BT-245, tombstone-style Catalin tabletop with louvers over speaker and pointed knobs, yellow body, **$800;** green body, **$1,400;** dark red body, **$2,200;** blue body, **$5,000;** very bright, marbled red body, **$7,000**

CH-256, "Strad," small Deco wooden table radio with violin-shaped top, 1939, **$200**

D-139, 10-tube Deco console with square dial and tuning eye, 1938, **$100**

F-133, 6-tube Deco tabletop, 1936, 2 contrasting bands around set, **$35**

L-141, L-143, square tabletops, mid-1930s, 5-tube radio with or without phono, **$35**

L-150, Deco 5-tube wooden chairside radio, pull out ashtray, **$75**

Snow White, pressed wood cabinet front shows Snow White and dwarfs, **$1,750**

Three Little Pigs, pressed wood front shows scene from Disney's *Three Pigs Versus the Wolf,* **$1,750**

U-5A, tombstone-shaped tabletop with Bakelite back and 2 knobs, brown or black body, **$150;** uncracked white body, **$200**

Empress

Bird House, 5-tube novelty radio kit, 1947, bird-house style cabinet, **$100**

ERLA (Electrical Research Labs)

DeLuxe Super Five, wide tabletop with 3 large dials on front Bakelite panel, lid lifts, 1925, **$75**

Standard Five, 5-tube wide wooden tabletop, 1925, 3 large dials on front, **$90**

FADA

5F50, 5F60, small Catalin tabletops, 1936, square inserted grill at left, square dial with two knobs, all yellow body and trim, **$750;** light green body and trim, **$900;** yellow body with tortoise grill, **$1,100;** yellow body with blue or bright green grill, **$1,500;** yellow body with red grill, **$2,000**

10, 11, 12, wide wooden cabinets with 3 wooden knobs and metal dial plate on front, lid lifts, 1928, **$60**

16, wide metal tabletop with 3 knobs and dial on front, lid lifts to expose tubes, 1929, **$50**

17, 1929 version of model *11,* **$60**

18, 20, similar to model *16,* **$50**

20T, 6-tube AM band simple wooden tabletop, late 1930s, **$25**

22, similar to model *16,* **$50**

32, wooden 4-legged console, 1929, double doors expose radio controls and grill, **$75**

32 Series, leatherette-covered portable, 1930s, front opens to expose metal face plate, 2 small Catalin knobs, **$45**

79, 6-legged highboy radio, early 1930s, 11 tubes, double doors open to expose radio controls, **$75**

FADA 5F60 Catalin radio, $750–$2,000.

109, wide Deco Bakelite tabletop with 4 ridges in top, small circular dial in front center, 1935, **$60**

110, 4-tube wooden Deco tabletop, mid-1930s, contrasting light and dark panels, **$65**

115, "Bullet," streamlined classic Catalin tabletop with flat left side, slots cut to form grill area, rounded right side, all yellow, pre-World War II, **$600;** all yellow with inserted yellow grill, **$1,200;** maroon with yellow trim or all light green, **$700;** maroon body with inserted yellow grill, **$1,800;** light green body with inserted grill, **$2,400;** yellow body and red trim, **$850;** yellow body with inserted red grill, **$2,000;** blue body and yellow trim, **$1,500;** blue body and inserted yellow trim, **$3,000**

130, 140, wooden tabletops, mid-1930s, rounded top and small wooden feet, **$50**

135, wooden tabletop, 1935, 5 tubes, square edges, **$25**

150CA, Deco console, 1935, 5 tubes, small round dial at top, large rectangular speaker cloth below, **$75**

160CA, 6-tube version of model *150CA,* **$75**

166A, kit radio, 1924, wide Bakelite panel with 3 large dials at left, 3 small knobs at right, **$75**

167, 6-tube, 2-band wooden tabletop, mid-1930s, rounded front top edge, modern look, **$85**

168, similar to model *167,* AM band only, **$75**

188, red, white and blue version of model *L-56,* all-original trim, **$5,000**

189, red, white and blue version of model *115* or model *1000,* all-original trim, **$5,000**

192A, wide wooden radio with 3 large knobs on front Bakelite panel, lid lifts to expose tubes, 1924, **$75**

200, "Bullet," Catalin radio using both model *115* and model *1000* parts, slots cut into body to form grill, all yellow, **$600;** maroon Catalin with yellow trim or all light green, **$700;** yellow Catalin body and red trim, **$850;** blue Catalin

FADA 1937 "Coloradios."

body and yellow trim, **$1,500;** bullet-shaped wooden body, tabletop, **$400**

209, Bakelite tabletop, 1941, 5 tubes, vertical louvers, white or brown, **$35**

242, "Coloradio," small 2-volt, 4-tube tabletop with 3 grill bars, 1937, brown or white Bakelite body, **$250;** black or red body, silver or gold bars, **$450**

246, similar to model *242,* 6-volt battery, brown or white, **$200**

252, "Temple," Catalin body with dial at top, slots form grill, pre-World War II, all yellow, **$450;** maroon with yellow trim, **$550;** all light green, **$800;** light green body, large speaker cloth on front, **$650;** light green with inserted grill, **$1,500;** blue body and yellow trim, **$1,800;** blue body and large speaker cloth on front, **$1,500;** blue body with inserted yellow grill, **$2,500;** wooden body, **$200;** cloth-covered wooden body, **$200**

254, "Coloradio," AC/DC radio with 4 overlapping grill bars, 1937, brown or white Bakelite body, **$90;** black body and silver trim, **$250;** red body and gold grill bars, **$450**

254T, similar to model *254,* walnut cabinet, **$35**

265A, simple version of model *480A,* 3 small knobs and no meter, **$60**

290C, 9-tube Deco console, 1937, multiband circular dial with 6 knobs below and tuning eye above, **$135**

290T, tall wooden Deco tabletop, similar to model *290C,* **$125**

454, Bakelite tabletop, 1938, 2 z-shaped grill bars molded with body, **$50**

480A, wide wooden tabletop with 5 small knobs and 2 dials plus meter on metal plate, 1926, **$60**

602, tabletop wooden radio with phono under lid, 1946, **$15**

605, 606, rounded Bakelite AM tabletops, mid-1940s, brown or white, **$35**

609, 610, small Bakelite tabletops, mid-1940s, vertical louvers at left, rectangular dial at right, **$35**

637, cloth-covered portable, 1946, 2 lids open to expose radio and phono, **$15**

652, "Temple," Catalin body, post-World War II, slots form grill, all yellow, **$450;** maroon with yellow trim, **$550;** all light green, **$800;** light green body, large speaker cloth on front, **$650;** light green with inserted grill, **$1,500;** blue body and yellow trim, **$1,800;** blue body and large speaker cloth on front, **$1,500;** blue body with inserted yellow grill, **$2,500;** wooden body, **$200;** cloth-covered wooden body, **$200**

659, similar to model *652,* shortwave band, all yellow or maroon with yellow trim, **$600;** all light green, **$1,000;** blue body and yellow trim, **$2,500**

700, "Cloud," Catalin tabletop, 1946, rounded sides, very large dial at right front, yellow or maroon body, **$500;** light green body, **$650;** blue body, **$1,000**

711, Catalin body tabletop, 1946, rounded corners, large cutout with inserted grill cloth and dial, all yellow or maroon, **$600;** light green body, **$800;** blue body, **$1,500**

740, small Bakelite tabletop, 1947, louvers wrap around left side, circular dial at right, white or brown, **$35**

790, large Bakelite tabletop, circa 1948, 4 knobs below AM/FM dial, "FADA" molded into grill, brown or white, **$65**

FADA 652 wooden "Temple," $200.

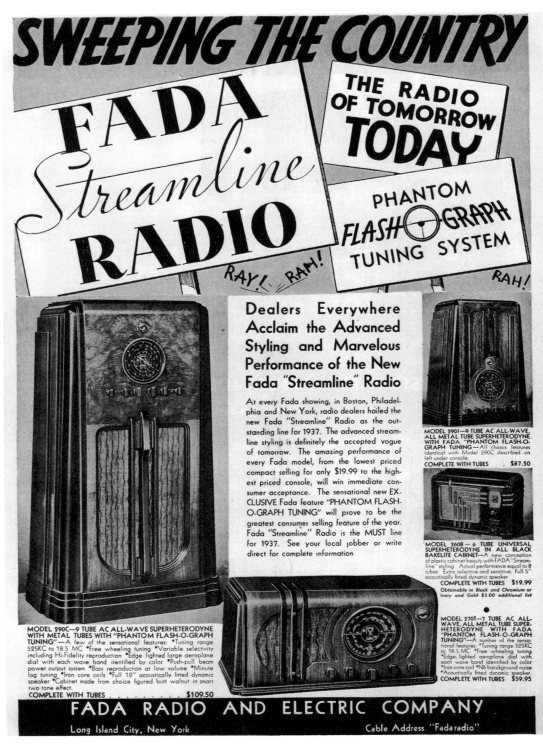

FADA 1937 wooden radios.

845, similar to model *700,* plastic body, various colors, **$150**

1000, "Bullet," post-World War II production of model *115,* slots cut into case to form grill, all yellow, **$600;** yellow body and inserted grill, **$1,200;** maroon or light green body, **$700;** maroon body and inserted yellow grill, **$1,800;** light green body and inserted grill, **$2,400;** yellow body and red trim, **$850;** yellow body with inserted red trim, **$2,000;** blue body and yellow trim, **$1,500;** blue body with inserted yellow grill, **$3,000**

1452, 6-tube wooden radio, mid-1930s, veneer panels, sold in both tabletop and console versions, **$50**

1462, wooden tabletop, mid-1930s, rounded top, 4 knobs and circular dial below intricate grill area, **$50**

1470, 7-tube, 4-band wooden radio, mid-1930s, sold in both tabletop and console versions, **$75**

F-55, similar to model *L-56,* no handle, all yellow or all light green, **$1,400;** maroon body, **$2,000;** yellow body and tortoise, blue or bright green grill, **$2,500;** yellow body and red grill, **$3,500;** green or blue body and yellow trim, **$5,000**

L-56, small rounded Catalin tabletop with handle on top, grill wraps around from left side to front, all yellow or all light green, **$1,000;** maroon body, **$1,400;** yellow body and tortoise, blue or bright green grill, **$1,700;** yellow body and red grill, **$2,500;** emerald green or blue body and yellow trim, **$4,000**

FADA 1000 "Bullet" Catalin radio, $600–$3,000.

FADA F-55 Catalin radio, $1,400–$5,000.

P-80, plastic portable with Catalin knob on front, lid flips up to reveal knobs and swirled grill, 1947, black, brown or maroon, **$45**

P-82, cloth-covered portable, 1947, simple 5-tube set with rounded top, **$15**

P-100, portable radio, 1947, alligatored front drops down to expose radio, **$25**

PL-24, 7-tube, 2-band portable, 1940, sliding front panel exposes speaker louvers and radio controls, **$15**

Farnsworth

CC-70, Deco console radio with 7 tubes, small elongated dial near top with push-button tuning, 1941, **$50**

CC-90, 9-tube version of model *CC-70,* **$50**

CK-58, CK-66, wooden radio-phonos, 1941, radio and controls on front, lid lifts to expose phono, **$25**

CK-73, 7-tube chair side, 1941, radio at front of top, lid lifts to expose phono, **$50**

CK-92, 9-tube Sheraton-style console, with radio and phono, 1941, **$150**

CK-111, Chippendale-style console, 1941, 11 tubes, deluxe phono, **$150**

CT-41, brown Bakelite tabletop, 1941, wrap around grill at left, oval dial behind window at right, **$35**

CT-42, 4-tube wooden tabletop, 1941, multiband, metal grill at left and rectangular dial at right, **$35**

CT-43, similar to model *CT-41,* gold-tone grill, **$45**

CT-50, rectangular Bakelite tabletop with grill bars across front and dial at top edge, 1941, **$25**

CT-51, similar to model *CT-50*, handle on top, **$25**

CT-52, similar to model *CT-50*, speaker cloth, **$25**

CT-53, similar to model *CT-50*, handle and grill cloth, **$25**

CT-54, wooden tabletop, 1941, long wrap around speaker grill along center, dial at top edge, **$35**

CT-59, plastic and cloth-covered portable, 1941, front lid swings open to turn set on and expose controls, **$35**

CT-60, suitcase-style portable, 1941, front lid flips down to expose radio controls, **$15**

CT-61, *CT-63*, similar to model *CT-50*, **$25**

CT-62, similar to model *CT-53*, **$25**

CT-64, similar to model *CT-54*, rectangular speaker cloth across front, **$35**

EK-102, Deco-style console, 1947, large rectangular speaker cloth, hidden AM/FM radio and phono at top, **$55**

ET-061, white Bakelite tabletop with applied blue, maroon, or black grill, 1947, **$75**

GP-350, brown cloth-covered portable, 1947, front lifts to expose large circular dial at right, metal mesh grill at left, **$35**

GT-051, streamlined Bakelite tabletop, 1947, rounded corners, large round dial at right, **$40**

Federal Telephone & Telegraph Co.

57, 58, large wooden tabletops, 1922, controls on front Bakelite panel, lid lifts to access 4 tubes, **$600**

59, 4-tube wooden set, similar to model *58*, whole lid lifts to expose components, **$750**

61, 6-tube set similar to model *59*, **$900**

110, tall wooden set, with 3 tubes, 1 large and 6 small dials on front panel, 1923, **$475**

141, wooden tabletop, 1924, doors open to expose controls, **$400**

Federal 57, $600.

A-10, 5-tube wide wooden tabletop, 1925, 3 large dials on Bakelite panel, **$125**

B-30, large wide wooden tabletop, 5 tubes with 3 dials on front, semicircular top, **$75**

C-30, 7-tube version of model *B-30*, **$75**

Jr., small crystal set with large pointer on front, crystal and screw posts on top, 1922, **$300**

Phonoradio, wide wooden cabinet on 4 legs, 1924, Bakelite panel and phono under double lid, **$175**

Freed-Eisemann

30, wooden tabletop with 2 metal dial plates and 5 knobs on front, 1926, **$65**

40, similar to model *30*, single metal dial plate, **$65**

50, deluxe wide wooden tabletop with drop-down front cover, **$75**

FE-15, wooden tabletop with 2 small and 3 large dials on front panel, 1925, **$100**

FE-65, 6-tube, 3-band wooden tabletop, 1936, 4 knobs below square dial, **$35**

NR-5, wide wooden tabletop with 3 dials on front Bakelite panel, 1923, **$75**

NR-6, similar to model *NR-5*, **$85**

NR-12, wide wooden tabletop with 2 large knobs on front, 1924, **$100**

NR-20, wide elaborate wooden tabletop with 3 large dials on front, **$100**

Freshman Q-15, $75.

Freshman

5-F-5, wooden tabletop, 1925, 3 large dials on front, wooden grill in front of enclosed speaker, **$50**

6-F-6, wooden tabletop with 3 large dials on front, lid opens, 1926, **$75**

7-83-5, console version of 1-dial Masterpiece Model, 1927, **$125**

21, metal tabletop, 1929, lid lifts off, contrasting painted areas on front and top, **$75**

Concert Model, similar to model *5-F-5,* grill and horn above Bakelite panel, **$125**

Masterpiece, "three dialer" with knobs on front panel, mid-1920s, lid lifts to expose 5 tubes, **$75;** 1 large dial on front metal plate, 6 tubes, **$50**

M-11, N-11, similar to model *21,* metal tabletop, **$65**

Q-15, wide metal tabletop with removable lid, circa 1928, **$75**

Garod

1B55L, "Drop Handle," Catalin radio with contrasting grill and knobs, handle drops into slot on top, all yellow, 1939, **$700;** yellow body with red trim, **$2,000;** maroon body with yellow trim, **$1,250;** brown body with tortoise trim, **$2,000;** green body with green trim, **$4,000**

5AP, "Companion," unusual Bakelite radio-phono, radio at front with exposed phono on top, white or brown, **$65;** pastel colors, **$85**

5D3, portable, 1947, front cover flips up to expose triangular dial and rectangular speaker cloth, various colors, **$45**

5RC1, "Radalarm," rounded corner plastic clock radio, 1948, small clock face at left, square dial at right, Lucite trim, **$25**

6AU-1, "Commander," Catalin radio, wrap around or flush, screwed-in grill, yellow or maroon body with yellow trim, **$600;** yellow body and red trim, **$1,200;** red body and yellow trim, **$1,400**

6B2, "Senator," tall Bakelite tabletop, 1946, horizontal grill bars over elongated dial, brown or white, **$25**

126, Catalin table radio with contrasting handle, 1939, 3 overlapping circles form grill, all yellow, **$1,200;** two-tone body with yellow and maroon, **$2,500;** red body with yellow trim, **$6,000**

711-P, wooden 7-tube tabletop, 1941, square dial and 3 knobs, phono under lid, **$15**

1450, "Peak Top," similar to model *1B55L,* 1939, handle sits on slightly pointed top, all yellow, **$800;** yellow body with red trim, **$2,500;** maroon or light green body, **$1,500;** brown body and tortoise trim, **$2,000;** blue body and yellow trim, **$6,000**

EA, wooden radio on tall spindle legs, 1926, 3-dialer tilts up to service radio, **$225**

EC, similar to model *EA,* 7 tubes, metal plate with 1 tuning wheel, **$225**

Heliphone, wooden crystal set, 1922, front opens to expose simple crystal, condenser and coil antenna, **$200**

Garod 6AU-1 Catalin "Commander," $600–$1,400.

Garod 1450 Catalin "Peak Top," $800–$6,000.

M, wide wooden tabletop with 3 large dials on front Bakelite panel, 1925, **$65**

R-212, wide wooden tabletop with 5 tubes, 3 large and 3 small dials on front, 1923, **$75**

RAF, wooden tabletop, 1923, 3 large knobs on front Bakelite panel, **$75**

V, wide wooden tabletop, 1924, lid lifts to expose components, **$55**

General Electric

50B, 50W, 1947, plastic clock radio with curved lines, square clock on left front, 2 knobs beneath grill, white, black or brown, **$15**

60, 1947, clock radio with circular tuning knob above rounded clock face, white or brown, **$15**

64, 1949 version of model *60,* brown Bakelite, **$15**

65, white-painted version of model *64,* **$15**

102, 1948, Bakelite tabletop with long louvers at top, and elongated dial below, white, brown or black, **$15**

107, similar to model *102,* wrap around louvers, **$15**

114, similar to model *102,* white or brown, **$15**

115, similar to model *102,* clear plastic insert forms grill, **$25**

123, 1949, wide brown Bakelite radio with oversized dial behind plastic window, **$15**

124, similar to model *123,* white Bakelite, **$15**

136, 1949, large white Bakelite tabletop, long AM dial between 2 knobs at front bottom, **$15**

143, 1949, pocketbook-style portable in maroon plastic case with molded handle, circular knobs at either side of front tuning dial, **$15**

145, 1949, coat-pocket portable, maroon plastic case, lid lifts to expose gold-tone controls, **$35**

150, 1948, plastic portable with long dial at top edge, textured finish on front and back, **$15**

160, 1949, plastic portable with rounded dial at top edge, maroon plastic and brass trim, **$15**

165, 1949, 5-tube plastic portable, long dial and 2 knobs below handle at top edge, **$15**

219, 221, mid-1940s, square wooden tabletops, AM/short wave bands, **$25**

250, mid-1940s, Bakelite portable, lid lifts to expose large elongated dial, **$35**

General Electric 250, $35.

260, 1947, deluxe aluminum-cased portable, lid lifts to expose 6-band dial and push-button tuning, **$65**

321, 1946, wooden tabletop, push-button tuning, metal grill at top, **$15**

401, 1950, plastic tabletop with dial behind clear plastic window at right, brown, white or red, **$25**

402, 1950, plastic tabletop with large grill area above elongated dial, **$15**

404, similar to model *402,* brown or white, **$15**

408, 1950, plastic tabletop with unusual semi-circular AM/FM dial protruding at front, **$35**

409, similar to model *408,* brown plastic, **$35**

410, 1950, square-lined wooden tabletop, rectangular metal grill, striped mahogany finish, **$15**

412, 414, simple plastic table radios, 1951, numbers light up when dialed, white, red or brown, **$25**

419, 1953, simple plastic tabletop, round dial at right front of grill, **$15**

422, 1951, simple plastic AM radio, elongated dial between 2 knobs on bottom, brown or white, **$15**

424, 1953, plastic AM radio with large circular dial in front center, **$15**

427, 1953, plastic tabletop with rectangular plastic dial set up from front grill, white, black or maroon, **$25**

General Electric 321, $15.

436, 1953, plastic tabletop, with AM/short-wave bands, **$35**

440, 1953, similar to model *408,* **$35**

500, 501, 1950, Bakelite alarm clock radios, circular clock face at left, tuning wheel at top of front, brown or white, **$15**

505, 506, 1950, Bakelite radio alarm clocks with rounded corners, tuning wheel at top of front, brown or white, **$15**

507, similar to model *505,* burgundy, **$25**

508, similar to model *501,* simulated blonde mahogany, **$15**

515, 1951, plastic clock radio with circular clock face at left, white, brown, black or red, **$15**

535, 1951, alarm clock radio with square clock face at left and square dial at right separated by ribs, maroon plastic, **$15**

546, 1953, plastic clock radio with vertical grill bars on front, square clock face in center, various colors, **$15**

555, 1953, plastic clock radio with square clock face at left, round dial at right, **$25**

560, 1953, square clock radio, large circular clock face in center with radio tuner on right side, brown or white, **$25**

564, similar to model *555,* green, red or white, **$35**

601, 1950 redesign of model *143,* **$15**

605, 606, 1952, plastic portables, handle and flip-up radio dial at top, various colors, **$35**

610, 611, 1951, portable with semicircular dial on front, handle at top, red or green plastic, **$15**

614, 615, pocketbook-style portables, circular dial on top under double handle, **$45**

635, 1955, flat coat pocket portable with folding handle on top and large circular dial at front right, **$35**

650, 1950, plastic portable, similar to model *165,* **$15**

A-52, 1936, 5-tube tall wooden tabletop with 4 knobs below wide multiband dial, **$85**

A-65, 1935, Deco console with vertical wooden grill, tiny 2-band dial, 4 knobs, **$100**

5 NEW AND SENSATIONAL
1936
GENERAL ELECTRIC
RADIO MODELS

they have everything in sales appeal and profit possibilities!

MODEL A-83. 8 metal tubes. Standard broadcasts, police calls, amateurs, aviation reports, foreign and domestic short-wave. 9-inch type stabilized dynamic speaker. Sliding-rule tuning scale. Speech-music control. Automatic volume control. 10 watts output.

MODEL A-54. A-c. and D-c. table or shelf model. 5 metal tubes, giving the equivalent of 7-tube performance. Standard broadcasts, foreign short-wave, amateurs, aviation, police calls. 6½-inch type stabilized dynamic speaker. Wide-vision dial. Red and black tuning scale. Automatic volume control. Gracefully styled cabinet. Standard finish: two-toned walnut-veneer. Special finishes: white and gold, black and gold, red and black.

MODEL A-52. 5 metal tubes, giving the equivalent of 7-tube performance. Standard broadcasts, foreign short-wave, police calls, aviation reports. 8-inch type stabilized dynamic speaker. Wide-vision dial. Red and black tuning scale. Automatic volume control. I.F. wave trap. Excellent tone. 5 watts output.

MODEL A-55. 5 metal tubes, giving the equivalent of 7-tube performance. Standard broadcasts, foreign short-wave, police calls, aviation reports. 9-inch type stabilized dynamic speaker. Wide-vision dial. Red and black tuning scale. Automatic volume control. I.F. wave trap. 5 watts output.

GENERAL ⓖⓔ ELECTRIC
THE ORIGINAL METAL-TUBE RADIO

APPLIANCE AND MERCHANDISE DEPT., GENERAL ELECTRIC CO., BRIDGEPORT, CONN.

MODEL A-85. 8 metal tubes. Standard broadcasts, police calls, amateurs, aviation reports, foreign and domestic short-wave. 11-inch type stabilized dynamic speaker. Sliding-rule tuning scale. Speech-music control. Automatic volume control. Remarkable sensitivity, selectivity, and reserve power. 10 watts output.

General Electric 1936 radios.

A-70, elaborate version of model *A-52,* dial in center front, **$100**

A-125, 1935, 5-band Deco console with elongated dial above wooden grill, platform-style base, **$100**

C-440, -450, -460, late-1950s, 5-tube plastic table clock radios with AM only, various colors, **$15**

F-51, 1937, Deco tabletop with rounded left side and circular speaker, chrome strips across front, **$85**

F-96, 1938, Deco console with multiband dials within rectangular cutout at top, 5 knobs plus push-button tuning, large oval speaker cloth, **$100**

GD-610, Deco wooden tabletop with rectangular AM dial and 1 knob at left under 5 push buttons on top edge, **$30**

H-79, 1940, Deco console, lid lifts to reveal radio and phono, **$50**

H-87, 1939, Deco console, rectangular dial and tuning wheels above push buttons and 2 knobs, **$65**

H-500, 1940, unusually designed Bakelite tabletop with circular tuning knob at top center, **$50**

H-600, typical 1940 Bakelite radio with rounded corners and 2 knobs below square dial at right, **$30**

H-632, 1939, wooden tabletop, speaker cloth at left and right front, 3 knobs and push buttons below square dial, **$45**

HJ-618, HJ-619, Deco wooden tabletops, rounded left side, push-button radio at right, lid lifts to expose phono, **$65**

General Electric HJ-618, $65.

General Electric J-62, $50.

J-62, 1940, square wooden tabletop in jewel-box style cabinet with handles on side, **$50**

J-718, 1941, wide console, small double doors at top conceal radio and phono, **$65**

J-805, 1941, Deco console, rectangular dial at top with AM/FM, push buttons and 4 knobs, **$75**

J-809, 1941, traditional wooden console, left door conceals pull out phono, right door conceals 3-band radio, **$35**

Jewel Box, small table radio with translucent tortoise-colored case and yellow knobs, fluted sides, lid lifts to expose radio, **$1,200**

General Electric H-500, $50.

L-570, rectangular Catalin table radio with contrasting long inserted grill across front, 2 knobs and handle, all yellow, **$500**; two-tone maroon or yellow, **$700**; tortoise or dark green body, **$1,000**; yellow body and blue trim, **$1,200**

LB-412, 1941, tall portable, front door exposes controls, two-tone brown, **$25**

LB-502, AC/DC version of model *LB-412*, blue and grey, **$35**

LB-603, 1941, two-tone brown portable, lid lifts off to expose radio controls, **$15**

LB-700, 1941, tall thin leatherette-covered portable with elongated dial above 2 knobs at top front, plastic grill at bottom, **$25**

LB-702, 1941, suitcase-style brown leatherette-covered portable, lid lifts to expose elongated dial and 3 knobs, **$15**

T105, T106, T115, T116, plastic 6-tube AM table radios, various colors, **$15**

T120, T135, late-1950s, AM/FM plastic table radios, various colors, **$25**

X-415, 1948, AM/FM 8-tube tabletop, unusual protruding grill at top, **$50**

General Television

5B5, similar to model *591*, plastic body and contrasting trim, brown or black with white trim, **$150**; green or red with white trim, **$300**

9B6, similar to model *5B5*, pierced-metal front and grill, **$50**

14A4, small Bakelite tabletop with louvers at left, square dial at right, mid-1940s, **$25**

17A5, similar to model *5B5*, wooden cabinet, no handle, **$45**

24B6, similar to model *5B5*, wooden cabinet with handle, **$45**

591, small Catalin radio with white plastic louvers, handle, dial trim and knobs, 1941, yellow body, **$500**; red Catalin body, **$1,000**; turquoise Catalin body, **$1,500**; brown or black plastic body, **$150**; green or red plastic body, **$300**

General Television 591 Catalin radio, $150– $1,500.

Gilfilan

10, wooden tabletop, late-1920s, 2 knobs and metal dial on front, **$75**

60, similar to model *10*, wooden tabletop, **$75**

GN-1, long wooden tabletop with 3 large dials behind center door, controls and storage behind 2 small doors, 1924, **$85**

GN-2, wide wooden tabletop with 3 large dials and meter on front panel, 1924, **$75**

GN-3, large wooden tabletop, 2 large and 1 small dial on front Bakelite panel, lid lifts, **$75**

GN-4, 5-tube console with 3 large dials and 2 tubes protruding from front panel, 1925, **$125**

GN-5, tabletop version of model *GN-4*, **$75**

GN-6, large wooden tabletop with all 4 tubes protruding from front panel, **$150**

Grebe (A.H. Grebe & Co.)

AC-6, wooden tabletop, with dial and 3 control wheels on front, 1928, **$175**

AC-7, AC version of model *Synchrophase 7*, **$200**

CR-3, long wooden tabletop with 3 large dials on front, **$550**

CR-5, tabletop with 2 large and several small controls on front panel, 1 tube visible through front, 1921, **$350**

CR-6, large tabletop with 4 large dials across front bottom, 1920, **$1,000**

CR-8, wide tabletop, 1921, 1 tube visible through front, **$400**

CR-9, 3-tube radio similar to model *CR-8,* built-in amplifier, **$350**

CR-12, wooden radio with 2 large coils and 4 tubes inside, 1923, **$350**

CR-13, wide wooden tabletop with 3 large dials on front, **$475**

CR-14, 3-tube radio, 1923, similar to model *CR-12,* **$450**

CR-18, wooden tabletop with 5 control wheels on front, 1926, **$600**

MU-1, "Synchrophase," large wooden tabletop with 6 control wheels on front Bakelite panel, 1924, **$175**

MU-2, 1925 version of Synchrophase, **$275**

RORD, 3-tube amplifier, 1920, **$375**

RORK, 2-tube amplifier, 1920, tubes visible through front, **$300**

RORN, 1-tube amplifier, 1923, 2 large controls on front, **$375**

Synchrophase 7, wooden tabletop with 2 control wheels and 2 small knobs in front center, 1927, **$175**

Hallicrafters

5R30, "Continental," rounded Bakelite tabletop with AM/shortwave bands, square grill at left, 1952, **$65**

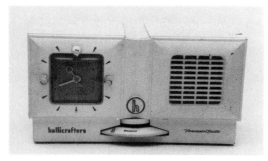

Hallicrafters 5R30 "Continental," $65.

5R50, similar to model *5R30,* square clock face at left, **$25**

404-S, large buffet-style console, 1947, large doors at center expose radio, **$45**

AT-1, 4-tube plastic tabletop, 1952, grill at left, square dial at right, **$15**

Atom, Bakelite clock radio, 1952, ridge in center separates clock at left and grill at right, wheel tuner below, **$35**

EC-404, Georgian credenza-style AM/FM console with push-button tuning, 1947, **$100**

TW-55, flat coat-pocket portable with folding handle on top, circular dial at front right, 1955, **$35**

Howard

200, 6-tube version of model *C,* **$75**

C, 1925, wide wooden tabletop, with 3 large dials on front panel, lid lifts, **$75**

Green Diamond Eight, wide metal radio with painted top, 3 small knobs on front, **$75**

Nuerodyne, similar to model *C,* 5 tubes visible through front panel, **$75**

International Radio Corp. (see Kadette)

Jewel

304, "Pixie," 1946, AC/DC battery-style portable, long handle, lid lifts to expose controls, **$35**

505, "Pin-Up," 1947, small clock radio with wrap around vertical grill bars, circular clock face at front center, tuning dial at right edge, **$45**

801, "Trixie," 1948, portable, lid lifts to expose Bakelite panel and radio dial, red, green or brown python, alligator, or tan leather, **$50**

814, "Tee-Nee," 1949, unusual plastic portable on long strap, rounded top and bottom with knobs on front, **$65**

901, "Trixie," 1949, similar to model *801,* **$50**

935, "Wakemaster," 1949, rounded Bakelite tabletop, round clock face at left, rounded dial at right, **$15**

949, "Golden," 1949, cloth-covered portable, large grill with round dial on front, **$15**

955, "Nugget," 1950, Bakelite tabletop with rectangular dial at right, brown or white, **$45;** various colors, **$75**

956, 1949, tabletop Bakelite radio with perforated grill at left, square dial at right, **$35**

960, 1949, Bakelite table radio, dial around front perforated grill, **$45**

5010, 1950, simple portable with black cloth cover, Plexon grill, brass trim, **$35**

5040, 1951, plastic tabletop, 2 radio-control wheels protrude through top front, circular clock face in center, **$30**

5100, plastic tabletop, 1951, simple lines with logo at left, oversized round dial and knob at right, **$15**

5200, 1952 redesign of model *5100,* **$15**

5250, 1952 redesign of model *5040,* **$30**

5310, 1955, flat plastic coat-pocket portable with fold-down handle and large circular dial in front center, **$35**

Jones (Jos. W. Jones Radio Mfg. Co.)

J-65, wooden tabletop, 1925, 2 large dials on front, 4 protruding tubes, **$175**

J-75, 5-tube wooden tabletop with sloping front Bakelite panel, lid lifts, **$75**

J-85, wooden tabletop with 3 large dials, 5 protruding tubes, 1925, **$175**

J-100, similar to model *J-75,* flush front panel, **$75**

J-175, 6-tube radio similar to model *J-100,* oversized cabinet and storage areas at left and right, **$75**

Jones/Melco

Flex-O-Dyne, wide wooden tabletop with storage area below Bakelite panel, 1923, **$175**

Melco Supreme, 4-tube wide wooden tabletop, 1923, lid lifts to expose components, **$75**

Kadette (International Radio Corp.)

35, 1937, tall wooden tabletop with horizontal grill bars over telephone-style dial, **$65**

40, "Jewel," 1936, solid-brown Bakelite tabletop, wide style with contrasting grill in center with 2 knobs, **$100;** lavender or green Plaskon, **$400**

41, similar to model *40,* yellow brown Plaskon, **$300**

43, similar to model *40,* ivory-speckled Plaskon, **$400**

44, similar to model *40,* red Plaskon, **$400**

47, similar to model *40,* black pearl Bakelite, **$200**

48, similar to model *40,* marbleized brown, **$150**

66, 1936, wide 6-tube wooden tabletop, grill slots above small square dial, **$45**

400, portable Deco wooden tabletop, similar to model *66,* **$45**

Junior, small 2-tube shirt-pocket size portable with Deco grill cutout, brown Bakelite or Plaskon, **$150;** red Plaskon, **$500**

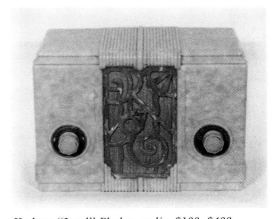

Kadette "Jewel" Plaskon radio, $100–$400.

Kadette 66, $45.

Kadette "Classic" radio, $750.

Kadette "Junior" Plaskon radio, $150–$500.

K10, K11, K12, K13, "Classic," large tabletops, 1936, designed by Sundberg and
Ferar, ivory body with blue, yellow,
green or rose trim, **$750**

K14, similar to model K10, brown body and
tan trim, **$400**

K15, similar to model K10, green body and
trim, **$900**

K16, similar to model K10, black body and
vermilion and ivory trim, **$1,250**

K21, "Modern Clockette," 1936, square 5-
tube walnut tabletop, large circular dial
in center resembles clock face, **$200**

K22, "Colonial Clockette," similar to model
K21, solid maple with hump top and ribs
down each side, **$200**

K23, "Sheraton Clockette," similar to model
K21, very squared-lines, mahogany
wood and gold dial, **$200**

K24, "Clockette," 1937, Crystlin plastic, yellow body and knobs, **$1,000**

K25, similar to model K24, green body and
trim, **$1,300**

K26, similar to model K24, blue body and
trim, **$3,000**

K27, similar to model K24, red body and
knobs, **$4,000**

K28, similar to model K24, swirled blue body
and knobs, **$3,000**

K-150, 1938, small Deco brown Bakelite tabletop, cameos of cadet at left and right,
$75

K-151, white Plaskon version of model K-
150, **$175**

Kadette L25 "Topper," $300.

THE KADETTE Clockette

PATENTS
APPLIED
FOR

The Modern

The Colonial

The Sheraton

THE RADIO IDEA OF THE HOUR!

The "Modern" Model 21—fashioned of rich figured and straight grained walnut contrasted in modern styling. Polished golden dial and ebony finished cradle.

The "Colonial" Model 22—Exemplifies the period in combining solid maple top and sides with quartered, matched figured maple front and brushed gold dial.

The "Sheraton" Model 23—cased in matched grain polished mahogany veneer with golden dial in harmonious contrast.

$19⁹⁵

COMPLETE WITH TUBES
AND ANTENNA

5-TUBES *in only half the space!*

Count on Kadette to come through with "timely" ideas! Conventional radios abound—but, as usual, Kadette steps out and does it different!

At the New York Show, the new Kadette Clockette stopped them. Yes Sir! No bigger than a small sized clock yet containing a powerful 5 *tube* chassis.

Clever designing is what did the trick. See how the tuning dial and grille are combined. A striking, new idea —lending to radio the charm and character of rare period clock designs —greater ease of tuning—large, full Dynamic Speaker with 100 per cent

operating freedom—and an uncrowded 5 tube chassis.

Three exquisitely beautiful "period" models. Dial rim of metal—handsomely finished in black and gold. Operates on AC or DC. Tunes 1600 to 540 kilocycles. Size 8" high— 7½" wide—5" deep.

Only Kadette dealers can cash in on this ingenious, fast selling idea. Here's the opportunity to give the public something different—something more beautiful—better performing—at a feature price.

Don't waste a minute—sell this radio idea of the hour!

INTERNATIONAL RADIO CORP., 514 William St, **ANN ARBOR, MICH.**

Creators of Quality Compacts

Kadette Clockette Series radios.

L25, "Topper," 1941, unusual Deco table-top, protruding speaker baffle on top, elongated dial on top edge, brown, white or brown and white, **$300**

Kellogg Switchboard and Supply Co.

502, 512, "Symphony," wide wooden table-tops with 3 tubes visible through front panel, 1923, **$225**

520, wide metal tabletop with removable lid, 1928, **$100**

Wavemaster, large tabletop with 4 knobs across front panel, circa 1925, **$75**

RFL, wide wooden tabletop with 2 knobs beside front dial, **$75**

Kennedy

60, 6-tube wooden radio, 1929, 3 small knobs on front, lid lifts, **$100**

110, "Universal Receiver," 1921, 1 tube in wooden cabinet, controls and dials on front panel, **$950**

210, large console on four legs, front metal plate with dial and knobs, **$150**

220, small wooden set with 1 tube and 4 coils inside, Bakelite control panel on front, **$700**

281, wooden tabletop with 1 tube, 3 large and several small dials on front panel, 1921, **$550**

521, 2-tube amplifier with Bakelite front panel, 1921, **$350**

525, 2-tube amplifier in tall wooden box with controls on front panel, **$400**

V, tabletop with sloping front panel, 1923, 3 protruding tubes, **$325**

VI, similar to model *V,* 4 protruding tubes, **$375**

X, large tabletop, 1923, similar to model *V,* storage area and built-in speaker, **$400**

XV, wide tabletop with sloping front panel, 1924, 5 protruding tubes, **$375**

King

30, 1925, large tabletop with 3 large dials on sloping front panel, **$75**

30-S, similar to model *30,* built-in speaker at right, **$85**

61, 6-tube tabletop with 3 large dials on front, **$75**

62, 6-tube wide tabletop with 3 knobs and dial on front, **$75**

71, 1926, wooden tabletop, large metal plate with two knobs and dial on front, **$75**

FF, wide metal cabinet with 3 knobs and dial on front, lid removes to expose 6 tubes, **$50**

Kitchenair

Kitchen Radio, 1940s, painted-metal radio with 1 glass and 1 metal shelf on each side, **$55**

Kodel

C-11, tall 1-tube radio, 1924, **$200**

C-12, larger 2-tube version of model *C-11,* **$225**

C-13, large 3-tube version of model *C-11,* **$250**

Logodyne, wide wooden tabletop, 1925, 3 large dials on front panel, **$75**

P-11, 1-tube portable, 1924, handle on top, front drops to expose controls, **$225**

P-12, 2-tube set similar to model *P-11,* **$250**

S-1, crystal set with knobs and crystal on front, sloping Bakelite panel, 1924, **$150**

Kolster (Federal Telegraph Co.)

6, "Model Six," wide wooden tabletop with dial and controls on front Bakelite panel, **$75**

6-D, 6-tube wooden tabletop with 3 small knobs and dial on front, 1926, **$75**

K-20, wooden tabletop with 3 knobs and carving on front, 1928, **$75**

Lafayette

1N420, battery- or AC-operated two-tone plastic portable, circa 1950, **$15**

1N422, similar to model *1N420*, AM and shortwave bands, **$15**

1N425, cloth-covered, battery-operated portable radio, early 1950s, **$15**

1N426, small Bakelite table radio with rounded corners, early 1950s, **$25**

1N540, square Bakelite AM tabletop, 1950, **$15**

1N819, square Bakelite AM-FM tabletop, 1950, **$15**

1N1207, 1N1209, 12-tube, AM-FM square consoles, early 1950s, double doors open to expose radio and pullout phono, **$50**

1N1210, 1N1211, similar to model *1N1207*, "Modern" blonde cabinets, **$75**

B-49, small 5-tube brown Bakelite tabletop, 1939, small square dial and 2 knobs at right, **$40**

B-50, similar to model *B-49*, white, **$45**

B86, Deco console, 1939, 11 tubes, 3-band rectangular dial, 3 knobs and push buttons, **$55**

B-101, Deco console with 9 tubes, 5 bands, push-button tuning with tuning eye, early 1940s, **$75**

B-102, similar to model *B-101*, Deco cabinet, lid lifts to expose radio and phono, **$125**

BB-22, brown Bakelite tabletop, 1940, 3 wrap around grill bars at left, tall foil dial and 2 knobs at right, **$65**

BB-23, similar to model *BB-22*, white, **$65**

BE-78, white Deco Bakelite tabletop, 1940, large rounded left side and grill, push-button tuning, **$75**

BE-79, similar to model *BE-78*, brown Bakelite, **$75**

C-1, battery-operated version of model *C-29*, **$35**

C-13, similar to model *C-29*, lid conceals phono, **$35**

C-16, 5-tube 2-band wooden tabletop, 1939, square dial and 3 knobs at right, **$30**

C-17, 8-tube version of model *C-13*, **$35**

C-19, similar to model *C-16*, tuning eye over dial, **$35**

C-20, 9-tube push-button console version of model *C-21*, **$45**

C-21, wooden tabletop with 6 tubes, 3 bands, tuning eye in dial, 1939, **$45**

C-29, 7-tube version of model *C-21*, **$45**

C-87, similar to model *C-16*, 6 tubes, large speaker cloth at left, **$30**

C-88, similar to model *C-87*, tuning eye over dial, **$35**

C-116, C-125, leather-covered 7-tube 3-band portables, early 1940s, **$25**

C-117, C-188, 7-tube 3-band wooden tabletops with tuning eye, **$65**

D-24, brown Bakelite tabletop, 1939, 2 knobs between left and right front grills, **$45**

D-25, similar to model *D-24*, white, **$45**

D-43, brown Bakelite push-button table radio, 1939, 2 knobs and vertical grill bars on front, **$50**

D-44, similar to model *D-43*, white, **$50**

D-56, similar to model *D-24*, longwave band, **$50**

D-57, similar to model *D-25*, longwave band, **$50**

D-58, unusually styled brown Bakelite tabletop, 1939, long horizontal dial with 2 push buttons and 1 knob on each side, **$65**

D-59, similar to model *D-58*, white, **$65**

D-60, battery-operated version of model *D-58*, **$55**

D-61, battery-operated version of model *D-59*, **$55**

D-72, brown Bakelite Deco tabletop with oval-shaped left side, 1940, **$65**

D-73, similar to model *D-72*, white, **$65**

D-76, AC-only version of model *D-72*, **$65**

D-77, AC-only version of model *D-73*, **$65**

D-131, square 4-tube Bakelite tabletop, white or brown, **$25**

D-133, early 1940s radio, top lifts to expose phono, **$15**

D-139, Deco Bakelite tabletop with rounded left side, early 1940s, 5 tubes, white or brown, **$75**

E-62A, Catalin radio with wrap around grill at left, 4 push buttons at top right, 1940, light green body, **$2,000**

E-63A, yellow body with tortoise trim, **$1,500**

E-191, leatherette-covered 4-tube radio, circa 1940, front opens to expose dial and controls, **$35**

FE-5, brown Bakelite tabletop with 5 push buttons below dial at right, 1940, **$50**

FE-6, similar to model *FE-5,* white, **$50**

FE-141, Bakelite Deco tabletop with rounded left side and push-button tuning, white or brown, **$100**

FE-143, 5-tube Deco tabletop, 1940, rounded left side, push-button tuning, white or brown, **$75**

FE-149, Deco console with 11 tubes, 5 bands, push-button tuning and tuning eye, early 1940s, **$100**

FE-153, similar to model *FE-149,* square Deco cabinet, lid lifts to expose radio and phono, **$125**

JA-7, wooden 6-tube tabletop, 1939, dial and 2 knobs at right, **$25**

JS-129, Deco console radio, cost $35 in 1940, 8 tubes, 3 bands with tuning eye, **$75**

JS-173, JS-183, wooden 8-tube tabletops with tuning eye, early 1940s, **$65**

JS-175, wooden tabletop, early 1940s, lid lifts to expose phono, **$75**

S-165, 5-tube square wooden tabletop, **$25**

Leutz

C, C-7, wide wooden tabletops, early 1920s, knobs across front panel with 2 meters at top of panel, **$1,000**

C-10, wide wooden tabletop with 2 large pointers and 2 meters on front panel, 1925, **$900**

Pliodyne-6, small wooden tabletop with 2 large and 2 small controls on front panel, **$100**

Super-8, similar to model *C-10,* **$750**

Super-10, similar to Super-8, 3 meters on front panel, 1928, **$650**

Super-Pliodyne 9, similar to model *C-7,* 1925, tabletop with Bakelite front panel, **$650**

Magnavox

A1, small wooden box, 1929, 1 tube and control on top, **$225**

AC2-C, similar to model *A1,* 2 tubes and controls on top, **$250**

Eton, wooden tabletop with large knob below dial window, 2 small knobs, **$100**

R3, 3-tube version of model *A1,* **$300**

TRF-5, wide wooden tabletop with large dial and 3 knobs on front, **$150**

TRF-50, similar to model *TRF-5,* built-in speaker below set, **$150**

Majestic

2C60, simple Deco console, 1940, 6 tubes, dial at top edge with push buttons and 2 knobs, **$35**

2C60P, similar to model *2C60,* center conceals pull-down phono, **$45**

3C90, unusually styled console, 1940, tall wooden ribs form grill, rectangular dial at top edge within ribbed shoulders, **$40**

5A410, 5A430, wooden tabletops, mid-1940s, small cutout dial at top edge, **$50**

5AK780, "Commander," square-lined chair side with radio at top, door opens to expose phono, **$15**

5C3, radio alarm clock, 1952, circular clock face in center with plastic louvers around clock, **$25**

5CAA, wooden tabletop, 1940, 6 tubes, 2 bands, speaker at rounded left side, **$25**

5T, square Bakelite tabletop, 1939, large clock face in center with concentric radio dial, black or white, **$150**

61, wide wooden tabletop, 1928, 7 tubes with dial and 3 knobs on front, **$65**

62, similar to model *61,* four legs, **$75**

Majestic 250 "Zephyr," $65.

Majestic 3C90, $40.

Majestic 5T, $150.

71, similar to model *61,* speaker below, 4 legs, **$100**

72, deluxe version of model *62,* front door exposes speaker over radio, 4 legs, **$85**

91, wooden console, 1929, 4 legs, radio over speaker, **$100**

92, similar to model *91,* double doors expose speaker over radio, **$125**

130, leatherette-covered portable, 1939, oversized dial and 2 knobs on front, **$50**

250, "Zephyr," Deco Bakelite tabletop, 1939, ribs across front and sides, dial at raised top edge, **$65**

511, square white Plaskon tabletop, 1938, contrasting circular grill and dial in center, **$300;** marbleized white body, **$400**

Charlie McCarthy, novelty brown Bakelite radio, figure of Charlie sits on left front, uncracked, **$1,000;** white-painted Bakelite, **$900**

Melody Cruiser, wooden novelty radio in shape of sailing ship, chrome masks, clean and complete, **$200**

Martian Manufacturing Co.

Martian Beauty, small set, 1924, tuning control on front, tube within coil visible at back, **$750**

Martian Big 4, crystal set, 1923, several inches high on miniature tripod, crystal and controls on top of large coil, **$275**

Martian Special, crystal set with large coil on board, lugs and crystal on sides, **$225**

T-3, wooden tabletop with 3 large knobs on front, lid lifts to expose 6 tubes, 1927, **$325**

Table Model, wide wooden tabletop with 7 tubes under lid, dial on front shows tuned frequency numbers in window, **$450**

Melco (See Jones/Melco)

Mir-Ray

"Rectangular Radio," large wooden tabletop with mirrors on both sides and front, stacked mirrors on top, silver with black mirrors, **$1,200;** blue mirrors, **$1,500**

"6-Sided Radio," off-white, 1936, wooden case with simple etched glass on front, oval dial with 3 knobs, peach or blue, **$1,000**

"8-Sided Radio," yellow-painted case with brown veins throughout, etched mirror front with dial and 2 knobs, blue or peach, **$1,500**

Motorola

3A5, plastic portable, 1941, lid lifts to expose grill and 2 large knobs, **$35**

5A series, "Playboy," plastic portable, lift-up front, mid- and late 1940s, **$50**

5C1, plastic clock radio, 1950, ribs separate dial and clock face, green, white or brown, **$25**

5H11, plastic tabletop, 1950, large circular dial and metal pointer with logo, **$25**

5J1, portable, 1950, lid lifts to expose contrasting Chinese-style grill, **$45**

5L1, "Music Box," plastic portable, 1950, 2 large circular controls on front, **$35**

5M1, "Playmate," portable, 1950, similar to model *5J1,* right-angle grill bars, **$45**

5X1, modern plastic tabletop, 1950, large circular dial, thick wire pointer and radio legs, black, white or brown, **$35**

5X2, similar to model *5X1,* shortwave band, **$35**

6L1, "Town and County," oversized plastic portable, circa 1950, **$15**

6X11, similar to model *5H11,* bent-wire dial, **$15**

7XM21, AM/FM tabletop, 1950, Bakelite set with large semicircular dial, green or brown, **$25**

8FM21, AM/FM console with unusual semicircular dial and pull-down phono behind door at bottom, 1950, blonde or mahogany, **$35**

9FM21, similar to model *8FM21,* doors open to expose dial and phono, **$50**

42B, "Escort Jr.," portable with oversized round volume and tuner under handle on top, 1952, **$15**

45P, "Pixie," portable coat-pocket style plastic radio with sub-miniature tubes, 1956, unbroken, **$75**

48L11, plastic portable with rounded sides, 2 large dials on front, handle on top, 1948, **$15**

50X1, typical Bakelite tabletop, 1941, rounded corners, square dial at right, **$15**

50XC1, "Circle Grill," Catalin tabletop with contrasting round grill, knobs and handle, 1940, red body, yellow trim, **$4,000**

50XC2, similar to model *50XC1,* turquoise body and yellow trim, **$5,000**

50XC3, similar to model *50XC1,* yellow body and cream trim, **$2,000**

50XC4, similar to model *50XC1,* brown body and turquoise trim, **$3,000**

51L1, "Music Box," 1951, plastic portable, green or maroon, **$25**

Motorola 5X1, $35.

Motorola 50XC1 "Circle Grill," $4,000.

51M1, "Playmate Jr.," portable with flip-up cover, 1951, maroon or green plastic, **$35**

51X15, "S-Grill," Catalin cabinet and knobs, 1940, radio front and handle in contrasting color, black body with red trim, **$5,000**

51X16, similar to model *51X15,* yellow body with green trim, **$3,000**

52, Catalin radio with inserted louvers and knobs in contrasting color, late 1930s, yellow body, tortoise trim, **$1,000;** maroon body or green body with yellow trim, **$1,400**

52B-2, "Escort," similar to model *42B,* green simulated alligator, **$15**

52B-3, similar to model *42B,* tooled leatherette, **$15**

52B-4, similar to model *42B,* grained tan leatherette, **$15**

52C, square-lined plastic tabletop with ribs between square clock and dial, 1952, yellow, white, brown or green, **$15**

52CW, "Pin-Up," plastic radio with large clock dial at top, radio controls on sides, 1952, designed to hang on wall, **$25**

52H, simple rectangular tabletop, 1952, large station numbers on clear plastic front, grey, green, white or brown, **$25**

52L, portable with handle, dials, and logo at top, grill on front, 1952, green, maroon, or grey, **$25**

52M, "Playmate Jr.," 1952, plastic lid lifts to expose large circular volume and tuner, **$35**

52R1, tabletop, 1952, large raised circle at left with logo, oversized tuning and volume knobs, red, **$35;** green, grey, maroon, white or brown, **$25**

52X, simple plastic tabletop, 1952, clear plastic knobs and top dial, white, maroon, or brown, **$15**

53H, large painted plastic tabletop, 1953, cylindrical protrusions for knobs on sides, pierced-metal grill, **$40**

53LC, large plastic portable with square clock face at left front, square dial at right, small and sub-miniature tubes, maroon, 1953, **$45;** grey or green, **$65**

55F11, wooden tabletop, mid-1940s, grill and elongated dial on front, lid lifts to expose phono, **$15**

55X11, 55X12, typical 1940s Bakelite tabletops, rounded edges, elongated dial near top edge, 2 knobs below, brown or white, **$35**

55X13, wooden tabletop, mid-1940s, rounded front corners, large grill cloth in center, **$25**

56X1, Bakelite tabletop, 1941, similar to model *50X1,* grill ribs wrap around left side, **$35**

56XAW, wooden tabletop, 1941, 5 tubes, square dial with 2 knobs and 4 push buttons at right, **$35**

Motorola 53LC, $45–$65.

Motorola 51X15 "S-Grill," $5,000.

Motorola 58F1, $45.

58F1, 58FRC, 5-tube wooden tabletop radio-phonos, 1941, wooden detailing around rectangular dial on front, phono under lid, **$45**

58L11, AC/DC battery version of model 48L11, **$15**

58R1, Bakelite tabletop, 1948, oversized dial and tuning knob at right, grill slots at left, brown, grey or white, **$15;** red, yellow or green, **$25**

62CW, square plastic clock radio, 1952, large square clock face with slot dial within face, mahogany-look, **$25**

62L, "De Luxe Town and Country," very square-lined portable, dial pops-up when pressed, grey, maroon or green, **$25**

62T1, wooden tabletop, 1941, rectangular dial with 3 bands, 4 knobs and push-button tuning, **$35**

62X, modern tabletop, 1952, large clear plastic dial across front top, green, white or brown, **$25**

63C, wide wooden clock radio with oversized oval clock face on front, knobs on sides, tan or brown, 1953, **$25**

63CW, similar to model 63C, square clock face, **$15**

63L, plastic portable with AM dial across front top edge, 1953, **$15**

63LS, similar to model 63L, shortwave band, **$30**

65T21, wooden tabletop, 1946, center grill cloth, elongated dial at right, **$15**

67F14, wooden upright radio-phono, 1948, pullout phono with built-in radio on top, **$15**

68F11, wooden radio-phono, 1948, tall elongated dial on front with phono under lid, **$15**

68L11, suitcase-style portable, 1948, dial within handle on top, unusual hard-finished case, square metal grill emblem, **$50**

69L11, 1949 version of model 68L11, plane with logo on metal grill over speaker cloth, **$90**

Motorola 62CW, $25.

Motorola 68L11, $50.

72XM, AM/FM plastic tabletop, 1952, numbers across top front, pointer over diamond-pattern grill, **$35**

77X, large Bakelite tabletop, grill extends around front and both sides, AM/FM dial at top, **$35**

78F11, radio-phono with pullout phono at front, radio on top of cabinet, 1948, **$25**

78F12, similar to model *78F11,* more traditional cabinet with lift-top phono on left, vertical radio dial at left, **$15**

78FM22, square console with AM/FM radio visible on right, door at left exposes phono, 1948, **$35**

79K21, square-lined console, 1949, large speaker cloth beneath unusual semicircular dial with oversized pointer, **$35**

83F1, wide walnut lowboy, 1941, 8-tube 3-band push-button radio, phono under lid, **$75**

85K21, Deco console, 1946, 8 tubes, 2 bands, long rectangular speaker cloth, **$35**

92-53, "Mantola," plastic tabletop, 1953, oversized circular dial and pointer on front, 2 knobs at bottom, brown, white or green, **$15**

103CK2, Deco console with clock and automatic-tuning radio dial, 10 tubes, 3 bands, 1941, **$250**

103K1, similar to model *103CK2,* no clock or auto-tuning, **$75**

Motorola 103CK2, $250.

107F31, traditional double door radio-phono, 1947, pullout phono at left, tilt-down AM/FM radio at right, **$15**

107F31B, blonde version of model *107F31,* **$15**

Mu-Rad Laboratories

MA-12, wide wooden tabletop, 1922, 2 large and 3 small dials on front, **$225**

MA-13, similar to model *MA-12,* 2 large and 3 small knobs, **$200**

MA-17, wide wooden tabletop with loop antenna on top, storage space below, complete, **$325**

MA-20, wide wooden tabletop, 1924, 3 large dials on front, radio only, **$85;** with original attached *MU-Rad* power converter, **$200**

Murdock

65, 75, wide wooden tabletops with large metal plate on front with 2 knobs, lid lifts, 1927, **$75**

CS32, CS33, wide wooden tabletops with 3 large dials across front, lid lifts to access components, 1924, **$175**

Neutrodyne, 5-tube wide wooden tabletop with 3 large dials across front, **$150;** built-in horn speaker on top, **$275**

Music Master

50, wooden tabletop, 4 protruding tubes and 2 large knobs on sloping front panel, **$175**

60, wide wooden tabletop with 3 large dials on Bakelite front panel, 1925, **$75**

100, wide tabletop with 3 large dials and 2 small knobs on inset, front sloping panel, **$75**

140, large wooden tabletop, Bakelite front panel with oversized dial in center of logo, lid lifts, **$125**

250, wide wooden tabletop with 3 small knobs and dial on Bakelite panel, circa 1926, **$75**

Neutrowound

C6, unusual wide wooden board with components and tubes covered by low contoured metal shield, mid-1920s, **$450**

Olympic

6-501, 6-502, Bakelite tabletops with sloping circular dial at right, 1946, white or brown, **$50**

6-504, wooden table set, 1946, radio controls on top right, lid lifts to expose phono on top left, **$15**

6-505, large Bakelite tabletop with elongated dial over grill slots, **$25**

6-506, wooden tabletop version of model *6-505,* **$30**

6-507, 5-tube wooden tabletop with dial on top edge, 1946, lid lifts to expose phono, **$15**

6-601, Bakelite tabletop, 1946, horizontal grill bars with elongated dial at top edge, **$50**

6-602, similar to model *6-506,* **$25**

6-606, cloth-covered portable, 1946, plastic grill and radio controls on front, handle on top, **$15**

6-617, wooden radio-phono, 1946, dial at top edge, lid lifts to expose phono, **$15**

7-532, rectangular Bakelite tabletop, 1947, long dial at front top edge, **$25**

8-451, 4-tube portable, 1948, lustrous polystyrene, lid lifts to expose radio, maroon, black or white, **$35**

450, plastic coat-pocket portable, 1955, fold-down handle, small circular dial at front right, **$35**

461, similar to model *450,* large dial at front right, **$35**

Ozarka

89, wide wooden tabletop, 1928, 2 tuning wheels and dial on front, **$700**

Junior, small wooden tabletop, 1925, 4 tubes protrude from sloping top, clean and complete, **$200**

Table Model, large wooden radio with 4 large dials across front panel, lid lifts to expose 4 tubes, 1924, **$150**

Paragon (See Adams-Morgan/Paragon)

Philco

15DX, large 11-tube console, 1932, grill with speaker cloth slopes upward, doors conceal controls, **$150**

37-630T, tabletop, 1937, 6 tubes, 3 bands with circular dial above tuning lever and 3 knobs, **$75**

37-630X, Deco console with 6 tubes and 3 bands, circular dial above tuning lever and 3 knobs, 1937, **$100**

37-640X, Deco console, 7 tubes, 3 bands, similar to model *37-630X,* **$100**

Philco 15DX, $150.

Philco 37-630T, $75.

37-650X, 8-tube version of model *37-630X,* **$100**

37-660X, 9-tube radio, similar to model *37-650X,* 6 ball feet on cabinet, **$100**

37-675X, 12-tube 5-band version of model *37-660X,* automatic tuning, **$150**

37-690X, 20-tube deluxe version of model *37-675X,* **$200**

46-200, Bakelite tabletop with rectangular grill at right, 1946, **$15**

46-250, Bakelite tabletop with rounded edges, ribs below dial form grill, 1946, white or brown, **$25**

46-350, cloth-covered portable with roll-up wooden front cover, 1946, **$15**

46-421, Bakelite tabletop with large oval speaker cloth and dial at top edge, 1946, brown or white, **$25**

46-1201, unusual sloping-front radio-phono, associated with Bing Crosby advertising, small door pulls down at front to allow insertion of record, **$45**

46-1213, traditional console, 1946, right door conceals vertical 3-band dial, left door drops down for phono, **$35**

47-1227, Deco console, 1947, large vertical grill bars cover phono, AM/FM, rectangular dial, **$35**

47-1230, AM/FM-shortwave version of model *47-1227,* **$35**

Philco 47-1230, $35.

48-300, 48-360, 1948 versions of model *46-350,* **$15**

48-475, wooden tabletop, 1948, 8 tubes, AM/FM, dial on large angled protrusion on top edge, **$25**

48-1201, 1948 version of model *46-1201,* **$50**

48-1260, console version of model *48-1201,* **$60**

48-1286, 11-tube AM/FM console, 1948, top door folds up to expose radio, center door conceals phono, bookcase on each side, **$35**

49-501, Bakelite tabletop, 1949, large area on left side shaped like boomerang, **$200**

49-503, "Transitone," small plastic tabletop with contrasting grill and circular dial, **$35**

49-603, unusual leather and Bakelite radio, 1949, opens in center, chassis concealed within brass screen, **$45**

Philco 46-350, $15.

Philco 49-501 "Boomerang," $200.

Philco 49-901, $65.

Philco 50-1727, $25.

49-901, unusual Bakelite tabletop, 1949, pierced-metal grill at left, drum on right pushed to turn on radio and spun to tune, white or green, **$65**

49-1401, wooden table radio with Bakelite top section and large area at left shaped like boomerang, **$50**

49-1606, wide console, 1949, AM/FM dial and 4 knobs, door below conceals phono, storage at each side, **$35**

50-527, clock radio, 1950, Bakelite case with circular clock face under tuning wheel, brown or white, **$15**

50-620, polystyrene portable, 1949, grill above AM dial on front, handle on top, green, brown or maroon, **$15**

50-1420, large flat Bakelite radio, 1950, lid at top left conceals phono, **$25**

50-1727, traditional AM/FM radio-phono, 1959, double doors over speaker cloth, **$25**

51-537, 1951 version of model *50-527,* **$15**

52-548, unusual plastic tabletop, 1952, large, protruding grill above long plastic dial, **$15**

84-T, simple cloth-covered portable, 1939, small dial, 2 knobs, **$15**

89C, simple portable with long strap, dial and knobs at top, rounded sides, 1940, **$30**

201XX, wide Deco console, 1939, dial and circular tuning knobs concealed under small panel, **$100**

217RX, similar to model *201XX,* push-button tuning and wireless remote control, complete, **$200**

Philco 49-1606, $35.

Philco 201XX, $100.

502, wooden tabletop, 1939, small dial in center front, lid lifts to expose phono, **$25**

511, wide metal tabletops, 1928, lid lifts to expose components, **$65;** hand-painted top and front panels, clean, **$175**

512, similar to model *511,* **$65**

842T, simple portable with plastic grill and square dial with 2 knobs on front, handle at top, leatherette-covered, 1941, **$15**

843T, 7-tube cloth-covered portable, 1941, drop-down front exposes square dial and 2 knobs, **$15**

844T, similar to model *843-T,* wooden roll-up front lid, **$15**

853T, AM/shortwave version of model *843T,* **$15**

854T, AM/shortwave version of model *844T,* 1941, **$15**

E-670, E-672, leatherette portable, 4 tubes, 1956, large grill on front with oversized dial at right, black or green, **$15**

E-675, deluxe version of model *E-670,* **$15**

E-676, similar to model *E-670,* large circular metal grill at center of front panel, **$25**

G-681, oversized portable with "Scan-tenna" handle, round dial at left with numbers above, **$25**

G-761, large plastic clock radio, 1958, square clock face sits above long dial, **$15**

G-963, plastic AM radio, 1958, 6 tubes, twin speakers, oversized dial in front near bottom, white or brown, **$15**

Philco E-676, $25.

Model G-761

Philco G-761, $15.

K-780, plastic tabletop clock radio, 1961, modern plastic dial at left, grill slots at right, **$15**

K-782, K-783, plastic clock radios with large clock face and dial at right, 1961, **$15**

K-785, flat AM radio, 1961, 2 large squares on top hold clock and speaker, **$15**

K-858, similar to model *K-785,* non-clock model, both squares hold speakers, **$15**

PT-48, square Bakelite tabletop, 1940, push buttons over square dial, **$25**

PT-87, 5-tube AC/DC version of model *842T,* **$15**

PT-88, 5-tube AC/DC version of model *843T,* **$15**

Pilot

Broadcast, 6-tube simple cathedral radio with semicircular dial, **$200**

Dragon, elaborate cathedral, similar to Broadcast, 8 tubes, **$250**

K108, wide wooden tabletop with large metal dial plate and controls on front panel, 1929, **$150**

Pilotone Universal, wide wooden tabletop with large dials on front, 1926, lid lifts to expose 5 tubes, **$175**

SG105, wooden tabletop, 1929, 2 metal dial plates and controls on front panel, **$150**

Super Wasp, 5-tube wooden radio, 1929, 2 metal dial plates and 4 knobs on front, 5 plug-in coils, **$175;** original wooden cabinet, **$275**

T-71, cloth-covered portable, 1940, front drops open to expose dial, **$15**

X-1451, 7-tube portable, 1940, large handle on top, large plastic grill on front with square cutout dial, **$15**

Porto

PB-520, "Baradio," large Bakelite tabletop with white handle and front grill, top holds glassware and liquor, complete, **$90**

Porto-Bar, similar to model *PB-520,* Bakelite panel where radio normally goes, complete, **$40**

Radak (See Clapp-Eastham)

Radiobar

107, simple Philco radio in Deco console, 1936, lid lifts to expose mirror and bar with glassware, **$550**

504, similar to model *107,* traditional console with 4 ball feet, complete, **$650**

507, similar to model *107,* Deco console with contrasting panels, complete, **$750**

510, deluxe version of model *504,* **$700**

515, similar to model *504,* double door above opens to expose bar, 4 doors below conceal controls, **$700**

RCA (Radio Corporation of America)

1R81, "Livingston," maroon plastic tabletop with large circular dial and pointer in front, **$15**

1X51, "Blaine," 1952, tabletop with semicircular dial, various colors, **$15**

1X591, "Gladwin," 1952, Bakelite tabletop with unusual grill louvers on front, elongated dial below, maroon or white, **$35**

2B400, "Super," 1952, thin portable, circular tuning dial takes up most of radio front, various colors, **$55**

2C521, 1952, square-lined plastic clock radio, **$15**

2US7, radio with long dial on front, 1952, square wooden lid lifts to expose phono, mahogany or blonde, **$15**

2X621, "Lindsay," 1952, Bakelite tabletop with grill across front and dial on top, maroon or white, **$25**

4X, 4X3, tall, 1936, Deco tabletops, 2 knobs on metal plates below speaker cloth, **$125**

4X4, similar to model *4X3,* white-painted finish, square edges, **$125**

6K10, 1936, Deco console, black-painted wood with circular speaker mesh and 2 grill bars, **$2,500**

6T10, 1936, tall Deco radio, circular speaker cloth with 1 grill bar running up over top, chrome tube forms stand, **$250**

6T86, 1950, buffet-style console, AM/FM radio plus phono for 45-, 33⅓-, and 78-RPM records, **$50**

8B41, 8B42, 1948, plastic portables, lid lifts to expose circular dial above long grill, black or brown, **$30**

8B43, similar to model *8B41,* red, **$50**

8BX5, 1948, large flat portable, alligator- or cloth-covered, round dial on front over grill, plastic sides, **$25**

8BX6, 1948, aluminum and Bakelite portable, dial behind lid at top edge, **$50**

RCA 4X3, $125.

RCA 8BX5, $25.

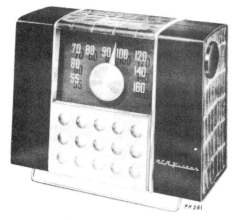

RCA 9BX56, $25.

8K11, similar to model 6K10, 8 tubes, **$3,000**

8T2, 1936, Deco walnut wooden tabletop, tuning eye over dial, **$75**

8T10, 8-tube version of model 6T10, **$350**

8T11, 1936, Deco black-painted wooden tabletop, square speaker mesh with 2 grill bars, chrome bar forms stand, **$1,500**

8V7, 1948, wide Deco wooden console, right lid conceals AM radio, left lid conceals phono, **$65**

8X521, 1948, maroon Bakelite tabletop, grill front, semicircular dial and pointer on top, **$35**

8X522, ivory version of model 8X521, **$35**

8X541, 8X542, 1949, wide Bakelite tabletops with circular dial in center front, knob on right side, various colors, **$25**

8X681, 1948, maroon plastic tabletop with large AM/shortwave dial around grill holes, protruding tuning wheels below, **$35**

8X682, similar to model 8X681, ivory, **$35**

9BX56, 1949, plastic portable, alligatored trim, front exposes large dial and pointer, **$25**

9K, 9K2, large Deco consoles with T-shaped dial, tuning eye and 5 knobs, **$150**

9K10, similar to model 9K, chrome strips form grill bars and connect to tubular chrome stand, **$3,000**

RCA 9K, $150.

9TX21, 9TX22, 1939, small Bakelite tabletops with cut-out grill at left, dial and 2 knobs at right, white or brown, **$15**

9TX23, Deco wooden version of model 9TX21, applied wooden sides, contrasting wooden panels, **$65**

9TX50, square version of model *9TX23,* right-of-center dial with grill slots on each side, **$25**

9U2, 1936, Deco console, nearly 3-feet high and 4-feet wide, 5-band 9-tube set, lid lifts to expose radio and phono, **$200**

9X571, 1949, square maroon Bakelite tabletop, concentric plastic cones on front, **$50**

9X572, similar to model *9X571,* ivory, **$50**

9Y51, 1949, Bakelite tabletop with dial at top edge, lid lifts to expose 45-RPM phono, **$45**

10K, wooden Deco console with 10 tubes, tuning eye, 5 knobs below, **$150**

10K11, 10-tube version of model *9K10,* **$4,000**

10T, 1936, 10-tube 5-band Deco walnut tabletop, 5 knobs below T-shaped dial, **$100**

10T11, black-painted version of model *10T,* chrome bar forms stand, metal mesh speaker grill, **$2,500**

45W9, 1950, AM/FM radio with large veneered doors, pullout 45-RMP phono, **$75**

54B, 1947, "Personal" portable radio, front door opens to expose chrome panel, grill and dial, **$45**

54B5, "Solitaire," 1947, deluxe portable, Catalin panel behind dial, gold plating on trim, **$75**

56X, 1945, typical Bakelite tabletop with dial at top edge and 3 knobs at bottom, **$25**

65AU, 1946, wooden tabletop, long radio dial over grill, 2 knobs, rounded lid lifts to expose phono, **$15**

65BR9, "Escort," circa 1947, large suitcase-style portable, round dial in center of cloth covering, rechargeable battery, **$35**

65U, similar to model *65AU,* **$15**

65U-1, similar to model *65AU,* sloping top, **$15**

66BX, 1947, rounded portable, plastic sides with large aluminum front and back, **$50**

66X1, 66X2, wide Bakelite tabletops, large area at top edge with dial, 3 knobs below speaker cloth, brown or white, **$15**

66X3, wooden tabletop with curved dial at top edge, large striped speaker cloth and 3 knobs below, **$15**

RCA 65AU, $15.

RCA 9X571, $50.

RCA 66BX, $50.

66X7, 66X9, 1946, wide black Catalin table-tops, curved dial at top edge, grill slots and 3 knobs below, **$300**

66X8, similar to model *66X7,* red Catalin body, **$500**

66X11, 66X12, wide tabletops, 1946, concentric squares for grill, brown or white, **$35**

66X13, wooden tabletop similar to model *66X3,* grill in front of speaker cloth, **$15**

75X11, 75X16, square Bakelite tabletops, vertical grill at left, dial behind clear panel at right, various colors, **$25**

75X17, 75X18, 75X19, similar to model *75X11,* hand-painted scene on cabinet and within dial, **$125**

91-B, 1934, metal portable with Deco grill, 3 tubes, silver finish with blue top, **$65**

96T4, 96T5, 1939, Deco wooden radios with electric 2-band tuning, 2 wooden bars across grill, push buttons, **$75**

96T6, simple version of model *96T4,* exposed grill cloth, **$25**

96X1, 96X2, 1939, Deco Bakelite tabletops, rounded left side, platform top, black, brown or white, **$125**

96X11, 96X12, similar to model *96X1,* push-button tuning, **$145**

102, 4-tube version of model *91-B,* **$75**

103, 1935, tall wooden tabletop, 3 knobs below circular dial, **$65**

119, wider 5-tube version of model *103,* **$65**

128, 1935, tall wooden 3-band 6-tube radio, curved top with shoulders, **$150**

143, elaborate version of model *128,* **$200**

221, 1934, 6-tube 2-band console, 4 short legs with tall grill below circular dial and 4 knobs, **$75**

224, 3-band 6-legged version of model *221,* **$75**

242, 1935, 8-tube Deco console, 6 legs, circular dial with 4 bands, **$150**

Aeriola Jr. (usually marked "Westing-house"), 1921, small wooden box, lid lifts to expose crystal, dial and instructions, **$275**

Aeriola, Sr., similar to *Aeriola, Jr.,* lid lifts to expose controls, 1 tube, **$175**

B411, 1952, thin portable with large circular dial on front, metal mesh grill below, **$35**

BX-6, 1950, portable, similar to model *66BX,* plastic on both sides and bottom, **$35**

BX-55, BX-57, "Reveler," 1951, plastic portables, dial at front top edge, alligatored trim, **$35**

C15-4, 1936, large Deco console with 8 tubes, 3 bands on oval-shaped dial, 5 knobs below, **$250**

D11-2, 1935, large Deco console with 11 tubes, 3 bands, lid conceals phono, **$200**

PX600, "Globe Trotter," 1952, plastic portable with handle on top, series of round holes on grill, **$25**

RA + DA, circa 1921, 2 small wooden boxes with 3 tubes, dials on front Bakelite panel, **$325**

Radiola II, 1923, portable wooden box, lid lifts to expose controls, leather handle on top, 2 inside tubes, **$225**; with *Balanced Amplifier,* 2 tubes protruding from similar box, complete setup, **$225**

Radiola III, 1924, wooden tabletop, 2 tubes protruding from Bakelite top panel, complete, **$75**

Radiola IIIA, 1924, wooden set, 4 tubes protruding from Bakelite top panel, complete, **$125**

Radiola 16, 1927, long wooden radio, dials on front panel, lid lifts, **$75**; with tabletop *Loudspeaker 103,* floral-embossed cloth on pressed wood octagonal speaker, complete, unripped, **$225**

Radiola 18, similar to *Radiola 16,* AC circuitry, **$75**; with *Loudspeaker 106,* large unit with cloth sides and 4 wooden legs, cloth unripped and complete, **$200**

Radiola 30, 1925, large console on 4 legs, door opens to pull out sloping front radio, **$350**

Radiola 60, long wooden radio with dial, 2 knobs and switch on front, lid lifts to expose tubes, **$125**

RCA Radiola 16, $75.

Radiola Grand, 1923, large tabletop, lid lifts to expose controls, **$600**

Radiola RS, 1923, wooden box, lid lifts to expose 2 tubes protruding from Bakelite control panel, **$275**

RC, RA and *DA* panels on single wooden box, complete, **$225**

T4-8, 1935, 4-tube simple cathedral tabletop, **$65**

T6-9, 1935, tombstone with simple arc-shaped dial and 4 knobs, **$65**

T9-7, T9-8, 1936, tombstones, arc-shaped dial and tuning eye, 3 bands, 9 tubes, **$150**

X551, 1950, Bakelite AM tabletop with large round dial and concentric speaker grill bars, maroon, **$35**

X552, similar to model *X551,* white, **$35**

Radio Shop (Echophone)

3, 1924, wooden tabletop, 3 tubes protruding from sloping front panel, **$250**

4, similar to model *3,* 4 protruding tubes, **$275**

5, large wooden tabletop, meter and controls on front Bakelite panel, lid lifts, **$200**

A, 1923, large wooden tabletop with 5 knobs on front, lid lifts to expose components, **$250**

J, "Junior," similar to model *A,* 3 knobs on panel, **$225**

Remler

40, 1936, small tabletop with dog logo in center of dial, black or white Bakelite, **$200**

Remler MP-5 tabletop, $150.

5500, "Scottie Pup," 1947, small Bakelite tabletop with vertical louvers in center, dog logo at top, **$200**

MP-5, small tabletop with logo of dog and handle on top, white or black, **$150**

Scottie Convertible, 1947, very small Bakelite radio, lid lifts to expose phono, **$200**

Scottie Mirror, empty mirrored cabinet with detailed grill and dog logo, complete with typical chassis, **$1,750**

Scottie Portable, 1948, "30th Anniversary," Bakelite face and handle colors match, brown leatherette case, **$150**

Sengbusch Self Closing Ink Stand Co.

Radio Desk Set, various colors of Plaskon or Bakelite, 1936, desk lamp with radio dials in center, clock on left, pen set to right, **$175**

Sentinel

195, small Catalin tabletop with tortoise-colored grill and knobs, push buttons on top, yellow or green, **$2,000**

228-P, 1941, 2-band cloth-covered portable, receives aircraft and beam signals plus AM, **$35**

247-P, 1941, tall swirled-plastic portable, front door opens to expose controls and speaker grill, **$35**

248, 1940, Catalin tabletop, grill wraps around left side, grooves run up and over top, yellow body, **$1,000**; red body, **$1,500**

249, 1941, 6-tube Bakelite tabletop, grill wraps around left side, white or brown, **$25**

262-P, 1941, portable, suitcase-style with leatherette covering, top front edge opens to expose radio controls, **$15**

284, 1946, Catalin tabletop with rounded corners, large grill area, and elongated dial and knobs at top edge, yellow or brown, **$750**; wavy grill, red body, **$1,500**; wavy grill, blue body, **$5,000**; outline grill, speaker cloth and applied grill ring, yellow body, **$1,000**; outline grill, red body, **$1,500**; outline grill, blue body, **$4,000**

293, 1946, Bakelite tabletop, center ribs form grill, white or brown, **$25**

294, mid-1940s, wooden tabletop with rounded sides and top, AM/shortwave bands, **$35**

312-P, 1950, lightweight plastic portable with dial at top edge, large gold-tone grill at front, green or brown, **$25**

314, 1949, rounded Bakelite case with wrap around ribbed grill below, dial at top edge, brown or white, **$45**

316, 1949, rounded plastic portable, handle on top, brown, red, white or green, **$15**

Sentinel 284 "Wavey Grill" Catalin radio, $750–$5,000.

Sentinel 314, $45.

331, 1949, Bakelite tabletop with large oval cutout on front, grill cloth at left, dial at right, **$45**

332, 1949, Bakelite tabletop, large grill cloth in front with dial at top edge, brown or white, **$35**

335-P, 1950, 4-tube plastic portable, white, brown, green or maroon, **$25**

338, 1950, plastic tabletop, 5 tubes with large pointer and dial at right, brown or white, **$15**

Setchell-Carlson

570, bed-side cylinder-shaped plastic radio, circa 1950, handle and dial across top, speaker detaches to fit under pillow, black, brown or white, **$45**; yellow or blue, **$75**

Silvertone (Sears, Roebuck and Co.)

3001, 3002, small rectangular tabletops with tuning wheel over large v-shaped speaker cloth with logo and knob, **$30**

4505, Deco Bakelite tabletop with wrap around grill and cloth at left, large tuner and small knob at right, black or uncracked white, **$100**

6109, large brown cylinder-shaped radio, large knob on one end, snap-off back at other end, unusual design, uncracked, **$750**

Silvertone 3001, $30.

Sleeper

70, 71, wide wooden radios, 1928, large metal dial plate on front panel, tabletop or console, **$75**

Scout 57, long wooden radio with 2 large dials on front center panel, 1925, **$75**

Scout Console, similar to *Scout 57,* four legs, **$75**

Sonora

KB-73, 1940, cloth-covered portable, round dial and 3 knobs across front, **$15**

KBU-168, 1941 version of model *KB-73,* radio behind front panel, **$15**

KD-75, similar to model *KB-73,* lid lifts to expose dial and knobs, **$15**

KE-151, similar to model *LCU-154,* no recording feature, **$15**

KF, 1941, small rounded plastic tabletop, two-tone colors, **$60**

KG-132, "Brownie," 1941, brown plastic portable, 4 tubes, front speaker, 2 knobs on left, handle on top, **$45**

KM, "Coronet," 1941, rounded-corner yellow Catalin radio with handle on top, green or maroon trim, **$1,500**

KNF-148, 1941, wooden tabletop, lid lifts to expose phono, **$25**

KT, "Cameo," rectangular Bakelite tabletop, brown or white, **$15**

KXF-95, circa 1941, massive 6-tube radio-phono, lid lifts to expose 10-tube push-button multiband radio and phono, **$75**

KW-152, similar to model *KE-151,* radio exposed on front, **$15**

LCU-154, 1941, leatherette-covered table-top, radio behind front door, recording phono under lid, **$35**

LD-93, 1941, wooden tabletop, lip at left edge, grill bars, 3 knobs under dial, **$25**

LP-161, 1941, molded-plastic portable, two-tone grey, front opens to expose small dial at right, 2 knobs, grill slots, **$30**

LP-162, "Jewel Box," flat wooden set, lid lifts to expose radio similar to model *LP-161,* **$35**

LP-163, tan leather version of model *LP-161,* **$15**

LR-147, 1941, brown portable with large grill and 3 knobs on front, elongated dial beneath, **$15**

RBU-175, Bakelite tabletop, typical 1947 style, elongated dial across front edge, 2 knobs at bottom front, brown, **$25**

RBU-176, similar to model *RBU-175,* white, **$25**

RDU-209, 1947, wooden tabletop, curved top, dial across front edge, **$25**

RMR-219, 1947, console, lid lifts to expose radio-phono, slightly curved lines, **$45**

RMR-245, similar to radio-phono model *RMR-219,* Deco lines and veneered panels, **$45**

RWF-78, similar to model *WGFU-242,* phono only, **$35**

RWF-238, similar to model *WGFU-241,* phono only, **$35**

RZU-222, 1947, sloping white Bakelite table-top, Deco lines, 3 knobs across bottom, elongated dial across front edge, **$35**

RZU-248, similar to model *RZU-222,* brown, **$35**

TW-49, 1940, unusually-styled Bakelite table-top with knob and push buttons on front, large tuner dial at top, **$75**

WAU-243, 1947 version of model *TW-49,* white or brown, **$75;** marbleized white, **$250**

WCU-246, 1947, plastic bed lamp, built-in radio with knobs on sides, **$50**

So New, So Different

and *Clear as a Bell*

THE NEW "NIGHTINGALE" BED LAMP-RADIO . . .

Smartest bedtime story ever told! A bed reading light that's kind on the eyes. A "Clear as a Bell" radio for bedtime entertainment. Styled like a dream in gleaming plastic. Compact, fits any bed. Packed with appeal for all of America—this SONORA "First" sells itself on your sales floor. You'll find SONORA'S "Fun in Bed" model a sure-fire seller!

Model WCU-246.
Ivory Plastic **$29.95**

MODEL RDU-209. Smartest table model on the market. Fashioned in rich walnut veneers. Powerful AC-DC Superhet **$39.95**

MODEL RBU-175. Features the modern plastic vogue everyone wants. AC-DC Superhet. Mahogany **$23.95**
Model RBU-176. Ivory. **$25.95**

Radio Originals

Look to SONORA for the *new* and *different!* Look to SONORA for sales-stimulating models that spark new business for you in every season of the year. Here's the kind of *original* merchandise that means steady good business for you!

MODEL RZU-248. A peerless plastic model of rare appeal. Powerful, sensitive Superhet. Mahogany **$32.95**
Model RZU-222. Ivory **$34.95**

THE SPARKLING NEW "GEMS"

Infinitely smart, refreshingly new—here are the most delightful of all small radios! Jewel-like in their perfection, the "Gems" are the perfect "extra" radio—yet they're truly good enough to serve as the "main" set in the home. For sheer radio cheer and charm in any room, there's nothing like the "Gems!" Available in three lovely colors to meet all the tastes of your trade.
Model WJU-253. Mahogany **$17.95**
Model WJU-252. Ivory **$18.95**
Model WJU-251. Buff-Burgundy Combination **$19.95**

MODEL WGFU-242. The popular "Serenade"—America's most distinctive table Radio-Phono. In Mahogany **$39.95**
Model WGFU-241. Ivory **$42.50**

THE "TOP-TUNER"

Here's a fast-selling SONORA original with irresistible eye appeal. Unique in its tasteful styling, rich with "Clear as a Bell" tone—*plus* push-button tuning! Sensibly priced to sell. Here's a model that's *new* and *different*—a table model sales-activator if there ever was one!
Model WAU-243. Ivory **$29.75**

(*Prices slightly higher in the Far South and West of the Rockies.*)

MODEL RWF-7B. The perfect Electric Phonograph—the best-seller in its field. "Clear as a Bell." Mahogany . . **$24.95**
Model RWF-238. Ivory **$26.95**

HOME RADIO ENTERTAINMENT AT ITS BEST
SONORA RADIO & TELEVISION CORP. • 325 NO. HOYNE AVE., CHICAGO 12, ILLINOIS

Sonora's 1947 line of radios.

WEU-240, 1947, Deco AM/FM tabletop, large square openings for speaker and dial, white Bakelite, **$65**

WEU-262, similar to model *WEU-240,* brown, **$50**

WGFU-241, circa 1947, Deco white Bakelite tabletop, radio controls at front, exposed phono at top, **$65**

WGFU-242, similar to model *WGFU-241,* brown Bakelite, **$65**

WJU-251, 1947, streamlined plastic portable with 2 large knobs on top, burgundy and cream, **$65**

WJU-252, WJU-253, brown or white versions of model *WJU-251,* **$45**

WLRU-219, WLRU-220, AM/FM versions of model *RMR-219,* **$45**

WLRU-245, similar to model *RMR-245,* AM/FM radio, **$45**

Sparton

5-AW-06, mid-1940s, small Bakelite tabletop with wrap around ribs, dial at top edge, **$25**

7-AM-46, 1946, Deco console, simple lines with multiband dial at top, **$25**

8-AM-46, similar to model *7-AM-46,* tuning eye, **$35**

7-BM-46, 1947, traditional-styled radio-phono, double doors at top front, **$25**

10-AM-76, 1947, console with unusual "Modern" styling, large wooden ribs across front center, doors at top open to expose radio-phono, **$200**

10-BM-76, 1947, console with elaborate veneer panels, double doors open to expose radio and phono, **$50**

100, 1947, Bakelite tabletop, elongated dial at top edge, black or white, **$25**

121, 1948, square wooden tabletop, AM/FM with large metal mesh grill above long dial and 4 knobs, **$25**

130, 1950, polystyrene tabletop, oval-shaped front with speaker cloth between large dials at right and left, **$35**

141X, 142X, 1948, wooden tabletops, simple style with large speaker cloth over AM/FM dial and 4 knobs, **$15**

201, 1947, wooden tabletop radio-phono, dial at top edge, phono under lid, **$15**

230, 232, 239, 1952 redesigns of model *130,* contrasting ring around front, black, maroon or ivory, **$35**

241, 1953, square wooden tabletop, 4 knobs below AM/FM dial, **$25**

242, similar to model *241,* blonde finish, **$25**

311, 312, 315, 319, 1953, variations of model *130,* 3 metal bars in center of speaker cloth, beige, maroon, green or ivory, **$35**

350, 351, 1953, rectangular 6-tube wooden tabletops with speaker cloth, dial at right and 2 knobs at bottom left, **$15**

409, "Seven-Sided," 1938, blue-mirrored radio, mirror insert over speaker, screened numbers on radio dial, **$1,500**

500, small yellow radio, Catalin body and knobs, blue cloisonne and chrome front, **$2,000;** red, yellow or green cloisonne front, **$3,000;** green Catalin body and brown cloisonne front, **$3,500**

506, "Blue-Bird," 1936, tabletop, circular blue-mirrored radio designed by Walter Dorwin Teague, chrome circles and knobs, **$2,000;** with original plateau mirror, circular blue mirror which sits under the radio for dramatic effect, **$2,250**

509, Canadian "Blue-Bird," large 6-sided wooden case behind blue mirror, 3 wooden knobs, bluebird on dial, **$2,000**

517, 1937, black- or white-painted wooden tabletop, 3 chrome strips over top, round dial with 3 knobs below, **$150**

537, walnut version of model *517,* no chrome over top, **$75**

557, "Three Knob," 1936, wide wooden tabletop with blue-mirrored panels on front and top, chrome trim, black-painted wooden case, **$1,750;** rose mirror and copper trim, brown-painted wooden case, **$3,000**

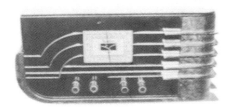

Sparton 558 "Four Knob," $2,500.

558, "Four Knob," similar to model *557*, elaborate front and top mirrors, blue with chrome trim, **$2,500;** rose mirror with copper trim, **$4,000**

1005, 1947, square-lined console with AM/FM, double doors at top open to expose radio and phono, double doors at bottom conceal storage area, **$35**

1007, 1947, square-lined console radio, double doors at top open to expose radio and rollout phono, **$25**

1037, 1948, square-lined radio phono with pull-down radio at right and pullout phono at left, **$15**

1039, similar to model *1037*, **$15**

1059, 1948, radio-phono with exposed radio at left, pull-down phono below, **$15**

1186, "Nocturne," circa 1936, 42″ blue-mirrored circle with chrome trim, knobs and legs, by Teague, **$12,500;** rose mirror and copper trim, **$17,500**

1300, 1953, very square-lined double-door console, left door opens to expose stor-

Sparton 1186 "Nocturne," $12,500–$17,500.

age space, right door conceals pullout phono and simple 6-tube radio, **$25**

1301, similar to model *1300,* blonde, **$25**

Splitdorf

Abbey, unusual large tabletop, 1928, control and dial on front, 6-sided lid lifts to expose metal-covered insides, **$100**

Polonaise, wide wooden 5-tube radio, 1925, 3 large and 2 small dials on front, **$75**

RV-590, wooden tabletop, 1926, similar to *Polonaise,* **$65**

RV-695, wooden tabletop with 2 large dials and 2 small knobs on front, **$65**

Stewart Warner

01-6E7, 1939, simple console, rectangular dial at front edge with multiband tuning, 6 push buttons and 4 knobs below, **$35**

01-9A7, 1940, 9-tube Deco console, push buttons below elongated dial, **$50**

07-5R3, 1940, Deco Bakelite tabletop, with rounded left side and wrap around grill, rectangular dial at right, **$60**

07-511, Deco tabletop, similar to model *07-5R3,* oversized plastic pointer at right with small knob below, **$75**

07-513, similar to model *07-511,* decals from Gulliver's Travels movie on top and right side, **$400**

07-513Q, Deco Bakelite tabletop, similar to model *07-511,* Dionne quintuplets names on front, decal of girls on top, **$500**

07-583Q, 1941, Deco Bakelite tabletop with rounded left side, vertical tuning at right, Dionne quintuplets decals, **$500**

6T8, 1940, square cloth-covered radio-phono, front drops down to expose radio controls, lid lifts to expose phono, **$15**

61T16, 61T26, 1946, Bakelite tabletops with rounded corners, large grill cloth, **$25**

62T16, 1946, wooden tabletop, wrap around grill cloth on left, push-button tuning, **$35**

Stewart-Warner 07-583Q "Dionne Quints," $500.

Stewart-Warner A51 "Air Pal," $75.

91-513, 1940, Deco tabletop with triangular-shaped body, dial, push buttons and knobs tilted upward, **$150**

325, wide wooden tabletop with dials on front, lid lifts to expose 5 tubes, **$65;** speaker model *415,* brass women on front, pot metal center, clean and complete, **$210**

365, similar to model *325,* **$65**

525, 1927, wide wooden tabletop, 3 knobs and dial on front, **$65**

705, similar to model *525,* larger cabinet, **$65**

801, 1928, metal AC tabletop, 2 dials and 2 knobs on front, removable lid, **$75**

1365, 1935, deluxe 7-tube Deco console, large round dial above 4 knobs, **$75**

1421, 1936, 5-tube Deco tabletop, circular dial and 2 knobs below elaborate grill, **$55**

1425, 1936, Deco console version of model *1421,* **$85**

9153-A, "Turnabout," 1950, green Bakelite tabletop with gold-tone trim, built-in handle allows set to become portable, **$45**

9160, 1952, small plastic tabletop with celluloid pointer, brown, white, grey, green, blue or red, **$35**

9161-C, 1952, plastic tabletop with rounded edges, large semicircular dial across front, yellow and black, white and red, or brown, **$35**

9162, 1952, clock radio with rounded sides, concentric clock face and dial at left, various colors, **$35**

9165, 1952, simple tabletop, perforated plastic front with dial and oversized pointer at right, red and tan or black and yellow, **$15**

9166-A, 1952, tabletop AM/FM radio with oversized circular dial, **$25**

9170, "Gadabout," portable, folding handle on top near dial and controls, **$35**

A6-1Q, similar to model *A51,* Dionne quintuplets decals on both ends, **$600**

A51, "Air Pal," 1947, rounded thin tabletop, 2 knobs and dial at top, molded grill bars at front, black, brown or white, **$75**

A61

"New Minstrel," 1947, large walnut console with tilted dial at top front, pullout phono below, speaker at bottom, **$25**

"Allegro," dark mahogany, **$25**

B51, 1949 version of model *A51,* grill cloth and metal x in front of speaker, **$40**

B92CR1LP, "Mt. Vernon," 1948, traditional square-lined console, AM/FM radio and phono behind doors at top, **$15**

B92CR3LP, "Manhattan," 1948, console with pullout phono at top left, exposed tilted-dial radio at top right, **$15**

Stromberg-Carlson

41, 6-legged console, lid lifts to expose automatic phono, **$300**

58-T, 1936, wooden tombstone, multiband octagonal dial, **$45**

61-H, 1935, wide wooden tabletop, octagonal dial above 3 knobs and lever, **$55**

YOU HAVE **SEVEN** HIGH FIDELITY
Stromberg-Carlsons
TO CHOOSE FROM

NO. 63
HIGH FIDELITY

NO. 62 HIGH FIDELITY

NO. 84 HIGH FIDELITY *

There is no danger of losing those profitable High Fidelity sales if you are a Stromberg-Carlson dealer. For this great line includes SEVEN High Fidelity models,—one of which is sure to suit your most particular prospect.

Look them over—they have everything. Real High Fidelity reproduction, eye appeal, the famous Stromberg-Carlson name and prices that ever-increasing-sales prove right.

This large group of High Fidelity instruments, together with the other models that make up the line with the longest price range in the industry, gives Stromberg-Carlson dealers unusual advantages in competition this season.

*Stromberg-Carlsons are priced from $59.50 to $985.
All prices slightly higher Texas, Rockies and West.*

STROMBERG-CARLSON TELEPHONE MFG. COMPANY, ROCHESTER, N. Y.

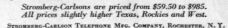

NO. 83 HIGH FIDELITY

NO. 70 HIGH FIDELITY *

NO. 72 HIGH FIDELITY *

NO. 74 HIGH FIDELITY *

* With the
exclusive
ACOUSTICAL
LABYRINTH

Stromberg-Carlson

1936 Stromberg-Carlson radios.

62, 63, circa 1936, Deco consoles, small octagonal dial on front with knobs below, some detail in grill area, **$65**

70, 72, 74, 1936, wide radios, controls behind small double doors, on six ball feet, **$100**

82, 83, deluxe versions of model *63*, **$85**

125-H, 130-H, 1936, wide tabletops, contrasting veneer, knobs below octagonal dial, **$45**

130-R, 140-H, similar to model *130-H,* Deco trim, **$65**

130-U, deluxe version of model *58-T,* 4 knobs below dial, **$65**

145-L, 150-L, 160-H, 1936, deluxe Deco consoles on ball feet, elaborate rectangular 5-band dial with 5 stepped knobs below, tuning eye, **$150**

145-P, 1936, unusual Deco radio-phono, radio section higher than phono, original turntable, **$250**

420-F, 1939, simple console with 7 tubes, rectangular dial with 6 push buttons and 4 knobs below, **$35**

420-PL, 1939, wide Deco console, radio with tuning eye and phono behind top doors, **$100**

430-M, 1939, Deco console with rectangular dial, push buttons and tuning eye, **$65**

505-H, 1940, simple wooden table radio, **$25**

515-M, circa 1940, Deco console, long dial and push buttons below long dial, **$55**

535, 1940, wide elaborate wooden radio-phono, various cabinets, **$65**

501, 502, 1926, wide wooden tabletops with sloping front panel, **$75**

601, 1925, 6-tube wooden tabletop, 2 large dials and volt meter on front, **$75**

635, 1928, wide wooden tabletop with dials and knobs on front, lid lifts, **$100**

1101-HB, "Dynatomic," 1946, Deco white-painted Bakelite tabletop, ribs wrap around front and both sides, thin elongated dial at top edge, **$65**

1101-HI, similar to model *1001-HB,* brown Bakelite, **$65**

1101-HM, "Sonnet," 1946, wooden tabletop with lyre-shaped grill cutout, **$35**

1101-HW, "Nocturne," 1946, wooden simple tabletop, similar to model *1101-HM,* grill slots, **$15**

1101-HY, "Etude Moderne," streamlined version of model *1101-HM,* **$25**

1135-PF, 1947, Georgian breakfront-style console with AM/FM radio and phono behind double doors, **$150**

1135-PL, "Autograph," classic-style version of model *1135-PF,* **$100**

1406-PLA, "Windemere," 1949, traditional blonde double-door radio-phono, speaker and record storage at bottom, **$30**

1406-PLM, similar to model *1406-PLA,* mahogany cabinet, **$30**

1409-M2M, "New World," 1948, modern blonde console, large double doors conceal push-button AM/FM radio and phono, **$65**

1409-M3A, "New Futura," similar to model *1409-M2M,* rounded corners, mahogany, **$55**

1409-PGM, "Hepplewhite," similar to model *1409-M2M,* traditional cabinet with simple squared lines, **$35**

BP-1, 1954, portable with folding metal handle, dial and knobs at top, grill slots on front, **$25**

EP-2, deluxe version of model *BP-1,* speaker cloth on front, **$25**

Sylvania

510H, 1950, Bakelite tabletop, horizontal louvers across front, raised area on top, black, brown or white, **$35**

518, 1955, rectangular clock radio, square clear clock face in center with radio dial at bottom edge, built-in night-light, **$15**

548, 1957, plastic clock radio, square clock face at left, radio dial on right side, tan, black, red or green, **$15**

1102, "Phone-Radio," 1957, rectangular plastic case, grill completely covers front, doubles as wireless intercom, red, white, green or black, **$25**

1202, "Twilighter," 1957, polystyrene rectangular tabletop with round dial in front, pierced-metal grill backlighted to illuminate room, pink, black or blue, **$45**

3401, "Prospector," 1957, 4-tube leather-covered portable, Geiger counter and compass on front, **$75**

5151, "Nocturne," 1957, plastic tabletop, similar to model *1102,* no intercom, **$15**

5485, similar to model *548,* on-and-off timer, appliance outlet, **$15**

Tele-Tone

117A, 1946, wooden tabletop, sides round out at front edges, **$25**

138, 1947, Bakelite tabletop, AM/shortwave, brown with dark brown inserted grill, **$45**

145, "Tag-A-Long," 1947, portable with plastic case, leather-look on edges, **$15**

148, "Dyna-Mite," 1947, small Bakelite tabletop with grill slots across front, dial at top edge, brown, **$25**

150, similar to model *148,* white, **$25**

157, 1948, small 5-tube Bakelite tabletop, brown, **$15**

158, 1949, 8-tube plastic AM/FM tabletop with long dial at bottom, tall grill slots, **$35**

159, 5-tube AM-only radio, similar to model *158,* **$15**

165, 1948, simple plastic tabletop, large round dial at right, **$15**

Tele-Tone 159, $15.

Tele-Tone 201, $15.

166, similar to model *157,* white-painted Bakelite, **$15**

184, 1949, Bakelite tabletop, large metal mesh grill on front with protruding elongated dial, black, brown or white, **$35**

195, 1950 version of model *165,* **$15**

198, wooden version of model *158,* **$35**

201, similar to model *184,* square holes in plastic grill, brown or white, **$15**

205, similar to model *195,* handle, **$15**

228, 1950, plastic portable, handle on top, large semicircular dial across front, maroon, green or beige, **$25**

230, circa 1950, plastic tabletop, 5 tubes, large circular dial, **$55**

232, similar to model *195,* **$15**

235, 1950, very simple and square-lined console, radio at top, pullout phono in middle, speaker cloth at bottom, **$15**

Trav-Ler

5015, 1948, Bakelite tabletop, top slightly raised, dial at top edge, **$35**

5022, 1950, portable with handle on top, square dial and 3 knobs on front Bakelite panel, **$30**

5028, 5029, alligatored leatherette-covered portables, similar to model *5054,* **$25**

5051, 1948, Bakelite tabletop, vertical grill bars wrap around top, **$25**

5054, 1948, small Bakelite tabletop, inserted grill matches knobs, **$35**

5060, 1950, Bakelite tabletop with long dial at top edge and 2 knobs on top front corners, **$35**

5066, 1948, Bakelite tabletop, dial at top edge, **$25**

5091, 1953, square wooden tabletop, large brass circular dial in center, clockette-style design, **$35**

5300, 1953, coat-pocket portable with fold-down handle on top, control wheels at left and right, **$30**

6053, 1950, wooden tabletop with oval mesh grill on front, lid lifts to expose phono, **$15**

War Reporter, 1939, Deco tabletop with painted circular grill at left, wrap around dial and 2 knobs at right, **$75**

Troy

5, 1935, wooden tabletop intricately cut silver mirror on front, brass dial and 3 Bakelite knobs, **$1,000;** blue-, green- or pink-mirrored front, **$1,500**

5+, redesigned model *5,* simpler dial within mirror at right front, silver mirror, **$750;** blue-, peach- or green-mirrored front, **$1,000**

5A, 1935, wooden tabletop, mahogany, maple, walnut or white, **$55**

45M, tabletop cut and etched thin silver glass front panel with square dial at right, 2 silver-painted knobs below, **$750;** blue-, peach- or green-mirrored front, **$1,000**

75-PC, 1936, wooden 5-tube tabletop, removable lid conceals phono, **$35**

Truetone (Western Auto Supply)

D2512, 1946, Bakelite tabletop with rounded edges, large metal grill on front, dial at top edge, **$25**

D2615, 1946, Bakelite on pedestal base, push-button tuning at front and tuning knob on right side, **$125**

D2620, 1946, large wooden tabletop, 2 wooden bars across speaker grill, dial at top edge, **$50**

D2621, 1946, wide wooden tabletop, top slightly raised, double loop in front of grill cloth, **$50**

D2630, mid-1940s, large Bakelite tabletop, ribs wrap around bottom, dial at top edge, **$35**

D2645, 1946, large wooden tabletop radio-phono with controls on top right, lid on left lifts to expose phono, **$15**

D2661, 1946, unusually styled Bakelite tabletop with large ribs on both sides, large square dial on front, **$45**

D3300, 1953, plastic coat-pocket portable with fold-down handle on top, large circular dial in center, **$35**

D3490, 1955, coat-pocket portable, similar to model *D3300,* very large dial, **$40**

Tuska

220, 1922, wide wooden tabletop with 4 dials on front panel, no tubes inside, **$675**

224, 1924, 1-tube wooden tabletop, 2 large dials on front, lid lifts, **$175**

225, wide single panel with knobs on front panel, lid lifts to expose 3 tubes, **$500;** model *224* and model *226* joined together, **$800**

305, "Superdyne," front panel similar to model *225,* 4 tubes, **$225**

Westinghouse

161, 1948, AM/FM wooden tabletop, dial forms arc at right front, 4 knobs below, **$15**

166, 1947, square-lined radio-phono, traditional-styled cabinet with double doors, **$25**

168, 1948, AM/FM radio-phono with phono under top door, large speaker cloth at top front, **$15**

169, 1948, deluxe traditional console with 4-band radio and phono behind doors, **$15**

190, 1949, square-lined console, elongated radio dial and knobs exposed at top, pullout phono behind center door, **$50**

LINE UP *with* Westinghouse

. . . and you'll never have a customer turn away

One customer wants a set with the new Precision Tuner. *You've got it in a Westinghouse.* Another wants All-Metal Tubes. *You've got them in a Westinghouse.* Another insists on beauty of cabinet design. *You've got it in a Westinghouse.* Another is shopping for big value at a low price. AND YOU'VE GOT THAT IN A WESTINGHOUSE.

Smart radio merchandisers are saying: "Stock fewer lines. Carry lower inventories. Stick to quality sets." Now, you can follow that sound advice, yet never have a customer turn away from your store. You have the right answer for every buyer, in the Westinghouse Precision Radio.

FEATURING

The **PRECISION TUNER**

An amazing control unit that automatically rules out the variables that distort tone, introduce noise and affect exact dial settings. Makes possible reception with true precision on every broadcast band

. . . with the new **ALL-METAL TUBES**

Westinghouse has the new metal tubes . . . just as it has *every* worth-while improvement in radio design and construction.

For complete descriptions and information see your nearest jobber or write Westinghouse Radio, Merchandising Headquarters, 150 Varick Street, N.Y.C.

Console WR-303. Standard, Police and European Short Wave Bands

Table Model, WR-201. "The Mighty Midget"—Standard and Police Bands

Table Model, WR-203. Standard, Police and European Short Wave Bands

Table Model, WR-205. Weather, Standard, Police, European Short Wave Bands. Precision Tuner and Metal Tubes

Console WR-304. Standard, Foreign and Police Bands. With Precision Tuner and Metal Tubes

Console, WR-305. Weather, Standard, Police, European Short Wave Bands. Precision Tuner and Metal Tubes

Midget, WR-100. Five tubes. Standard and Police Bands

Midget, WR-101. Six tubes. Standard, Police and European Short Wave Bands

Table Model, WR-204. Standard, Foreign and Police Bands. With Precision Tuner and Metal Tubes

Console, WR-306. Four Bands, Weather, Standard, Police and European Short Wave. With Precision Tuner and Metal Tubes

Prices Start with Mighty Midget at $19.95 up to Super Deluxe at $139.50
(Slightly higher west of the Rockies)

Westinghouse *Precision Radio*

Westinghouse radios from 1936.

82

309P5, 1950, green plastic portable, knobs and dial on front, **$15**

312P4, 1950, brown plastic portable with white grill, elongated dial at top edge, **$15**

313P4, similar to model *312P4,* white case and brown grill, **$15**; red case and black grill, **$35**

315P4, similar to model *312P4,* black case and red grill, **$35**

316C7, 317C7, 1950, double-door consoles, left door opens to expose large grill cloth with dial, pullout phono and bookcase behind right door, **$35**

318T5, 1950, black plastic tabletop with large dial at left side, **$15**

320T5, similar to model *318T5,* white plastic, **$15**

321T5, 1950, large black Bakelite AM table radio, concentric rectangles form grill, **$25**

322T5, similar to model *321T5,* maroon, **$25**

323T5, similar to model *321T5,* white, **$25**

324T7, 1950, AM/FM black Bakelite radio, large rectangular shape with rectangular dial at bottom, **$25**

325T7, similar to model *324T7,* white, **$25**

326C7, 1950, large 4-door console, radio and pullout phono behind top doors, bookcase and speaker behind lower doors, **$25**

327T6, 1951, 5-tube plastic radio, below elongated dial large grill, **$15**

328C7, 1951, wide console, double doors conceal pullout phono and storage space at right, large semicircular dial at left, **$30**

345T5, 1951, 4-tube maroon and white plastic tabletop, large circular dial and oversized pointer, **$15**

348P5, 1951, 5-tube plastic portable with oversized circular dial on front, folding metal handle, maroon and grey or green and tan, **$25**

350T7, 1951, 7-tube wooden tabletop, AM/FM semicircular dial across front, **$25**

354-T7, similar to model *328C7,* exposed radio above pull down phono, **$15**

355T5, 1951, maroon plastic clock radio, round clock face at left, tuning knob at right edge, **$15**

356T6, ivory version of model *355T5,* **$15**

470R12, "Symphony Hall Modern," similar to model *480C12,* blonde finish, high spindle legs, **$65**

480C12, "Symphony Hall," 1955, high fidelity double-door console, large speaker cloth behind left door, radio and pullout phono behind right, **$30**

482PR5, 1955, suitcase-style radio-phono, speaker cloth completely covers front, controls on right side, lid conceals phono, **$30**

503T4, 1955, plastic AM radio with large dial at front right, very simple set, **$15**

523T4, "Star Value," 1955, square plastic tabletop with oversized knob at front right, **$15**

536T6, brown plastic AM radio, grill covers front of set, elongated dial and 2 knobs at bottom, **$15**

541T5, 1955, television-styled clock radio, round clock face within oval area at left, **$35**

546T5, similar to model *541T5,* shut-off feature, **$35**

547T5, 1955, clock radio, clock face covers most of front, elongated dial and 2 knobs below, **$35**

Aeriola Jr., 1921, small wooden box, lid lifts to expose crystal, dial and instructions, **$275**

Aeriola, Sr., similar to *Aeriola, Jr.,* lid lifts to expose controls, 1 tube, **$175**

H-104, H-105, 1946, large wooden tabletops, wooden grill forming front slopes in, push-button tuning, **$50**

H107, 1946, wide console, left door pulls out phono, right door opens to expose radio and controls, **$15**

H-110, 1946, 7-tube console, large speaker cloth at top front, long dial below, double doors at bottom open to expose pullout phono, **$35**

H-125, H-126, 1946, unusual Bakelite table-tops, refrigerator-shaped with flip-up handle, various colors, **$75**

WR-62K1, "Carryette," 1941, suitcase-style portable with exposed speaker cloth and square dial above 3 knobs, **$15**

WR-102, 1936, simple rectangular wooden tabletop, square speaker area next to square dial, **$25**

WR-173, 1940, small Bakelite tabletop, ribs across front and sides, brown or white, **$25**

WR-175, circa 1940, square Bakelite table-top, vertical ribs across front and top, **$25**

WR-209, 1936, wooden tabletop with oval dial and 3 knobs across front, **$35**

WR-214, 1936, Deco tombstone with tuning eye above multiband oval dial, 4 stacked knobs below, **$75**

WR-272, 1940, Deco wooden tabletop, 6 tubes, long dial with push-button tuning, contrasting veneer, **$50**

WR-274, 1939, 7-tube wide wooden tabletop with round push buttons, **$55**

WR-310, 1936, wooden console, wide "modern" look, intricate grill and cloth, **$85**

WR-311, 1936, Deco console, multiband circular dial with 4 knobs below, **$55**

WR-314, similar to model *WR-310,* simpler grill and tuning eye, **$75**

WR-316, AC/DC version of model *WR-311,* **$55**

WR-374, 1939, Deco console, 8 tubes, rectangular dial with push buttons and tuning eye, **$65**

WR-375, 1940, Deco console with 6 tubes, 3 bands, simple styling with push-button tuning, **$50**

WR-388, 1941, Deco wooden tabletop with contrasting panels at top and bottom, push buttons and 3 knobs, **$40**

WR-470, 1939, wooden tabletop with 5-tube multiband radio with push buttons on front, lid conceals phono, **$35**

WR-474, 1939, wide Deco console with 8-tube radio and phono under lid, **$100**

WR-676, 1940, small suitcase-style portable, cloth covered, dial and controls under handle, **$15**

Wurlitzer

Four, wide wooden tabletop, 1928, large pointer and dials on front Bakelite panel, lid lifts to expose 6 tubes, **$125**

Six, wide wooden tabletop with 2 oversized dials and 2 small knobs on front Bakelite panel, **$125**

Nine, Ten, 6-tube wooden tabletops, 1928, 3 large pointers on front, lid lifts, **$125**

Zenith

3R, 4R, wide wooden tabletops, 1926, battery operated, Bakelite front panel, **$300**

4B313, 4B314, 6-tube Bakelite tabletop, 1939, **$30**

4B317, World's Fair radio similar to model *5R317,* **$200**

4K402, leatherette-covered portable, 1940, front door drops down to expose controls, **$15**

4K600, "Pocketradio," 4-tube Bakelite coat-pocket radio, 1941, lid lifts to expose chrome trim, **$45**

5D011, square wooden tabletop, 1946, cloth on left front, large circular dial on right front, **$15**

5D027, Bakelite version of model *5D011,* **$35**

5R312, 5-tube Bakelite tabletop, 1939, rounded speaker area at left, push-button tuning, **$85**

5R317, wooden version of model *5R312,* glass rods in cabinet front, **$175**

6D015, unusual Bakelite tabletop, 1946, grill and dial form large semicircle, brown or white, **$45**

6D030, wooden version of model *6D015,* **$25**

6D311, 6D315, "Wavemagnet," Deco Bakelite tabletops, 1939, large antenna attachment on back, **$85**

6D317, 6-tube version of model *5R317,* **$100**

Portable televisions from the 1940s to the 1970s. **Top to bottom, left to right:** *Symphonic "Mini TV," Model TPS-5050, $45; Motorola "Astronaut," Model 19P1, $75; Sentinel Model 400TV, $85; Philco 51-T1604, $45; JVC "Videosphere," Model 3240, $100; Sony 8-301W, $125.*

Portable radios from the 1940s and 1950s using miniature and sub-miniature tubes, and transistors. **From top, row 1:** *Emerson "Miracle Wand," Model 847, $75; Admiral 7L12 with solar battery, $150.* **Row 2:** *Westinghouse Model H-589, $50.* **Row 3:** *Motorola 53LC clock radio, $45; Heathkit Model X1, $65.* **Row 4:** *Emerson "Transistor III," Model 843, $85; Emerson "Transistor Pocket Radio," Model 838, $125; DeWald K-701-A, $300.* **Row 5:** *Emerson 888, $65; Sylvania "Thunderbird," $200; Zenith "Royal 500," $85; Emerson "Vanguard," Model 888, $125.*

Transistor radios shown in both shirt-pocket and key-chain size. **From top, row 1:** *Sony TR-63, $450; Boy's Radio, $45; Toshiba "Lace," Model 5TR, $145; General Electric P850, $10.* **Row 2:** *A Ross "Diamond Micro" ($40) sits atop a Toshiba 6TP-385 ($50); Toshiba 6TP-31, $65; Sony TR-610, $75.* **Row 3:** *Sears Model 7216, $35; Hitachi TH-621, $125; Hitachi TH-666, $85; Sony 1R-81, $85; Emerson Model 707, $45.*

Novelty transistor radios come in all shapes and sizes. **From top, row 1:** *Television shape, $15; Popeye, $65.* **Row 2:** *Sunglasses with built-in radio, $60; Typical can shape, $15; Paint can, $20.* **Row 3:** *Whiskey bottle, $25; Globe-shaped paper and metal radio, $25; Cathedral style, $15.*

A grouping of novelty and early transistor radios makes an attractive and colorful collection. **From top, row 1:** *Microphone shape, $30; Typical large bottle shape, $25; Pinocchio, $55.* **Row 2:** *Pepsi Cola dispenser, $25; General Electric Model P771A, $15; Emerson "Mercury," Model 899, $45.* **Row 3:** *Sylvania 4P14, $50; Money Talks radio, $25; RCA Victor 1-BT-2, complete with charger, $145.* **Row 4:** *Emerson "Eldorado," Model 911, $45; Westinghouse "Escort," Model RS21P, $15; Channel Master Model 6514, $25.* **Row 5:** *Continental Model 160, $50; Arvin Model 60R23, $35; Silvertone Model 211, $20.*

An array of radios from the 1930s includes furniture-style console radios, Art Deco wood and chrome models, and Bakelite and Catalin tabletops. **At left:** Atop a RCA Model 224 console ($75) sits an Addison Model 2A, $1,000 **(left),** and a FADA "Coloradio," Model 242, $450. In front of the console is a DeWald 502-A Catalin, $400. **At right (top);** A typical chrome-trimmed Majestic, $75; **(center):** Detrola "Super Pee Wee," $400; **(bottom):** Kadette "Clockette," $1,300.

*The large console radios of the 1930s eventually gave way to the smaller tabletop radios and televisions of the 1940s and 1950s. **At left:** In front of a Philco 37-630X console ($100) is a Crosley JMB "Book Radio," ($100). **At right (top):** Pilot television Model TV-37, $150; **(center):** Kadette "Junior," $500; Olympic 446, $65; **(bottom):** Bulova "Bantam," Model 670, $45; Zephyr Model RN-7, $45.*

The space age and high technology designs of the 1950s gave a whimsical look to many radios and televisions of that period. **Top to bottom:** *Philco 17" Predicta "Debutante," $200; Mickey Mouse clock radio, $45; Motorola "Pin-up," Model 52CW, $25; Crosley D-25, $65; Delco "Sportable" transistor, $100; Admiral Model 811, $15; Motorola 5XI, $35.*

ZENITH
America's Most Copied Radio
—again a year ahead!

GOING OVER BIG! That's the news we get from dealers and distributors everywhere on the sensational new 1937 Zenith line. For instance: *"Never witnessed a more enthusiastic acceptance of any radio line,"* wires one. . . . *"More thrilled than ever before in my radio career,"* telegraphs another. . . . *"Booked largest amount of business in our history,"* says yet another. Everywhere Zenith enthusiasm is growing. Little wonder! For Zenith's 1937 line is by all odds the finest ever manufactured. Every model is top quality—the biggest value in radio at its respective price. Here's why: Zenith operates on a low margin of profit. Every cent goes into the product itself. No P.M.'s—no spiffs—no lavish cruises to get business. The clearly evident superiority of the product is what makes the sales. Yes—Zenith is going places and doing things. Why not you? See your Zenith Distributor.

Some of the 42 Zenith Models

ZENITH 10-S-160
10 tubes. Tunes American and foreign stations, police, amateur, aviation, ships at sea. Auditorium 12-inch Electro-Dynamic Speaker. 42 inches high. **Price $139.95.**

ZENITH 8-S-154
8 tubes. Tunes American and foreign stations, police, amateur, aviation, ships at sea. Auditorium 12-inch Electro-Dynamic Speaker. 41 inches high. **Price $89.95.**

ZENITH ZEPHYR 6-S-147
6 tubes. Tunes American and foreign stations, police, amateur, aviation, ships at sea. 10-inch Electro-Dynamic Speaker. 23 inches high. **Price $84.95.**

ZENITH COMPACT 6-D-117 (AC-DC)
6 tubes (including ballast tube). Tunes broadcast stations, police, amateur, aviation. 5-inch Electro-Dynamic Speaker, Tone Control. 8¾ inches high. **Price $34.95.**

ZENITH 6-S-128
6 tubes. Tunes American and foreign stations, police, amateur, aviation, ships at sea. 8-inch Electro-Dynamic Speaker. 22 inches high. **Price $59.95.**

ZENITH FARM RADIO 6-B-129
6-tube Superheterodyne. Tunes American and foreign stations, police, amateur, aviation, ships at sea. 8-inch Zenith Dynamic Speaker. Operates on single 6-volt storage battery. 22 inches high. **Price $69.95.**

ACOUSTIC ADAPTER
and other 1937 FEATURES

Acoustic Adapter
The only device now made that adjusts for perfect performance in any size room.

Lightning Station Finder
Twirl the control and the pointer speeds to the station you want. No more slow, laborious knob twisting.

Big Black Improved Dial
With the "Squared Circle" and "Tell Tale" Controls. Zenith's most imitated feature again improved.

Split-Second Re-Locater
Only means yet devised to re-locate short wave foreign and domestic stations.

Voice-Music-High Fidelity Control
Voice control adjusts for natural speaking voice. . . . *High Fidelity* for startling realism. Three additional important adjustments.

Exclusive Features Patented
THEY SELL THE SET EVERY TIME

The only Radio adjustable for perfect reception in any size room in the house

————(Prices slightly higher in West and Southern States)————

ZENITH RADIO CORPORATION
CHICAGO, ILLINOIS

1937 radios by Zenith.

6D410, 6D411, rounded Bakelite tabletops with grill bars extend over top, 1940, **$35**

6D413, 6D414, similar to model *6D410,* push buttons, **$25**

6D426, 6D429, wooden tabletops, 1940, small push-button dial, **$40**

6D510, simple Bakelite tabletop, 1941, large rectangular dial and handle on top, **$15**

6D525, 6D526, similar to model *6D510,* wooden cabinet, **$35**

6D614, 6D620, large square Bakelite tabletops, 1942, brown or white, **$35**

6G001Y, 7G004Y, transoceanic portables, 1946, concentric semicircular dials similar to model *6D015,* **$45**

6-S-27, tabletop, tombstone with round dial, 5 bands and 6 tubes, 1936, **$135**

6-S-137, 6-tube "Zephyr" Deco tombstone, 1937, wooden ribs around radio, **$250;** original bone white- or black-painted finish, **$350**

6S302, 6S304, square wooden tabletops, 1939, phono built into top, **$75**

6S340, semicircular Deco chair side, 1939, tall wooden ribs on side, 6 tubes, **$150**

6S341, similar to model *6S340,* horizontal ribs on lower half of cabinet, **$250**

7-D-168, "Zephyr" Deco console with wooden ribs around set, 1937, **$275**

7G004Y, see *6G001Y*

7G04, Bakelite AM/FM tabletop, left corner forms dial with oversized pointer, 3 knobs below, **$25**

7G605, "Trans-Ocean Clipper," multiband portable with push buttons and sailboat or plane on grill cloth, 1942, **$125**

7-S-28, 7-tube version of model *6-S-27,* **$175**

7-S-232, cathedral with large oval dial, circa 1938, similar to radio on TV series "The Walton's," **$500**

7S490, radio-phono, 1940, semicircular left half of radio, lid lifts to expose phono, **$125**

8H023, large square Bakelite tabletop, 1946, semicircular dial with old and new FM bands, brown, black or white, **$50**

8H034, similar to model *8H023,* wooden cabinet, **$75**

8G005Y, multiband Transoceanic portable, 1946, large square dial with pop-up antenna, **$50**

8-S-531, elaborate tabletop with 8 tubes, grill offset at left, round dial with white push buttons on either side, 1941, **$100**

8S661, 8-tube Deco console, 1942, large rectangular black dial with black push buttons on either side, **$75**

9H079, 9H081, square radio-phonos with radio controls on slanted top and pullout phono in middle, 1946, **$50**

9-S-30, 9-tube version of model *6-S-27,* **$175**

9-S-54, 9-S-55, Deco consoles, 1936, 9-tube chassis with round dial, **$175**

9-S-232, 9-tube version of "Walton's" radio, model *7-S-232,* **$750**

10-S-147, Deco "Zephyr" chair side, 1937, end-table style, **$350**

10-S-155, Deco console, 1937, large dial, mahogany finish, **$275;** finished in black- or white-paint, **$450**

10-S-160, similar to model *10-S-155,* **$275**

11, 11E, 12, 6-tube wooden tabletops, late 1920s, rotary dial on sloping front panel, **$125**

12-A-58, 12-tube economy version of model *16-A-63,* **$275**

12H090, 12H092, 12H094, square console, 1946, double doors at top conceal pullout phono and pull-down radio, **$50**

12-S-232, 12-tube version of "Walton's" radio, model *7-S-232,* **$875**

12S370, 12S371, Deco consoles, 1939, 12 tubes, round dial with white push buttons on either side, **$400**

14, similar to model *12,* built into elaborate console with double doors and 4 legs, **$300**

15, 15E, 8-tube wooden tabletops with rotary control on front, late 1927, complete with antenna, **$175**

15U269, Deco multiband console with 15 tubes and oval dial, 1938, **$500**

Zenith's first "Trans-Oceanic" 7G605, $125.

15U270, similar to model *15U269*, traditional cabinet on 4 short legs, **$575**

15U272, similar to model *15U269*, Georgian-style cabinet, **$600**

15U273, similar to model *15U269*, elaborate Louis XV cabinet, **$650**

16, 16E, similar to model *15*, built into huge Spanish-style wooden console with veneered double doors, **$275**

16-A-61, 16-A-63, "Stratosphere," large Deco consoles with 16 tubes, circa 1936, 6-band dial and "shadowgraph" tuning, **$1,500**

52, 53, 54, 9-tube wooden consoles on 4 short legs, 1930, large rotary dial between 2 knobs above speaker grill, **$150**

55, elaborate Italian Renaissance version of model *52*, oversized cabinet and remote control, **$350**

60, 61, 62, 64, lowboy 9-tube radios, circa 1930, rotary dial, veneered panels or doors on front, **$150**

67, elaborate lowboy version of model *61*, **$350**

71, 72, 73, wooden lowboy cabinets, 1931, 9 tubes, doors or panels conceal controls, **$125**

75, elaborate version of model *71*, 4 ball legs, lid lifts to expose radio and phono, **$450**

210, 230, cathedral-style Zenette (economy) wooden tabletops, 1933, **$250**

220, economy highboy cabinet, circa 1933, **$100**

250, 9-tube Zenette cathedral, 5 knobs below small dial, **$250**

701, economy wide 5-tube tabletop with 1 knob on each side of grill, 1934, **$75**

705, 706, 707, small wide 6-tube tabletops, 1934, grill in center front with small dial over right knob, **$125**

711, similar to model *705*, 2 dial windows with "shadowgraph" tuning, **$125**

715, elaborate large 8-tube tombstone tabletop with intricate grill, 1934, **$250**

760, 765, elaborate 6-legged consoles, 1934, 9 tubes, twin speakers, "shadowgraph" tuning, **$225**

960, 961, economy 6-tube consoles, 1935, **$125**

970, 975, 6-legged wooden consoles, **$170**

808, simple 6-tube economy tombstone tabletop with Deco panels, 1935, **$175**

809, similar to model *808*, rounded corners and chrome trim, **$225**

811, Deco tabletop, 1935, 6 tubes, rounded left top edge, grill forms arc from center to right, **$225**

829, Deco set similar to model *809*, 7 tubes and elaborate chrome grill, **$225**

835, very large deluxe version of model *809*, 10 tubes, **$275**

960, 961, simple 6-tube consoles, 1935, circular 3-band dial, **$150**

975, similar to model *960*, period highboy cabinet with 6 legs, **$150**

G500, Transoceanic portable multiband with square dial, 1950, **$50**

H500, Transoceanic with rectangular dial and push buttons to right, 1951, **$65**

J402, pocket-book style AM portable, 1952, large emblem on front, dial, knobs and handle at top, **$35**

J733, similar to model *K622*, AM/FM, **$25**

K515, plastic clock radio, 1952, rounded sides, brown or black, **$15**

K518, deluxe version of model *K515*, timer, **$15**

K622, clock radio with square clock face and dial, 1952, **$15**

Stratosphere, "Big Black Dial," massive console, 1930s, 25 tubes, possibly the most impressive Zenith console sold, **$4,500**

Super-Zenith VII, 6-tube nearly 4-foot-long tabletop with front Bakelite panel, storage area inside, 1926, **$125**

Super-Zenith VIII, similar to *Super-Zenith VII*, 4 mahogany spindle legs, **$150**

Super-Zenith IX, deluxe version of *Super-Zenith VIII*, wooden compartments for built-in loudspeaker and battery boxes, **$250**

Super Zenith X, elaborate floor model on 4 legs, mid-1920s, battery operated, **$275**

T600, Transoceanic portable with rectangular dial and horizontal scales, push buttons to right, 1954, **$65**

Zeneth Model A, 6-tube cathedral, 1931, "Zenette" economy line, **$250**

Zeneth Model B, more elaborate version of *Zeneth Model A,* **$300**

Zeneth C, D, lowboy cabinets with Model A chassis, **$150**

Chapter Two
TRANSISTOR RADIOS

Early Radios

In the late 1940s, Bell Telephone Laboratories produced point-contact transistors, and Raytheon and Texas Instruments were able to manufacture cheap transistors by the early 1950s. Tube and transistor hybrid radio sets were quickly marketed, and soon Regency, a little-known maker of electronic components, brought out the Regency TR-1 all-transistor radio at Christmas time in 1954, and the rest is history.

Early transistor radios have displaced even Deco and Catalin radios as the 'hottest" group of radios now being collected. Many collectors, investors, and dealers are capitalizing on the early transistor radios, mostly those made from 1954 to 1964. In what has become a surprising trend even to radio veterans, dozens of these early transistor sets are selling for unbelievable prices, with some of the rarer radios (especially in unusual colors) being sold for $50 to $500. Because the early transistor radios went from being valued at a few dollars to hundreds of dollars so quickly, they can still be found at nearly every major flea market and antiques show at well below their collector value.

Although the earliest sets are not always easy to spot, there are a few distinguishing features that most share. Transistor radios which have the Conelrad Civil Defense markings at 640 and 1240 on the dial, small triangles or the letters "CD," are usually among the earliest sets. Transistor radios which have soft plastic or nylon cases with rounded edges usually have more value than later sets which have hard plastic cases and very square corners.

A quick look inside will often reveal push-in transistors and a metal tuning capacitor in the earliest sets; plastic-covered transistors and tuners soldered to printed circuit boards are usually in the later radios. Early Japanese sets are collectible, but Sears and many other American companies used Japanese components and cases by the late 1960s, and normally Japanese-made sets for U.S. manufacturers are shunned by collectors.

Some times, just the brand name is an indication of the set's popularity. Pick up any Regency, Raytheon, Sonora, Hoffman, or Mitchell transistor radio and you have a collectible set. Other collectible features include radios with built-in solar batteries or plug-in solar power packs, "micro" sized sets (about 1 cubic inch), brightly colored sets, and radios with chrome trim, especially the chrome trim which resembles a stylized rocket ship.

There are two other related groups of radios which have gained in popularity and value as the early transistor radios have increased in price. The "sub-miniature" tube radios and the "hybrid" sets. Sub-miniature tube sets use tubes which were designed for the early hearing aids and are about the diameter of a pencil, but only an inch in length. These radios were the last-ditch effort to miniaturize tube-type radios and were sold from 1945 (the Belmont "Boulevard" 5P113 was the first) until all-transistors sets captured the market.

By the mid-1950s, "hybrid" radios were developed. A hybrid was a radio with both tubes and transistors. They were a short-lived attempt to keep the cost and size of radios down, while taking advantage of vacuum tube power and transistor popularity. But as prices plummeted, all-transistor sets quickly displaced both the sub-miniature tube and hybrid sets.

Remember, as with the Deco radios, condition is of utmost importance. Prices are given for internally and externally clean sets with no cracks or chips, working or not. A corner crack or chip, or battery damage inside, can cut these prices in half. Early transistor radios which are truly mint and still in the original box can be worth twice the stated prices. Generally, leather cases, earphones, and other accessories do not add significantly to the value. As with most collectibles, more important sets will often be bought, even if in rough condition, but the common models or common colors may not sell unless they are nearly perfect. (Model numbers can usually be found somewhere on the back of the set.)

Admiral

4P21, 4P24, large radios, with oversized dial at right, metal handle, 1957, black or tan, **$60**

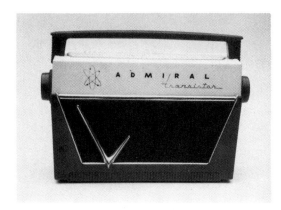

Admiral 7L12, with solar pack, $150.

4P22, 4P28, similar to model *4P21,* red or turquoise, **$85**

6M3, shirt-pocket radio with circular window for station numbers, 1962, **$10**

7L12, 7L18, first solar-powered radios, large red or turquoise plastic set with metal V on front, circa 1956, complete with solar pack, **$150**

7L14, 7L16, similar to model *7L12,* tan or yellow plastic, **$125**

7M11, similar to model *4P21,* black or tan, **$50**

7M12, 7M18, similar to model *7M11,* red or turquoise, **$75**

8C2, "Clipper," large wide radio with leatherette covering, 1961, 3 bands, directional antenna under handle, **$10**

231, oversized portable with large plastic handle, 1958, metal front with 2 knobs and tuner, **$75**

528, 531, large portables, 1958, similar to model *231,* **$75**

561, 566, cordless table radios, 1959, two-tone with large knob at front right, **$15**

581, coat-pocket set, 1959, recessed volume control above large tuner at right front, no handle and no earphone jack, **$50**

691, "Jupiter," grey economy version of model *703,* **$20**

692, red economy version of model *703,* **$45**

703, "Saturn," coat-pocket set with volume control in grill at left, large clear dial at right, 1960, white, **$20**

Admiral 691 "Jupiter," $20.

708, similar to model *703,* light green, **$45**

711, "Polaris," deluxe version of model *703,* gold-tone trim, **$45**

739, "Palomar," large grey leatherette-covered set, 1959, volume at left and tuner at right, **$20**

742, 743, "Meteor," similar to model *739,* red or white leatherette, **$20**

Admiral 742 "Meteor," $20.

Admiral 811 "Oriole," $15.

751, 757, "Celestial," large leatherette-covered portables with gold-tone metal grill on front, 1959, **$25**

793, "Starette," small tabletop with AM/ clock radio dials at right front, 1960, **$10**

811, 816, "Oriole," cordless clock radio versions of model *561,* **$15**

Airline

GEN-1106, wide leatherette-covered portable with large plastic tuner at right, handle on top, 1958, **$60**

GTM-1108, tan leatherette-covered radio, 1957, large dial at right, strap, **$65**

GTM-1109, large plastic set with vertical bars across front, large knob at right, 1958, white, **$60;** turquoise, **$85**

GTM-1201, tall coat-pocket radio with wire handle, large dial below grill, 1960, **$15**

GEN-1202, wide coat-pocket with metal grill to left, logo and station window across front, 1962, **$20**

GEN-1215, small radio, 1962, front plastic covers open to expose radio and controls, **$25**

Arvin

61R13, pink plastic shirt-pocket 1961, grill below offset V-shaped metal area with large tuner, **$20**

Airline GEN-1106A, $60.

Airline GTM-1201, $15.

61R16, green version of model *61R13,* **$20**
61R19, black version of model *61R13,* **$15**
61R39, shirt-pocket with metal grill and arc-shaped window on front, 1962, **$10**

61R48, large coat-pocket with leather at top, bottom and sides, **$20**

2564, tabletop, with large grill area at left, 2 irregularly shaped knobs at right, 1959, **$35**

5561, plastic AM/clock radio with large square dial at left, 2 knobs at top right, 1959, pink or green, **$25**

7595, oversized plastic radio, 1960, large tuner knob at right, wire handle, **$15**

8571, similar to model *9574,* covered in grey tweed, **$50**

8572, green or tan leatherette version of model *9574,* **$50**

8573, turquoise or red version of model *9574,* **$85**

8576, tall set with square wrap around grill at bottom, black, 1958, **$60;** turquoise, **$100**

8584, oversized set with large handle on top, recessed controls over grill, 1958, **$60**

9562, large leatherette set, 1957, long dial and knobs on top under handle, complete with "Arvin" logo on front, **$100**

9574, unusually shaped large vinyl-over-aluminum set, 1957, knobs on each side, plastic handle on top, cream or tan, **$50**

9577, tall set with hourglass-shaped front covering, ivory or black, 1957, **$100;** pink, **$75**

9595, deluxe version of model *7595,* fancy grill, **$20**

Arvin 61R13, $20.

Arvin 8584, $60.

Arvin 9562, $100.

Arvin 9574, $50.

Bulova 670 "Bantam," $45.

Bell

Kamra, similar to Kowa *Ramera,* combination radio and hidden 16mm camera, uncracked, **$75**

Boys's Radio (various manufacturers)

2-TR, 2-transistor shirt-pocket Japanese radio, usually two-tone plastic with rounded corners, marked "Boy's Radio" on back, **$45**

Bulova

250 Series, shirt-pocket sets, copy of Regency TR-1 (first transistor radio), brass dial at top right, logo at left, plastic case, **$300,** leather case, **$350**

260 Series, large leatherette-covered sets, 1957, snap-open back exposes printed circuit board, **$50**

270 Series, leatherette-covered sets with large grill across front, **$75**

670, "Bantam," small shirt-pocket, 1961, metal front with small glass "jewel" (glass diamond) above perforated grill and logo, **$45**

715, large leatherette-covered radio, 1961, handle on top, **$15**

742, shirt-pocket with metal grill below recessed controls, 1961, **$20**

792, wide coat-pocket, 1961, station numbers across upper right front edge, **$25**

Capehart

11P7, large leatherette set with knobs on sides, large gold-tone grill, 1957, marked "transistor V66," **$200**

Channel Master

6448, "Micrette," tall thin miniature radio with perforated grill on front left with logo, small window at front right, **$25**

6501, coat-pocket radio with perforated metal grill and large window for tuner numbers, 1959, **$20**

6502, two-tone plastic shirt-pocket set made in Hong Kong, chrome front includes grill and station window, **$10**

6506, rectangular shirt-pocket radio with grill to left and large square at right with station numbers, **$20**

6512, 6514, wide coat-pocket radios, 1960, chrome lever under window to switch from AM to shortwave, **$25**

Continental 160, $50.

Continental

160, tall coat-pocket set, 1959, rectangular metal grill below 2 large dials, wire handle, **$50**

TR-100, shirt pocket radio with round metal speaker below volume/tuning area, wire handle, 1960, **$30**

Channel Master 6448 "Micrette," $25.

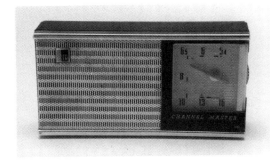

Channel Master 6506, $20.

Continental TR-208, $35.

TR-200, shirt-pocket set with metal grill below V-shaped station number window, 1959, **$30**

TR-208, two-tone shirt-pocket set, 1959, strip with tuner across front, 2 jacks at top edge, **$35**

TR-300, wide coat-pocket radio with metal grill at left, plastic area at left with vertical tuner, **$30**

Crosley

JM8, 1956, "book radio," hybrid transistor/ sub-miniature tube set, lift-up front exposes metal grill and controls, **$100**

Crown

TR-333, shirt-pocket with wrap around metal grill below recessed tuner knob, 1958, white or black, **$35;** other colors, **$60**

TR-610, large set with metal handle, large tuner at right front, 1959, **$35**

TR-666, wide radio with perforated metal grill at left and station numbers in a line, 1959, **$35**

TR-820, wide coat-pocket set with wire handle, large tuner knob at right, **$20**

TR-830, wide coat-pocket radio with large tuner knob over recessed volume wheel at right, 1959, **$20**

Crosley JM8, $100.

Delco "Trans-Portable," $100.

Delco

Sportable, 1958 Oldsmobile or Pontiac portable car radio, 2 knobs on chrome end, plays in or out of car, **$100**

Trans-Portable, 1959 Oldsmobile, Buick or Pontiac radio with wide chrome face and tuner, recessed volume on side, plays in or out of car, **$100**

DeWald

K-544, small leatherette-covered radio with dial on right front, numbers stamped into front, 1957, **$75**

K-701-A, large swirled plastic radio, 1955, Dewald's first transistor set, large dial at front below grill, collapsible handle on top, **$200**

K-702-B, leatherette-covered version of model K-701-A, **$50**

DeWald K-701-A, $300.

L-414, oversized leatherette-covered radio with handle on top, 2 knobs on right side, 1958, **$45**

L-546, coat pocket sized leather-covered set with recessed volume knob above tuner at right front, 1958, **$35**

L-703, oversized leatherette portable with 1 knob on each side, 1958, **$45**

DuMont

RA-902, large leatherette radio with leather strap, 1957, crest at lower left, control knobs at right, **$100**

Emerson

555, scarce coat-pocket set with large grill at left, see-through tuner at right, 1959, **$85**

707, plastic shirt-pocket, 1962, large circular area near top with "707" and station numbers, **$45**

838, wide coat-pocket set with plastic grill and large knob at right, 1955, "hybrid" with sub-miniature tubes and transistors, marked across top "Transistor Pocket radio," **$125**

842, large leather-covered set with huge tuner at top front center, 1956, **$50**

844, leatherette version of model *847*, **$35**

847, oversized plastic radio, 1956, large "Miracle Wand" handle on top, knobs to left and right of grill, **$75**

Emerson 707, $45.

Emerson 847, $75.

849, Emerson's first all-transistor radio, wide coat-pocket with 2 metal inserts at right with tuner window and logo, **$125**

855, 1957 version of model *842*, **$50**

856, 1956 redesign of model *838*, marked across top "Transistor II," sub-miniature tube and transistor hybrid, **$125**

868, *869*, versions of Miracle Wand model *847*, large tuner at center front, **$45**

Emerson 555, $85.

Emerson 849, $125.

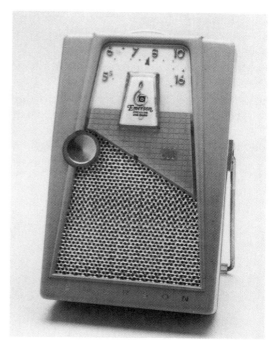

Emerson 888 "Explorer," $85.

Emerson 868, $45.

888

"Atlas," similar to Pioneer model, random pattern and no logo on grill, black, grey or white, **$85**

"Explorer," coat-pocket with perforated grill below window with station numbers, black, grey or white, **$85**

"Pioneer," coat-pocket, 1958, grill with logo and diamond pattern below oversized knob, black or white, **$85**

"Satellite," leather-covered coat-pocket, 1958, grill with random holes on front, **$95**

"Transtimer," large brown leather set, front drops to expose clock, tuner and speaker, complete and clean, **$75**

"Transtimer II," black version of *Transtimer*, 1958, **$85**

Emerson 888 "Pioneer," $85.

"Vanguard," similar to *Pioneer* model, grill slots cut into case, rocket at center right, black or white, **$85**

Models in colors other than grey, white or black, **$150**

911, "Eldorado," coat-pocket set with large plastic gold-tone grill, pull-up handle at top, 1959, very clean, **$45**

999, scarce tall shirt-pocket with large tuner in upper left, recessed volume at upper right, 1958, **$100**

General Electric

675, black set with square grill holes and inverted pyramid-shaped depressions on left, large dial on right, 1956, GE's first transistor set, **$75**

676, similar to model *675,* ivory, **$100**

677, similar to model *675,* red, **$125**

678, similar to model *675,* aqua, **$125**

P15, 1958 version of model *P715,* **$65**; radio complete with battery charger, **$100**

P671, similar to model *P760,* collapsible handle on top, **$20**

P710A, rectangular radio with grill slot at left, large dial at right, 1957, **$35**

P715, P716, long metal coat-pocket sets, 1956, tuner and volume at right, **$65**

P715, radio complete with battery charger, **$100**

P725, large plastic set, 1957, large plain metal grill on front, **$35**

P745, coat-pocket set with grill slots at left, large tuner and recessed volume control at right, 1958, black with gold trim, **$25**

Emerson 888 "Vanguard," $85.

General Electric 675, $75.

Emerson 911 "Eldorado," $45.

General Electric P15, $65.

General Electric P715, $65.

General Electric P800, $20.

P746, similar to model *P745,* turquoise with white trim, **$45**

P760, oversized two-tone plastic portable with knobs on sides, plastic handle on top, 1958, **$20**

P776, leatherette set with metal grill on front, two knobs at top front, 1959, **$15**

P785, P786, wide black or white coat-pocket sets with perforated plastic grill below long tuner, 1959, **$35**

P788, similar to model *P785,* blue, **$50**

P797, oversized leatherette portable with metal grill in centerr, 1959, **$15**

P800, oversized radio with slot grill at left of large dial, 1960, **$20**

P806, common 1959 coat-pocket radio with metal grill painted with random pattern on left, tuner at right, white, **$15;** blue, **$25**

P830, grey shirt-pocket set, metal grill covers bottom front, long dial at top, 1959, **$30**

P831, similar to model *P830,* blue, **$50**

P850, small shirt-pocket with key ring attached to top, 1962, **$10**

General Electric P807 (similar to P806), $15.

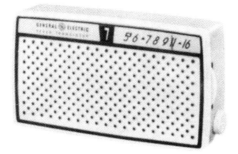

General Electric P785, $35.

General Electric P850, $10.

Global GR-900, $45.

Global

GR-900, oval-shaped shirt-pocket with clear plastic section at top front above perforated metal grill, black or white, **$45;** colors other than black or white, **$65**

Hallicrafters

TR-88, large leatherette radio with name across bottom, two knobs across top, 1957, **$100**

Heathkit

X-1, large blue plastic tabletop kit radio, gold-tone metal grill, handle molded into top front, **$65**

XR-1L, large leather-covered kit radio with diagonally cut grill slots, knobs on sides, 1959, **$30**

XR-1P, plastic version of model *XR-1L,* two-tone blue with gold-tone trim and grill, **$45**

XR-2L, kit radio built into oversized leatherette case, large slot grill on front, knobs on sides, 1960, **$20**

Heathkit X-1, $65.

XR-2P, brown plastic version of model *XR-2L,* **$40**

Hitachi

TH-621, tall plastic shirt-pocket, 1958, tuner above slot grill, recessed volume knob on right, white or black, **$75;** other colors, **$125**

Hitachi TH-621, $75.

Hitachi TH-666, $65.

TH-660, shirt-pocket, metal grill front has window for station numbers, 1961, **$30**

TH-666, tall shirt-pocket with painted metal grill below clear plastic-covered volume and tuner, 1958, white or black, **$65;** red and grey, **$85;** oversized speaker box, **$145**

WH-761, shirt-pocket radio with AM and shortwave bands, 1961, **$25**

Hoffman

P410, large flat radio, 1957, circular grill at left and square clear dial at right, **$150**

Hoffman 706, $225.

P411, similar to model *P410,* solar battery pack, **$225**

706, coat-pocket set, 1958, solar battery on top, complete and working, brown, black or tan, **$225;** pink, red or turquoise, **$300**

Kowa

Ramera, coat-pocket plastic radio, Kowa 16mm camera built into front, uncracked, **$75**

Lafayette

FS-112, shirt-pocket with wrap around metal grill on lower half, 1958, black or white, **$35;** other colors, **$60**

Kit, radio in square leather case, aluminum chassis slips in end which snaps closed, two knobs at other end under handle, 1957, **$45**

KT-119, kit radio with large knob marked "Micro Super" at right front of leatherette case, 1957, **$35**

Lafayette kit, 1957, $45.

Magnavox AM-2, $150.

Magnavox

AM-2, 1957 redesign of model *CR-729,* "Magnavox all-transistor" on 1 line, **$150**

AM-22, wide shirt-pocket with perforated metal grill at left, metal window at top right above recessed volume control, **$55**

CR-729, coat-pocket radio with large metal grill, "all-transistor" on line above "Magnavox," 1957, **$200**

IR1006, Japanese-made sub-miniature square black plastic radio with chrome trim, long dial across top, **$20**

Magnavox 1R1006, $20.

Mantola M-4D, $250.

Mantola (Madison Industries)

M-4D, copy of Regency *TR-1* shirt-pocket radio, 1955, metal dial at top right with "orbiting electron" logo, recessed volume to left, ivory or black, **$250;** red or other colors, **$350**

Micronic Ruby (See Standard)

Mitchell

1101, leather-covered pocket radio, 1956, copy of Regency *TR-1* with mesh grill, **$300**

1102, alligatored version of model *1101,* **$350**

1103, white-colored version of model *1101,* **$400**

Mitchell 1101, $300.

Motorola

6X28, wide coat-pocket with vertical ribs up and over set, 1958, white or brown, **$85;** blue or pink, **$100**

6X31, similar to model *6X32,* logo across slotted plastic grill, **$100**

6X32, wide coat-pocket, 1957, painted metal grill, flip-up handle/stand, **$100**

Motorola 6X31, $100.

6X39, wide radio with flip-up handle/stand, 1958, coat-pocket with AM/Weather band, plane logo with "Weatherama" on front, **$125**

7X23, wide coat-pocket with flip-up handle and stylized chrome rocket, 1959, blue, **$85**

7X24, similar to model *7X23,* brown or white with gold trim, **$75**

7X25, tall coat-pocket with wire handle, 1959, large dial above grooved front, **$25**

56T1, oversized shirt-pocket, 1956, metal front with fabric-covered back, perforated metal grill, flip-up handle, **$75**

66T1, wide coat-pocket with oversized dial at lower right, flip-up handle at top, 1957, **$100**

76T1, 76T2, oversized fabric-covered portables, large plastic handle on top, **$50**

L12, large wide set with "Power 8" between two knobs across front, vinyl handle on top, 1960, **$10**

L13, L14, similar to model *L12,* large plastic handle, **$10**

X11, small shirt-pocket with all metal front, oval window over oval logo, **$35**

Motorola X11, $35.

X12, wide plastic coat-pocket, 1959, recessed knobs at right, **$75**

Olympic

447, large radio with white plastic grill on front, two knobs below top handle, 1955, transistors soldered into tube chassis, **$100**

666, coat-pocket set with oversized tuner over "Olympic 666" logo at front right, 1958, **$100**

766, tall coat-pocket, 1958, leatherette covered, **$40**

768, plastic coat-pocket set with collapsible handle on top, large metal tuner, **$65**

771, coat-pocket set, 1959, large flip-up handle, logo across front, **$75**

779, shirt-pocket set with large circular grill in center, 1959, grey, tan or black, **$50;** red or blue, **$75**

780, shirt-pocket radio with grill at bottom, 2 recessed knobs, black, grey or tan, **$40;** red, **$65**

781, simple shirt-pocket with metal grill at bottom, circular window shows station numbers, black or tan, **$35;** red or blue, **$50**

Olympic 780, $40.

808, wide coat-pocket, 1960, 2 knobs at right, handle on top, **$20**

1100, 1200, large multiband tabletops with High Fidelity, 1960, **$15**

Philco

T-3, "Veep," portable with earphone (no speaker), 1958, 3 recessed knobs on front, **$85**

T-4, coat-pocket radio with large tuner dial at right front, black and white, 1958, **$60;** aqua, **$85**

T-4J, similar to model *T-4,* earphone jack, black, **$75**

Philco T-3, "Veep," $85.

Philco T-4, $60.

T-5, coat-pocket set with numbers appearing in window on front, 1958, black and white, **$60;** pink and black, **$85**

T-6, leather-covered large portable with plastic tuner knob on front, 1958, **$25**

T-7, first Philco radio, coat-pocket set, 1956, painted metal grill at left, usually black and white, **$60;** other colors, **$125**

T-7X, 1958 redesign of model *7-T,* plastic case in front of speaker, **$50**

T-9, large multiband with flip-up front, band scales and 4 knobs on exposed radio front, 1959, **$150**

T-70, large coat-pocket set with wire handle, foil decal above grill, V at top shows tuner numbers, black or grey, **$25;** various colors, **$35**

T-75, large leatherette portable with large tuner dial in front, 1958, **$35**

T-88, wide coat-pocket set with unusual style, 1962, large knob on front, long dial shows on front and top, **$35**

T-500, similar to model *T-5,* black and white, **$60**

T-600, large plastic tabletop version of model *T-6,* black and white, **$25**

T-700, T-800, square plastic set with metal handle-support, 1958, **$50**

T-701, similar to model *T-700,* large handle on top, **$35**

T-900, large plastic tabletop with vertical bars across front, dial at lower right, 1958, **$25**

T-1000, tabletop with square clock in center, square speakers on either side, **$50**

Philco T-70, $25.

Philco T-75, $35.

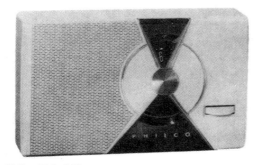

Philco T-7, $60.

Philco T-600, $25.

RCA (Radio Corporation of America)

1-BF-32, coat-pocket set with metal trim, large tuner and recessed volume on right, 1959, radio only, **$60;** radio plus charger base, **$125**

1-BT-2, "Transicharg," coat-pocket set, 1959, complete with oversized cloth-covered battery charger, **$145**

1-BT-3, similar to model *1-BT-2,* flip-up handle, complete with charger, **$145**

1-BT-41, leatherette-covered set with metal grill on front, 1958, **$45**

1-BT-58, large leatherette "Globe trotter" radio with long AM scale on front, knobs on sides, handle on top, 1958, **$25**

1-MBT-6, large multiband portable with flip-up map which exposes 7 band set, 1958, **$175**

RCA 1-MBT-6, $175.

7-BT-9, coat-pocket set with grill at left, large dial at right, 1955, RCA's first transistor radio, **$150**

7-BT-10, large leather-covered set with handle, long dial across top edge, 1955, **$50**

8-BT-7, 8-BT-8, two-tone plastic sets, late 1956, large knob at front right, two-tone grey or black and white, **$50;** turquoise and white or pink and white, **$75**

8-BT-10, similar to model *7-BT-10,* **$35**

9-BT-9, wide plastic set with logo across bottom, 1957, **$75**

RCA 1-BT-2 with simple charger, $145.

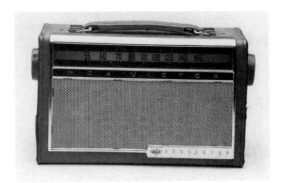

RCA 1-BT-58, "Globe trotter," $25.

RCA 8-BT-7, $50.

RCA 9-BT-9, $75.

Raytheon T-100, $300.

Raytheon

8-TP-1, Raytheon's first set, 1955, large leather-covered radio with oval metal grill
on front, 2 knobs on top, **$150**

T-100, Raytheon's first pocket set, 1956,
metal tuner at right front, molded-in
logo at left, **$300**

T-150, redesigned version of model *T-100,*
metal shield logo at left over "Deluxe,"
$250

T-2500, 1956 redesign of model *8-TP-1,* large
rectangular grill in front, **$125**

Regency

RP-3, leather-covered portable phono, made
to work through model *TR-22,* **$125**

TR-1, the *first* all-transistor radio, shirt-
pocket size with large tuner at right
above grill formed by perforated cabinet,
designed by Painter, Teague, and Pe-
tertil, ivory or black, **$300;** other solid
colors, **$375;** marbleized brown, **$500;**
marbleized green, **$750**

TR-1G, similar to model *TR-1,* label inside
marked "TR-1G" or "TR-1/TR-1G,"
ivory or black, **$200;** other than ivory or
black, **$300**

TR-4, 1957 redesign of the model *TR-1/TR-
1G,* ivory or white, **$150;** other colors,
$200

TR-5, long leatherette-covered radio, 1957,
gold-tone dial at right front, **$125**

TR-6, large leatherette-covered radio, 1957,
square logo at upper left front corner,
controls on side, **$75**

TR-11, simply styled radio with tuner at top
front, 1959, **$85**

TR-22, oversized leatherette portable with
large grill on front, **$75**

Regency TR-1, $300.

Regency TR-1G, $200.

Regency TR-5, $125.

Regency XR-2A, $200.

TR-99, shirt-pocket with "World Wide" on logo over metal grill, 2 knobs across top front, 1960, **$100**

XR-2A, small red 2-transistor set with earphone (no speaker) and on/off lever at top, 1958, **$200**

Roland

4TR, large portable with large plain front, 2 recessed knobs near top, 1959, **$65**

5TR, large tabletop with 2 recessed knobs at top, simple grooved front, 1960, **$20**

6TR, tall radio with leatherette covering, 1957, 2 large knobs on top under strap, **$75**

7TL, 7TW, large portable on wire legs, 1959, scale between 2 knobs across top, **$100**

71-288, wide plastic coat-pocket with alarm clock built into left front, 2 small knobs across bottom, **$45**

TC-10, TC-11, wide radios with wire handle, 1960, 2 small knobs on front, plastic around clock at left, **$35**

TR-8, "Bi-Fidelity," large brief case-style set with 2 large knobs under leatherette handle, **$20**

TW-6, "Twin-Speaker Bi-Fidelity," large portable with 2 large round grills on front, recessed tuner at top lip under metal handle, **$75**

Roland TC-10, $35.

Ross Diamond Micro, $40.

Sharp TR-182, $85.

Ross

Diamond Micro, small plastic radio with metal front and perforated metal grill, 2 knobs on right side, **$40**

RE-210, "Micro Ten Transistor," small square plastic set made in Hong Kong, metal grill on front, 2 knobs on right side, **$25**

Sears

7216, small plastic set, about 3″ high, front has metal grill and window to show station numbers (actually a Channel Master model *6448*), **$35**

Sentinel

CR-729, metal front radio with large dial at front right, 1957, white or black, **$150;** red, turquoise or coral, **$200**

Sharp

TR-182, wide shirt-pocket with metal grill on front, cutout window shows station numbers, 1958, ivory or black, **$85;** other colors, **$100**

Silvertone

208, "All Transistor 500," wide coat-pocket with grooved grill at left and dial and metal insert with logo at right, flip-up handle, **$20**

217, "Transistor 600," oversized leatherette case with controls at sides, 1960, **$15**

220, "All Transistor 700," oversized radio with leatherette body and metal front, **$15**

1201, large shirt-pocket radio with V at top exposing tuner wheel, 1961, **$10**

2201, shirt-pocket with small squares formed on grill area, 1962, **$10**

2202, shirt-pocket set, 1962, logo on metal grill, recessed tuner wheel at right, **$10**

2205, similar to model *3205,* no strap, **$10**

2206, 2207, similar to model *3206,* no strap, **$20**

2208, 2210, "Medalist," wide black plastic coat-pocket sets with metal grill below tuner window, **$10**

2209, 2211, blue versions of model *2208,* **$20**

3205, small shirt-pocket black plastic radio with metal grill and small window near top for station numbers, carry strap at top, **$10**

3206, 3207, similar to model *3205,* gold or blue, **$20**

7228, large set with perforated metal grill on front, leatherette-covered sides, pull-up handle, 1958, **$35**

Silvertone 2201, $10.

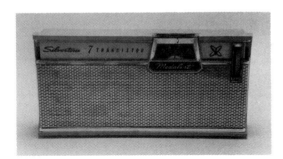

Silvertone 2209, $20.

8204, 8208, tall radios with grill on front, metal handle supports radio, 1957, grey or black, **$50**

8206, similar to model *8204,* coral, **$125**

8220, unusual oversized two-tone set with large front grill, tuner on right side, round volume control under thick metal handle, 1958, **$75**

8228, 8229, oversized table radios, 1958, 3 knobs at right front beside twin-speaker grill, brown or white, **$35**

9202, tall coat-pocket set with slots cut into front forming grill, recessed volume and semicircular tuner window at top, 1958, grey, **$35**

9203, similar to model *9202,* pink, **$65**

9204, 9206, tall coat-pocket sets, 1959, metal grill at bottom, grey or black, **$30**

9205, similar to model *9204,* pink, **$75**

9226, multiband radio with flip-up lid which exposes controls, chart and dials, 1960, **$150**

Sonora

610, wide plastic radio with grill slots at left, tuner at right center with recessed volume control above and logo below, 1957, **$175**

TR-281, tall coat-pocket with wire handle, perforated metal grill on front, brass dial at top front, volume on top at right, **$150**

Sonora TR-281, $150.

Sonora 610, $175.

Sony

ICR-100, first integrated circuit radio, 1966, **$150**

ICR-120, redesign of model *IRC-100,* very small set in black and chrome with 2 knobs on top, complete with charger, **$125**

Sony ICR-100, $150.

Sony IR-81, $65.

IR-81, sub-miniature set about 2″ wide, black plastic with metal grill and logo, **$65**

TFM-151, first transistor FM set, 1958, common, **$25**

TFM-825, coat-pocket AM/FM set with long dial on left edge, 1965, **$10**

TR-55, Sony's first and most desirable set, 1955, coat-pocket, "transistorized" across top, oval dial, large knob on front, **$750**

TR-63, shirt-pocket with oversized tuner at top left front, 1957, advertised as "world's smallest," very popular set, black or ivory, **$275;** other colors, **$400**

TR-86, shirt-pocket with wrap around metal grill below logo and large tuner, 1959, **$125**

TR-610, small pocket set with large circular metal grill below tuner window, wire handle, 1958, **$75**

TR-650, coat-pocket set with oversized circular grill, 1965, **$20**

TRW-621, shirt-pocket with clock in upper left corner, 1961, **$85**

Sony TR-63, $275.

Sony TR-650, $20.

Sparton

CR-729, Sentinel *CR-729* with Sparton logo, black or white, **$175;** red or turquoise, **$200**

Standard (Micronic Ruby)

SR-F22, 1958, shirt-pocket radio with large tuner and recessed volume control above wrap around metal grill, **$75**

SR-F410, wide shirt-pocket radio, oval metal grill on front, controls on right side, **$25**

SR-G430, "Micronic Ruby," sub-miniature set with pointed metal grill, 1965, ruby red plastic with gold trim, **$75**

Standard SR-F410, $25.

SR-G433, less expensive plastic version of model *SR-H437,* 1965, metal slot grill on front, 2 plastic knobs on right side, **$35**

SR-H46, small square "Micronic Ruby," black or red plastic, flush logo on front, long metal plate with logo on top, 2 knobs on right, **$100**

SR-H436, similar to model *SR-H438,* perforated metal grill across front, **$65;** gold-tone metal and trim, black plastic case, **$85**

Standard SR-H437, $65.

Standard SR-Q460F, $150.

SR-H437, "Micronic Ruby," with circular logo on front, 1965, black plastic case with chrome trim, **$65;** ruby red with gold-tone trim, **$75**

SR-H438, wide sub-miniature radio, 1965, large chrome slot grill covers most of front, black plastic case, **$65;** gold-tone metal with black plastic body, **$85**

SR-J770F, wide coat-pocket FM/AM radio, plastic set with perforated metal grill at left, circular station windows at right, **$10**

SR-Q460F, black plastic miniature AM/FM radio, flip-up antenna on left, chrome tuner on right, **$150**

Sylvania

4P05, small shirt-pocket with arc-shaped station window on front, **$10**

Sylvania 4P14, $50.

Sylvania 3102 "Thunderbird," $200.

4P14, wide coat-pocket radio with slot grill on front with volume knob and station number window, partially opens to insert batteries, **$50**

5P10, 5P11, deluxe versions of model *4P14,* **$50**

7P12, coat-pocket radio similar to model *4P14,* 1960, stands vertically on wire handle, **$50**

3202, 3203, 3204, coat-pocket sets with collapsing plastic handle on top, large tuner at right front, 1957, **$50**

3305, deluxe two-tone version of model *3203,* **$65**

Toshiba

5TR, "Lace," shirt-pocket with lace fabric beneath clear grill, tuner in upper right corner, black or white, **$100;** other colors, **$145**

6TC-485, set opens in center to expose watch on left half, radio on right, 1962, **$75**

6TP-31, small shirt-pocket with chrome front, semicircular window for tuner pointer, **$65**

Toshiba 5TR "Lace," $100.

Toshiba 6TP-31, $65.

6TP-309, shirt-pocket, 1960, perforated metal grill at bottom, window in large metal V, **$50**

6TP-385, wide two-tone plastic shirt-pocket with perforated chrome grill, 2 recessed knobs on right side, **$50**

6TR-92, globe-shaped table set with elaborate design around upper half, clean and complete, **$125**

6TR-186, wide shirt-pocket with grill at left, 2 recessed knobs at right, 1959, white or black, **$50;** other colors, **$75**

7TP-303, shirt-pocket set with metal V across grill, **$40;** with oversized speaker/power supply, **$100**

Toshiba 8TM-294, $65.

8TM-294, large wide radio with checkerboard metal grill across front, clear plastic tuner with station numbers on both edges, **$65**

8TM-3005, wide coat-pocket with AM and shortwave scale under windows at top, control knobs on sides, **$25**

9TM-40, unusually styled-shirt pocket, 1961, metal grill on lower section, top with tuner smaller than bottom, **$100**

Trav-Ler

TR-250, TR-251, tall coat-pocket with wire handle, 1957, metal grill on front, brass dial at top front, volume on top at right, **$150**

TR-280, TR-281, 1958 version of model TR-250, "all-transistor" across bottom, **$75**

TR-601, shirt-pocket set, 1961, large perforated metal grill beneath 2 recessed controls, **$30**

TR-620, TR-625, all plastic coat-pocket sets with tuner pointer visible through large clear plastic window at right, **$20**

Toshiba 6TP-385, $50.

Trav-ler TR-620, $20.

Truetone

D3614, "Deluxe 4," wide coat-pocket set, 1957, metal shield logo at left, metal tuner at right, **$200**

D3715, wide coat-pocket radio with volume below tuner on front right, 1958, **$150**

D3716, large leatherette-covered radio with 2 knobs at front top, 1957, **$75**

DC3050, coat-pocket with AM/shortwave bands across top edge, 1959, **$15**

DC3052, wide coat-pocket with metal V and station window at right, 2 knobs on right side, **$30**

DC3164, shirt-pocket with small circular window for station numbers on front, 1962, **$10**

DC3884, oversized leatherette portable with 2 knobs on front, 1958, **$25**

DC3886, larger version of model *DC3884,* **$25**

Westinghouse

H-587, H-588, wide coat-pocket sets, 1957, large clear plastic tuner with numbers at right front, grey or black, **$35**

H-589, similar to model *H-587,* red, **$50**

H-602, very large leatherette-covered radio with metal grill in center under 2 knobs, circa 1957, **$35**

H-610, wide grey plastic coat-pocket set with large dial at front right, 1957, **$30**

H-611, H-612, similar to model *H-610,* blue or yellow, **$45**

H-617, H-618, similar to model *H-610,* square-holed grill, grey or black, **$30**

H-619, similar to model *H-617,* red, **$45**

H-621, H-622, oversized plastic radios with metal handle over 2 knobs, 1958, lays flat or stands up, **$75**

H-651, H-653, wide coat-pocket sets with square and circular grill holes, recessed volume control below tuner at right, 1957, **$60**

H-652, similar to model *H-651,* turquoise, **$80**

Westinghouse H-619, $45.

Westinghouse H-617, $30.

H-655, coat-pocket set, 1959, white and grey with grill over large tuner, metal handle, **$30**

H-656, similar to model *H-655,* white and red, **$40**

H-685, tabletop radio with clock to left and dial at right, 1959, **$15**

H-697, similar to model *H-656,* two-tone finish, **$35**

Westinghouse H-693, $55.

H-693, 1959 version of model *H-652*, brown
with gold trim, **$55**; green and gold or
pink and gold, **$75**

Zenith

Royal 50, shirt-pocket with clear pointer over
station numbers, 1961, **$10**

Royal 150, small shirt-pocket with grained
plastic case, 1962, **$10**

Royal 200, tall rectangular plastic set with
large tuner dial above grill, **$15**

Royal 300, shirt-pocket Royal series, 1958,
small circular tuner window at front
right, **$35**

Royal 450, large portable with metal handle at
top, 1959, **$35**

Royal 500, Zenith's first shirt-pocket set,
chassis number on battery compartment
7XT40, hand wired, black or maroon,
$100; other colors, **$175**; printed circuit board chassis *7XT40Z*, **$65**

Royal 500E, similar to *Royal 500*, plastic area
around circular speaker has perforated
look, **$35**

Royal 500H, tall coat-pocket with large oval
brass grill beneath and in front of controls, **$100**

Royal 500H2, similar to *Royal 500H*, electrical redesign, **$75**

Royal 500RD, similar to *Royal 500*, "Long
Distance" below logo, **$50**

Royal 555N, square black plastic radio with
chrome trim, flip-up plastic handle with
solar batteries, **$125**

Zenith Royal 500, $100.

Royal 700, oversized leatherette portable with
2 knobs on front, 1958, **$25**

Royal 750, similar to *Royal 700*, **$25**

Zenith Royal 500H, $100.

Zenith Royal 555N, $125.

Zenith Royal 755 (similar to Royal 750), $25.

Royal 760, "Navigator" version of *Royal 700,* signal-strength antenna under handle, **$35**

Royal 800, large radio with pop-up handle at top, large round speaker, 1957, Zenith's first transistor radio, black or ivory, **$125;** other colors, **$175**

Royal 900, wide tabletop, clear plastic left side with tuner and volume knobs, **$15**

Royal 950, "Golden Triangle," set sits on gold-tone base with speaker on one side, clock on second side, and radio on third side, **$150**

Royal 1000, large "Trans-oceanic" portable with 8-band scales, front and back open, **$100**

Novelty Radios

The love of novelties is high in most collectible fields, and radio collectors have also felt the call. An inexpensive and amusing collection can be assembled very quickly if the radio collector sets his sights on novelty transistor radios. Although today most novelty radios come from Hong Kong or even China, there were lots of early examples from Japan and a few from the United States.

In general, the major product brands of soda, beer, and food stuffs have swamped the marketplace with novelties, but often even these premiums will be in short supply within a few years of their offering. Many interesting new sets can be bought for the cost of the product, a stamp, and possibly a few dollars; many of the older novelty sets do command a much higher price. Many collectors also buy or trade with other collectors from other parts of the country (or world) who may have easy access to radios featuring products not distributed locally.

Some people collect by theme, for example all forms of transportation, from the Model T Ford to the 1960s Mustangs. Cartoon characters, from the He-Man series to Superman and Little LuLu, have been immortalized in novelty radio form. Some of the early Japanese sets resemble guns, golf balls, even bugs, and a well-rounded collection might include as many different types and styles as can possibly be found and bought.

Luckily, premiums are being designed, produced, and distributed right now, and a clever collector does not pass up the opportunity to buy a new novelty radio. Today's passed-by commonplace radios might lead you on tomorrow's futile search.

Novelty Transistors

Adam and Eve, 2 tall black plastic radio halves with chrome sex organs, halves push together, **$100**

Alligator, long green plastic radio in the shape of a reptile, produced by General Electric, **$30**

Apple, fruit-shaped small plastic radio with stem on top, **$20**

Automobile

Rolls Royce, plastic body with chrome and brass trim, **$15;** pewter or brass body, trimmed in plastic and plated plastic, **$35**

Model "T" Ford or similar antique car, plastic with metal-plated trim, **$15**

Old touring car, plastic with chrome or brass-plated trim, **$15**

1960s car manufacturers' promotion, well-detailed Ford or GM automobile from the period with quality radio in bottom, **$50**

Avon Skin-So-Soft, plastic bottle-shaped radio with controls on back, painted logo, **$20**

Backgammon, rectangular radio with painted game board, checkers and dice inside, **$20**

Ball

Simple plastic ball by Panasonic with cutout for dial, large metal knobs, **$15**

Round red ball with "76" (gasoline station) logo, **$25**

Barbie Radio System, oversized plastic bust of Barbie doll with remote speakers, complete, **$25**

Avon Skin-So-Soft, $20.

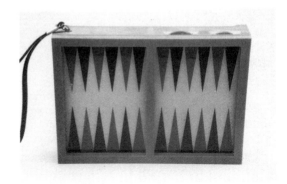

Backgammon, $20.

Automobile, antique car, $15.

Baseball

Simple white plastic baseball style radio, **$20**

Japanese-made Toshiba baseball, mounted on 3 baseball bats, complete, **$85**

Batman, plastic radio showing top half of super-hero's body, very clean, **$65**

Battery

Small car battery-shaped radio with decals, about 4″ wide, **$30**

Car battery, large radio with good detailing, about 12″ long, **$100**

Flashlight battery-shaped radio, brand logo on decals, **$20**

Beer

Bottle-shaped radio with decal of brand type, **$20**

Simple can-shaped radio, decals to simulate can of beer, **$15**

Big Bird (Sesame Street)

White plastic head-shaped radio with molded and painted details, **$30**

Flat bird's-head shaped radio with paper decal on front, **$15**

Binoculars, Japanese Bakelite or plastic opera-glass size set with controls on top, **$60**

Bowling Ball, black ball-shaped radio set atop 3 crossed pins, complete, **$60**

Battery, flashlight battery shape, $20.

Bozo, clown's head with hair and collar, very clean, **$65**

Bugs Bunny

Plastic bunny seated or standing on plastic base, **$20**

Plastic radio shaped like top half of Bugs with carrot in hand, clean, **$50**

Cabbage Patch Kid, child on plastic base, **$20**

Camel, "Tune-a-Camel" radio in camel shape, **$15**

Camera-Radio, Kowa *Ramera* or Bell *Kamra,* coat-pocket radio with 16mm spy radio built in, **$75**

Camera, inexpensive black plastic camera-shaped set with flashlight and radio built in, **$20**

Cannon, plastic and metal cannon-shaped radio, **$30**

Care Bears

Semicircular plastic radio with plastic sticker of bear, **$10**

Small plastic bear-shaped radio with heart or smile on stomach, **$15**

Cathedral Radio, old-fashioned beehive-shaped brown plastic set, **$15**

Champagne Bottle, oversized radio in the shape of a bottle of bubbly, various brands, **$45**

Cathedral, $15.

Charlie the Tuna

Bike radio, flat blue radio with "Sorry Charlie" and fish outline, **$40**

Blue plastic radio in shape of standing fish, **$60**

Cigarette Pack

Pack-shaped plastic radio, lid flips up to give access to controls, **$40**

Oversized rectangular radio, brand markings on wrap around decal, **$25**

Coca-Cola Can, soda-can shaped radio, **$15**

Coke Bottle, tall bottle-shaped radio, **$20**

Coke Cooler, small cooler-shaped transistor radio with "Drink Coca-Cola," **$65**

Cookie, Nabisco Oreo cookie-shaped plastic radio, **$25**

Cookies, rectangular radio with Keebler's Animal Crackers label, **$30**

Cow, "Tune-a-Cow" radio in cow shape, **$15**

Cracker Jack, box-shaped radio with decals, **$30**

Dick Tracy, wrist radio, for child's arm, complete (several versions), **$65**

Dollar Bill

Clear plastic block with bills inside, **$15**

Money-shaped wide rectangular simple plastic radio with decal on top, **$20**

Donald Duck, plastic radio in shape of Donald's head and cap, very clean, **$65**

Duck, "Tune-a-Duck" radio in duck shape, **$15**

Ernie, Sesame Street boy in bath tub, **$15**

Elephant, "Tune-a-Elephant" radio in pachyderm shape, **$15**

Football, brown plastic football-shaped radio, **$25**

Fred Flintstone, plastic radio in shape of cartoon character's head, very clean, **$65**

Frog, "Tune-a-Frog" radio in frog shape, **$15**

Garfield (the cat)

Plastic rectangular radio with Garfield clawing at side of set, **$15**

Plastic radio shaped like the face of Garfield with broad smile, **$40**

Gasoline Pump

Tall and thin plastic radio in shape of old-fashioned gas pump, **$30**

Rectangular modern pump-shaped radio with square logo on front, **$10**

Gasoline Pump, modern style, $10.

Globe, paper globe on base, $25.

Girl

  Black-skinned sexy blonde in nightgown, unusual, **$100**

  Sexy girl in shear nightgown, radio controls on breasts, complete, **$50**

Globe

  Dateline on clear plastic top half, imitation marble base, **$20**

  Plastic globe radio mounted on a plastic base, **$20**

  Paper or composition globe radio on wooden or plastic base, **$25**

  Oversized table radio, Toshiba model *6TR-92* with elaborate design around upper half, **$125**

Golf Ball, white plastic golf-ball shaped radio, **$35**

Golf Club, small Japanese-made radio in shape of club and partial shaft, **$45**

Grenade, green plastic ammo-shaped set, **$30**

Gumby, large flat green plastic radio in Gumby's shape, **$25**

Gun, derringer-shaped plastic radio, realistically-detailed small Japanese set, **$60**

Hamburger, plastic radio shaped like hamburger or cheeseburger on bun, **$15**

Hand, "Hamburger Helper" hand-shaped radio with big red nose in palm, **$30**

Harp, tall plastic radio in musical instrument shape, brass and gold-tone trim, **$45**

He-Man, face of cartoon warrior on plastic base with logo on front, **$20**

Helmet, football-helmet shaped radio with various team logos, **$20**

Hi-Fi, wide radio/record player stereo-shaped unit with speakers or storage space, **$15**

Holly Hobbie, plastic radio with young girl, **$20**

Hot Dog, plastic radio in shape of hot dog on roll, **$15**

Huckleberry Hound and Yogi Bear, plastic radio in shape of side-by-side faces, **$60**

Huckleberry Hound, plastic radio shaped like face of "Huck" with bow tie, **$50**

Ice Cream Bar, plastic radio shaped like a pop on a stick with bite taken out, **$30**

Golf Club, $45.

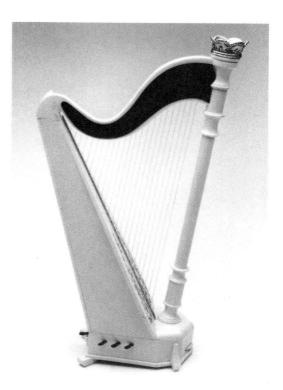

Harp, $45.

Ice Cream Cone, food-shaped plastic radio, **$30**

Keg, large brown plastic keg-shaped set with volume at tap, **$35**

Ketchup, red plastic bottle-shaped set with logo on front and top, **$25**

Knight

Bust of knight in armor, face plate lifts, complete, **$35**

Standing knight in armor with letter opener/sword, complete with opener, **$25**

Ladybug, small radio in bug shape, wings open, complete, **$15**

Light, blue fireman's-light shaped radio with dial around bottom, **$20**

Lion, "Tune-a-Leo" radio in lion shape, **$15**

Lipton Cup-of-Soup, box-shaped radio with decals, **$30**

Little Sprout, Green Giant's child-shaped radio, **$35**

Lock, plastic Master-lock shaped radio in silver and black finish, **$30**

Little Sprout, $35.

Lion, "Tune-a-Leo," $15.

Locomotive, old-style train engine, black plastic body with gold or silver trim, **$20**

Loop, Panasonic plastic radio, loop opens to fit around wrist, **$15**

Love

Plastic radio forming the letters "L-O-V-E," various styles and colors, **$15**

Pendant radio with metal mesh grill, "Love" painted on grill, **$20**

LuLu, face of famous cartoon girl, Little LuLu, complete with pigtails, **$65**

Mayonnaise, Miracle-Whip brand jar-shaped radio with decals, **$30**

Michael Jackson, rectangular radio with paper label on front picturing performer, **$15**

Mickey Mouse

Figure of Mickey reclining on large blue arm chair, **$20**

Plastic form of Mickey on front of large radio, **$20**

Radio in shape of mouse's face with big black ears, **$30**

Money Talks, $25.

Mork from Ork, white plastic egg-shaped radio with Mork's face in window, **$15**

Mouth, Blabber Mouth shows lips and teeth on square white radio, **$12**

Mustard, jar-shaped radio with Gulden's mustard decals, **$30**

Oil, can-shaped radio, decals of various oil brands around sides, **$15**

Outboard Motor, large plastic boat-motor shaped set on metal stand, **$60**

Owl

 Very detailed large plastic standing bird with brass trim, jeweled eyes are controls, **$40**

Mayonnaise, Miracle-Whip jar, $30.

Mickey Mouse, mouse's face, $30.

Reclining Mickey on yellow rectangular radio, doors in front, complete, **$25**

Small square blue radio with Mickey's head and ears built into set, **$12**

Microphone, old-fashioned desk-microphone shaped plastic radio on base, **$30**

Money Talks, wide plastic set with $1.00 decal, Washington's tongue moves, **$25**

Owl, very detailed, $40.

Small yellow plastic radio with basic owl shape, little detailing, dials form eyes, **$10**

Pacman, round yellow plastic radio in circular video cartoon character's shape, **$20**

Paint Can, can-shaped radio with label and handle of various paint manufacturers, **$20**

Panda, plastic panda-bear shaped set in white and black, **$20**

Peace, pendant radio with metal mesh grill, "Peace" painted on grill, **$15**

Pendant, black plastic oval with jewel on front, large gold-tone chain, **$35**

Pen, "Radibo," small plastic ballpoint pen with radio built into top portion, **$25**

Pepsi Bottle, bottle-shaped radio with Pepsi decals, **$25**

Pepsi Can, soda-can shaped plastic radio with Pepsi decals, **$15**

Pepsi Dispenser

Tall rectangular plastic set with plastic decals, shape of modern soda-can machine, **$25**

Old-fashioned soda-fountain shaped radio, 3 taps and plastic glass, complete, **$100**

Panda bear, $20.

Paint Can, $20.

Pepsi Dispenser, modern machine, $25.

Phonograph, old style gramophone with large horn, complete, **$15**

Piano, grand piano, lid opens, detailed Japanese set, **$65**

Piggy Bank, plastic pig-shaped radio, **$20**

Pillsbury Doughboy, white plastic "boy" with blue eyes and logo, **$30**

Pinocchio, radio shaped like head of whittled youth complete with hat and bow tie, **$55**

Planters Peanuts, can-shaped plastic radio with Planters logo on blue decal, **$20**

Polaroid Film, square blue plastic radio, paper labels with brand information, **$15**

Popeye, plastic set in the shape of sailor's head with pipe, **$65**

Pound Puppy, soft stuffed dog on top of simple plastic radio, **$15**

Pyramid, "Tetra," large pyramid-shaped set with AM on one face and FM on other, **$25**

Radio

Plastic set forming the letters "R-A-D-I-O," various styles, **$15**

Old-fashioned radio formed in ceramic, simple modern radio placed in bottom or back, **$10**

Raggedy Ann and Andy, plastic radio shaped like side-by-side children, **$25**

Railroad Crossing, large black plastic radio with train station signs, **$25**

Raisin, set shaped like California Raisin character holding a microphone, **$30**

Robot, various designs of robot or transforming robot shape, **$20**

Piggy Bank, $20.

Planters Peanuts can, $20.

Polaroid Film, $15.

Rocket Ship

Large plastic tabletop in shape of rocket on base, **$15**

Small two-tone plastic spaceship with earphone (no speaker), actually a crystal set, **$65**

Saucer

Large "flying saucer" black plastic Toshiba wall radio with gold trim, **$100**

Small "flying saucer" with clear top which exposes components, **$30**

Scooby Doo, plastic set shaped like cartoon dog's face with tongue, **$50**

Secretary, old-fashioned secretary-shaped set with bookcase, radio built into back, **$25**

Shell, yellow clamshell-shaped plastic radio with Shell motor oil company logo, **$75**

Ship

Old sailing ship with plastic body, masts and lines, on plastic base, complete, **$35**

Yacht or speedboat in plastic and painted metal, **$55**

Shoe, radio shaped like lady's high-heeled shoe, **$20**

Skate, small plastic skate-shaped radio, **$20**

Smurf, plastic radio in shape of blue elf's head with large white hat, **$20**

Snoopy

Large white plastic dog-shaped radio with black sketched details, **$25**

Smurf, $20.

Snoopy, $25.

Rocket Ship, $15.

Radio shaped like dog laying on top of red and white plastic doghouse, complete, **$25**

Snorks, strange looking plastic radio shaped like yellow head of cartoon character, nozzle-shaped top, **$20**

Soap Powder, rectangular box-shaped radio with logo on applied decal, **$25**

Soccer Ball, European football-shaped plastic radio, **$15**

Soda Can, can-shaped plastic radio with decals of various brands of soda pop, **$15**

Space Ship, various styles of plastic radios resembling plastic rockets on plastic bases, **$20**

Spark Plug, large Champion brand grey and white plastic spark plug, **$65**

Spice Rack, brown radio, doors open in front to expose storage area, **$20**

Spiderman

Simple round red plastic radio in shape of web with eyes, **$10**

Oversized red radio in shape of "Spidey's" head, **$45**

Spray Can, tall aerosol-can shaped radio with decals, various logos, **$30**

Sputnik, globe-shaped radio with clear plastic top, control knobs on sides, **$30**

Stagecoach, old-fashioned coach with plastic body and metal trim and wheels, **$25**

Statue of Liberty, metal statue on plastic base which conceals simple radio, **$35**

Steam Boat, large plastic paddle boat with plastic body and metal and metal-plated trim, **$35**

Spiderman head, $45.

Sunglasses, sunglasses with miniature radio built into both arms, **$60**

Superman, flat radio resembling top half of body with fists clenched, very clean, **$65**

Tape Measure, Stanley Powerlock chrome-plated plastic radio, **$25**

Teacher's Highland Cream, tall whiskey bottle with paper label, **$45**

Telephone

Old style candlestick-telephone shaped radio, **$15**

Radio shaped like French styled phone, movable headset, **$15**

Television, TV-shaped radio with room for photo, **$15**

Tire, car-tire shaped black plastic radio with chrome-plated rim, **$30**

Toilet, small plastic toilet-shaped radio with lift-up seat, **$15**

Toilet Paper, oversized plastic radio with paper dispenser attached, **$10**

Tom and Jerry, large face of cat with mouse standing at side, **$85**

Soccer Ball, $15.

Tropicana, $20.

Tony the Tiger, orange tiger-shaped radio with logo at bottom, **$30**

Tropicana, orange fruit-shaped radio with straw, **$20**

Van deGraff Generator, brown plastic base with large black plastic ball on top, **$20**

Watch

Armitron watch with radio tuner on front, working, **$25**

Large wristwatch-shaped wall-hanging radio, **$30**

Whiskey, small dark plastic bottle-shaped radio with brand decals, **$25**

Wine Cask, large brown plastic cask-shaped radio, **$25**

World Timer 747, large plastic cylinder, globe and time zones at top, **$25**

Yago Sangria, tall bottle-shaped set with decals of drink, **$30**

Chapter Three
VINTAGE TELEVISIONS

History

Since the mid-1980s, television collecting has been recognized as an "acceptable" associated hobby at most radio meets and in most radio clubs. Although there are individuals who have always liked the television sets of bygone eras, formal structure and pricing became well established only recently. There are two distinct influences on the pricing of vintage televisions: television collectors, who look for early and historically significant models; and 1950s collectors who search for "retro" items and buy the more modern televisions (which are generally shunned by vintage television collectors). The model number can be found on the back of the set or on the metal chassis.

Although many novice collectors only know to look for "Channel 1" televisions (post WWII sets), there are many other important sets. Unusually styled sets from the 1940s and 1950s, with 7″ to 20″ picture tubes, are included in the important vintage televisions as defined by hobbyists. Large-screen wooden televisions from the mid-1950s to mid-1960s, and the "space-age" look plastic or metal sets that have been mar-

keted over the years, are important to design-oriented collectors.

The purpose of this chapter is to clarify what are and what are not collectible vintage televisions. Interestingly, vintage televisions need not work to be of value; generally, old tube-type televisions will not work, or not work safely, when found.

Most collectible televisions fall into four basic groups:

1. *Mechanical.* (Current value—$500–$5,000.) The earliest televisions were produced in the late 1920s and early 1930s. These mechanically-operated televisors were sold both as kits and finished sets, and were sold with and without electronics. They usually have a neon bulb (or at least a socket for one) which would shine through a spirally-perforated metal or paper disc which was spun by a motor. The image was viewed through a magnifying lens or was projected onto a small ground-glass screen. These sets are often overlooked because they are so rudimentary.

2. *Pre-war electrical.* (Current value—$1,000–$6,000.) These televisions usually contain a very long, funnel-shaped picture tube, almost always 5″, 9″, or 12″, and often contain as many as five chassis inside with electrical components. Sold as kits or pre-built sets, the majority of these televisions were made in the mid and late 1930s, with the majority sold at about the time of the 1939 World's Fair. RCA, GE, and dozens of other major manufacturers were producing and selling these early televisions, as both console and tabletop sets. Most of these pre-war sets have a push-button or "click" type tuner with one, three, or five channels, although some were modified in the 1940s with a thirteen-channel tuner.

3. *Early black-and-white post-war sets.* (Current value—$25–$500.) Look for televisions in unusually styled wooden cases made from 1945–1949, usually with 7″, 10″ or 12″ picture tubes and with tuners for channels 1–13 or 2–13. The very square sets from the early 1950s are usually shunned, as are most of the metal and Bakelite cabinets from the late 1940s and 1950s.

4. *Early color sets and color adapters.* (Current value—$250–$3,000.) In the early 1950s, many companies experimented with color television. (GE actually tried color experiments in the late 1930s, but pre-war color televisions are virtually non-existent.) Nineteen inch and smaller round picture-tube color television sets from 1955 or earlier are of value to many television collectors. The cabinets are quite large and very heavy and look strange with such small picture tubes. Also, any color adapter or color wheel, contraptions which were added to a black-and-white television to produce a true color image, is valuable. However, most magnifiers, antennas, and stick-on polarizing filters from the period have little value.

Admiral

C2516, 24″ console, 1954, simple square lines, **$20**

F2817, double-door console with 27″ tube, 1954, **$20**

L2326, huge combination with 21″ screen behind left door and pullout radio-phono behind right door, 1952, **$20**

LHS21H54, LHS21H62, 21″ HiFi remote-control consoles, 1959, **$20**

P17E31, painted metal tabletop with handle on top, 1959, **$35**

P17F2, plastic 17″ portable with controls at right front, 1959, **$10**

SH21H39, SH21H44, stereo HiFi consoles with phono behind doors below 21″ screen, 1959, **$20**

T2316, T2317, square-lined wooden TVs with 21″ picture tube, 1952, **$20**

4H15, 4H126, large combinations with TV and pull-out phono plus AM/FM radio, 1949, **$15**

8C11, 10″ combination (chassis *30A1*), 1948, large, heavy and unpopular, **$25**

14R12, 14″ Bakelite tabletop, 1951, 2 large knobs below screen, **$25**

16R12, 16″ version of model *24R12,* **$25**

17T11, 7″ brown or black Bakelite tabletop, 1948, **$100**

19A11, similar to model *17T11,* **$100**

20A1, 20Y1, 10″ tabletops, 1949, **$75**

20B1, 20Z1, 12″ wooden TVs, circa 1948, **$75**

20T1, 21B1, 14″ Bakelite consoles, very square lines, 1949, **$25**

20X11, 10″ Bakelite tabletop, square lines, ribs molded into sides, **$65**

Admiral 20X11, $65.

20X122, 10″ Bakelite console, 1948, small and quite popular, **$200**

22X12

    Bakelite console with 12″ screen, 1949, square lines, square speaker grill, **$25**

24R12, large Bakelite console, 1950, 14″ rectangular screen with square block grill, **$35**

30A14, 30B15, 10″ wooden consoles, 1948, **$75**

32X15, 32X35, 12″ wooden combinations with TV behind right door, slide-out radio-phono behind left door, 1950, **$25**

321F46, 321K46, large combinations with 20″ screen, 1951, "Tele-Bar" and glassware concealed behind right door, **$150**

Air King

Model 1200, 1937, 12″ mirror-in-lid pre-war with radio, large credenza with TV image projected up onto left-hand lid, **Rare**

A-711, A-712, 1950, wooden tabletops, 12″ screen, **$35**

A-1000, 1948, 10″ wide wooden tabletop

Air King A-1001, $100.

with grill cloth in right and left panels, 4 knobs across bottom, **$100**

A-1001, 1949, 10″ wide console, screen a bit forward of wooden cabinet, **$100**

A-1001A, 1949, 10″ console with flat front, screen over 4 knobs and large grill cloth, **$75**

A-1016, 1949, 16″ console, very square lines, drop-down door at center conceals controls, **$50**

A-2000, 1949, 10″ square wooden tabletop with screen slightly offset to left, **$75**

A-2001, 12″ tabletop version of model A-2000, **$75**

A-2002, 12″ console version of model A-1001A, **$75**

12C1, 12T1, 12″ wooden TVs, 1949, **$75**

16C1, 1950, simply styled 16″ console, 2 knobs below screen, **$25**

Andrea

KTE-5, 5″ kit TV, 1937, metal chassis complete with front panel and 5″ funnel-shaped picture tube, **$2,500**

1-F-5, 5″ factory assembled pre-war TV, 1937, complete set including the original wooden cabinet, **$3,500**

2F12, 8F12, large 12″ pre-war mirror-in-lid consoles, 1939, 5-channel tuner, may have 3-band radio and phono, rare, **$4,500**

C-VJ12, console version of model *T-VJ12,* **$75**

CO-VJ12, combination version of model *T-VJ12,* double doors in front of screen and phono, **$75**

C-VK12, 12″ console, continuous tuner to right of screen, **$100**

C-VK15, 15″ wooden TV with 13-channel continuous tuner with FM radio dial below screen, 1948, **$75**

CO-VK12, 12″ combination with double doors concealing continuous tuner at right of screen, pullout phono below, 1948, **$75**

BUILD YOUR OWN TELEVISION

SIGHT and SOUND RECEIVER!

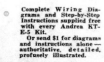

Andrea Television Kit, rear view, assembled.

Andrea pre-war 5" televisions.

Andrea T-VK12, $100.

CO-VK16, 16″ combination, tuner similar to model C-VK15, **$75**

T-VJ12, 12″ console with screen out and up a bit, long TV/AM radio dial below, 1948, **$125**

T-VK12, 12″ wide wooden tabletop with continuous 13-channel tuner and FM radio dial on right side of screen, 1948, **$100**

Ansley

701, "Beacon," 10″ wide wooden tabletop with 13-channel tuner, 1948, grill cloth and mesh on left and right panels, 4 knobs at bottom, **$75**

12″ wooden tabletop, 1949, continuous tuner (similar to DuMont sets), **$65**

Bellevue, blonde finish, modern combination version of *Somerset* model, **$25**

Projection TV

Set resembles an end table, small door exposes projection lens, 1948, **$25**

"Revere," combination with radio and phono, in double-door cabinet, 1949, **$100**

Somerset, 12″ combination, 1948, double-door set, TV on left, radio and phono on right, **$25**

Arvin

15-550, large color console with plain front, 15″ round picture tube, 1954, scarce, **$450**

Arvin 2160, $25.

2160, simple console version of model 2161, 1950, **$25**

2161, 16″ square-lined TV with 2 knobs below screen, **$35**

3120, 12″ wooden tabletop, 1950, simple style, 2 knobs below screen, **$35**

4080T, 8″ metal tabletop, 1950, slightly rounded top, cabinet painted mahogany, green, or blonde, clean and complete, **$100**

8211, 8213, 21″ tabletops, 1953, 2 knobs below screen, **$10**

9210, similar to model 9218, double doors, **$10**

9218, 21″ console, 1953, screen above 2 knobs, **$10**

9240, 24″ console version of model 9218, **$10**

Arvin 4080T, $100.

Automatic

TV-707, 7″ blonde wooden tabletop, 1948, screen in center with grill slots on each side, **$200**

TV-709, 7″ mahogany version of model *TV-707,* **$200**

TV-710, scarce 7″ console in mahogany, 1948, screen centered in top half, speaker grill below, **$500**

TV-712, blonde version of model *TV-710,* **$500**

TV-P490, leatherette-covered 7″ portable with lid and handle, built-in magnifier, 1948, **$350**

TV-1049, -1050, -1055, 10″ TVs, 1949, **$75**

TV-1249, 12″ wooden tabletop, 1949, rounded edges, **$75**

TV-1250, console version of model *TV-1249,* **$25**

TV-1649, -1650, 16″ TVs, 1950, square lines, **$50**

5006-T, 16″ wooden tabletop, simple styling, 1949, **$25**

Baird Shortwave and Television Corporation

K-26, mechanical TV, circa 1932, amplifier, motor, lens and lamp, **$1,500**

Belmont (See Raytheon/ Belmont)

Bendix

235B1, blonde version of model *235M1,* **$75**

235M1, 10″ mahogany tabletop with double doors which conceal plastic bezels around screen and push-button tuner, 1949, **$75**

325M8, 10″ combination version of model *235M1,* TV at upper right, phono and radio at upper left, storage space and speaker below, **$50**

2001, 10″ tabletop, 1950, rounded corners, 3 knobs below screen, **$100**

2020, 12″ version of model *2001,* **$85**

2025, 12″ square-lined tabletop, 1950, 3 knobs below screen, **$65**

2051, 16″ square-lined tabletop, larger version of model *2025,* **$50**

3001, 10″ console version of model *2001,* **$50**

3030, 12″ console version of model *2001,* **$50**

3051, 16″ square-lined console, similar to model *2051,* **$35**

6001, 16″ console with double doors, similar to model *2051,* **$20**

6100, 16″ combination, 1950, similar to model *2051,* **$20**

Capehart/Farnsworth

GV-260, 10″ tabletop, 1947, controls beside and below screen, front top rounded with mesh grill, scarce, **$200**

2T216, 3T216, square wooden tabletops with 21″ tube, knobs below screen, 1953, **$20**

8C215, 21″ wooden console, 1953, 2 large knobs below screen, **$15**

22C215, similar to model *8C215,* triple speaker in bottom grill, **$15**

321M, square-lined tabletop, 1950, 16″ screen with 4 knobs below, **$15**

325F, console version of model *321M,* colonial styling with double doors, **$415**

651-P, 661-P, deep wooden tabletops with 10″ screen, 1948, lid swings to side to allow access to chassis, **$75**

Capehart 651-P, $75.

3001, 3002, wooden tabletops, 1950, **$35**

4001, 12″ combination with AM/FM radio and phono, **$65**

CBS-Columbia

U22C05, console similar to model *22C05,* UHF added, 1955, **$25**

U23C49, UHF version of double-door console model *23C49,* **$25**

10FM, 12FM, wooden tabletops, 1948, actually Videodyne TVs with CBS logo, **$150**

10TV, 12TV, wooden tabletops, 1948, actually Videodyne TVs with CBS logo, **$150**

12CC2, experimental console TV with color drum mounted inside, 1951, **$3,500**

20C, wooden console with simple styling, 20″ screen, 1950, **$20**

20C3, 20″ console in French Provincial styling with double doors, 1951, **$25**

20M, metal tabletop with 20″ screen, 1950, **$15**

CBS-Columbia 12CC2, $3,500.

20T, wooden tabletop version of model *20C,* **$25**

22C05, 22C07, 21″ black-and-white wooden consoles, circa 1955, **$25**

22T09, 22T19, 21″ wooden tabletops, 1955, similar to model *22C05,* **$25**

23C49, similar to model *22C05,* area at bottom for records, **$25**

23C59, similar to model *22C05,* double doors, **$25**

CBS-Columbia 22C05, 22C07, $25.

205C1, very large and heavy console, 1955, 19″ round color picture tube, **$250**

205C2, similar to model *205C1,* double doors, **$250**

Cleervue

Hollywood, unusual 1947 console, 15″ screen turns above wooden box-like TV, 4 long wooden legs, **$400**

Regency, console with 15″ tube, 4 knobs below, double doors conceal screen, 1947, **$75**

Color Converter Inc.

Model 100-1, "COL-R-TEL," large Formica-covered unit with 3-color transparent acetate wheel inside, complete with small converter chassis, **$600;** without electronic box or chassis, **$400**

Other period kits or homemade color wheels with housing, motor and colored acetate, **$75**

Crosley

AC10, wooden console, 1965, 21″ screen, 4 narrow legs, **$10**

AT10, AT70, tabletop versions of model *AC10,* **$10**

DC10, DC12, DC14, DC16, console model wooden TVs, 1965, controls in long strip on top of cabinet, **$10**

DT12, tabletop version of model *DC10,* **$10**

EU-30, 30″ huge console TV (actually a DuMont *RA-119*), **$250**

F-17TOL, square tabletop with 17″ screen above 3 large knobs, 1954, **$10**

F-21COB, F-21COL, console with 21″ screen, 1954, similar to model *F-17TOL,* **$10**

F-21TOL, 21″ version of model *F-17TOL,* **$10**

F-27COB, 27″ version of model *F21-COB,* **$10**

G-17TO, "Super V," square-lined wooden tabletop, 1955, controls on right side, **$20**

Crosley G-17TO, $20.

307-TA, "Spectator," 13-channel 10″ wooden tabletop, 1948, screen in center with 2 knobs at lower left and 2 knobs at lower right, **$100**

348-CP, "DeLuxe Spectator," 10″ combination, 1948, Swing-a-View picture tube above tilt-out controls and radio, pull-out phono, **$175**

9-403, 10″ wooden tabletop, 1949, continuous tuner to left of screen, **$60**

9-407, 12″ wooden tabletop, 1949, metal mesh surrounds screen, continuous tuner control and window to right of screen, **$65**

9-409M, 12″ console, 1949, double doors, controls to left and right of screen, **$35**

Crosley 348-CP, $175.

Best Christmas sales ever with Crosley...

Designed and built to give the clearest TV picture

Christmas for Crosley TV dealers promises to be the biggest in history because Crosley has what the public wants—bright, steady, clear pictures in gorgeous cabinets that match fine furniture. Crosley's outstanding features do a *double job* for you. They help you make sales; they minimize repair and replacement problems.

Features like these build the popularity of Crosley TV:

- ELECTRONIC PICTURE STABILIZER, for extra steadiness
- MICRO-ADJUSTED CIRCUIT, for faithful image reception
- UNDISTORTED PICTURE, assured by 4 to 3 aspect ratio
- HEAVY-DUTY CONSTRUCTION, for heavy-duty service
- CONTINUOUS TUNER, most trouble-free tuning method
- REPEATED FACTORY INSPECTIONS, to meet top standards

10-401

A handsome 10″ picture tube table model, encased in smart, durable cabinet of molded mahogany plastic. With simplified tuner that selects bright, clear pictures in a single operation.

10-414

A magnificent new TV console encased in rich mahogany veneer. With a huge 16″ picture tube that gives brilliant, lifelike reception. (Model 10-416 similar to the 10-414 pictured here, but without doors).

9-425

The "PORTA-VISION," lightweight, *portable* TV, that gives clear, lifelike pictures on a bright 7″ picture tube. Cased in brown leatherette.

FULL-YEAR CATHODE RAY TUBE GUARANTEE
The big picture tube, heart of each Crosley TV set, is guaranteed for a full year.

NOTE: With the continuous tuner in Crosley TV, future provision can be made to secure reception on proposed UHF channels based on present standards.

Crosley televisions from 1949.

9-414, 10″ console, 1949, double doors, controls to left and right of screen, **$60**

9-419, 12″ tabletop, continuous tuner to right of screen, **$100**

9-420M, 10″ mahogany console, 1949, continuous tuner to left of screen, **$75**

9-424B, 10″ blonde console, 1949, similar to model *9-420M,* **$100**

9-422, 16″ console with simple styling, 1949, **$35**

9-425, 7″ portable tabletop with lid and handle, 1949, **$125**

10-401, 10″ Bakelite tabletop with large plastic mask around screen, 1950, not very popular, **$50**

10-414, large wide 16″ console with double doors, 1949, **$75**

10-416, similar to model *10-414,* no doors, **$75**

10-419, 12″ TV, 1950, square cabinet with 2 knobs to right of screen, **$25**

10-420, console with plastic mask around 12″ screen, 1950, very large, **$65**

Crosley 11-443, $65.

10-428, 14″ TV with simple square lines, 1950, **$35**

10-429, 16″ console, plastic mask around screen, **$25**

11-443, 19″ console, 1951, rounded front with large plastic mask around screen, **$65**

11-445, simple square-lined 16″ console, 1951, **$25**

11-446, 16″ version of model *11-443,* **$50**

Daven

Essential, TV kit, 1931, includes lamp, disc, and motor, complete, **$1,000**

Crosley 9-420M, $75.

Daven "Essential" kit, $1,000.

Television Receiver, large wooden cabinet, 1932, 2 knobs under square screen in front, **$2,000**

DeWald

BT-100, 10″ tabletop, 1948, wide set with screen in center and grill on both sides, 6 control knobs below, **$75**

CT-101, 16″ console, 1949, **$25**

CT-102, -103, 10″ wooden TVs, 1949, **$65**

CT-104, 12″ console with simple styling, **$65**

DT-102, 10″ wooden tabletop, 1949, **$75**

DT-120, 12″ wooden tabletop, similar to model *DT-102,* **$60**

DT-160, 16″ tabletop, very plain styling, **$35**

DeWald BT-100, $75.

DeWald DT-160, $35.

DT-190, 19″ simple console, 1950, **$25**

ET-140, square tabletop with 14″ rectangular picture tube, 1950, **$20**

ET-171, large console, 1951, 17″ screen at top, pull-out phono in lower section, **$45**

DuMont

80, early version of model *180,* 1937, controls in 2 rows below screen, **$3,000**

180 through *183,* 14″ pre-war tabletop, 1937, 4-channel tuner, **$2,500**

180X through *183X,* pre-war console, 1937, **$3,500**

195, 20″ pre-war tabletop produced in very limited quantity in 1941, **Rare**

RA-101

Custom rack-mounted chassis with 20″ picture tube, 1946, no cabinet, **$35**

Hampshire, 20″ blonde version of *Westminster* model, **$500**

Plymouth or *Revere,* 15″ console with double doors, 1946, **$45**

Westminster, huge mahogany combination set with 20″ mechanically-raised tube, **$65**

RA-102

Club, large grey-painted tabletop with 12″ screen and controls behind door, **$200**

DuMont 180, $2,500.

DuMont "Clifton," $600.

Clifton, unusually shaped 12″ console, 1947, stepped top, **$600**

RA-103

Chatham, 12″ trapezoidal tabletop, 1947, round continuous tuner with Channels 1–13 plus radio, common but popular, **$145**

12″ console, round or square tuner window, **$25**

RA-103D, square-lined cabinet version of *Chatham* model, square tuner window, Channels 2–13, **$25**

DuMont "Chatham," $145.

DuMont RA-105, $35.

RA-105, 15″ television, very square lines, circa 1949, **$35**

RA-106, RA-109, large screen TV in square-lined cabinet, 1950, **$35**

RA-119, "Royal Sovereign," huge 30″ console with double doors, 1952, **$400**

DuMont RA-164, $35.

Emerson

527, 10″ console, front surface tilted back, unusually designed TV, 1948, rare, **$400**

545, unusual 10″ tabletop with screen centered and a bit forward of cabinet, 6 knobs and 13-channel tuner below, 1947, **$150**

571, 10″ square wooden tabletop, 1948, rounded corners, 4 knobs below screen, **$100**

585, 10″ combination with pull-out phono, double doors in front of screen, **$75**

600, 7″ portable 1949, leatherette-covered, handle on side, **$125**

606, 10″ console version of model *571,* **$75**

608, 16″ console, 1948, tops lifts to allow picture tube assembly to swing up and out, **$150**

609, small projection console, pop-up ground glass screen, 1949, **$100**

611, 10″ tabletop with square lines and flat top, 1948, painted glass screen, 4 knobs across bottom, **$75**

614, Bakelite tabletop with 10″ porthole-look screen, 1950, ribs across front and sides, **$75**

619, 10″ console, circa 1948, screen and 4 knobs tilted out, square lines, **$75**

621, 10″ wooden tabletop, 1948, vertical tuner windows to right and left of screen, **$75**

622, 10″ combination with book storage, similar to model *621,* **$65**

624, similar to model *611,* rounded top, **$100**

628, 10″ wooden tabletop with hump-top case, 1948, vertical tuners similar to model *621,* **$85**

630, 12″ double-door combination with porthole-look screen, similar to model *621,* **$65**

631, 16″ tabletop, rounded top, 1950, porthole-look screen, **$65**

637, 10″ wooden tabletop, 1 knob in each of 4 corners, **$75**

638, console version of model *611,* **$75**

639, 7″ wooden tabletop version of model *600,* 1949, **$100**

644, 12″ tabletop, porthole-look screen, 4 knobs in corners, **$75**

Emerson 621, $75.

Emerson 628, $85.

Emerson 608, $150.

Emerson's 1952 televisions.

Emerson 631, $65.

647, 12″ console, similar to model *644,* **$65**

648, 10″ Bakelite tabletop, rounded corners, ridges to left and right of screen, **$75**

649, tall wooden projection console, 1949, fixed plastic screen at top front, **$75**

650, 12″ wooden tabletop, 1949, large glass screen, simple lines, **$65**

651, 16″ tabletop version of model *650,* **$35**

654, 12″ console version of model *650,* **$45**

662, 14″ Bakelite tabletop, 1950, rectangular picture tube, **$25**

663, 14″ wooden tabletop, similar to model *662,* **$35**

666, 16″ combination, very square lines, 1950, **$10**

669, 19″ console, 1950, double doors conceal screen, **$10**

1030, 1032, leatherette-covered portables with handle, 1955, 14″ screen, lid opens to expose controls, **$10**

1104, 1106, wooden tabletops, 1955, 21″ screen with controls on right side, **$15**

1444, 21″ wide console with stereo radio-phono beneath right door, 1959, **$25**

1472, large portable, 1959, 17″ screen, handle on top, controls on right, **$20**

1504, painted metal 17″ portable, 1959, handle on top, controls on right, **$35**

Empire State (See Western Television)

Espey

Training kit, simple TV with 3″ green tube, 1947, 7 knobs below screen and speaker, sold without cabinet, **$350**

FADA

R-1050, 16″ version of model *S-1030,* **$25**

S-1015, 12″ wooden tabletop, 1949, Bakelite mask, 4 knobs below screen, **$35**

S-1030, square-lined wooden tabletop with 4 knobs below screen, 1950, **$35**

S20C10, console with 20″ screen on left and 4 knobs behind small door, 1951, **$20**

TV-30, 10″ tabletop, 1947, similar to RCA *630TS,* metal mesh on both sides of screen, **$125**

799, 13-channel version of model *TV-30,* glass plate in front of screen, **$125**

880, 4′-high projection TV, 1948, Deco-style with stepped front and top, **$225;** original projection model with very square lines, flat front and top, **$45**

899, similar to model *TV-30,* **$125**

925, 16″ tabletop, 1949, screen trim is slightly out in front and at top, **$65**

930, 12″ wooden tabletop, similar to model *925,* screen trim out in front and at top, **$85**

940, 12″ console version of model *930,* **$75**

965, 16″ console version of model *930,* **$55**

FADA 899, $125.

FADA 965, $55.

Farnsworth (See Capehart/ Farnsworth)

Garod

Model 100, rare 5″ pre-war TV kit, 1938, single channel, sight only (no speaker), complete with cabinet, **$3,500;** assembled with tube, bare chassis, **$1,500**

10TZ, 10″ tabletop, 1949, AM/FM radio below porthole-look screen, **$165**

12TZ, 12″ version of model *10TZ,* **$150**

15TZ, 15″ version of model *10TZ,* **$125**

900TV, 910TV, 10″ tabletops, 1948, 2 large circular knobs with 13-channel tuner and AM/FM radio dial, 7 control knobs below, **$175**

920TV, 10″ tabletop with screen above 13-channel tuner and long AM/FM tuner window, 1948, **$125**

930TV, blonde version of model *920TV,* **$125**

1000TV, 12″ tabletop version of model *900TV,* **$150**

1020TV, 12″ version of model *920TV,* **$100**

1030TV, 12″ version of model *930TV,* **$100**

1200TV, 12″ double-door combination version of model *900TV,* **$100**

1672, 1673, large wooden consoles, 1950, 16″ screen, **$20**

1974, 1975, similar to model *1672,* 19″ screen, **$20**

3912, 12″ combination with 4 doors, 13-channel push-button tuner, slide-out phono and AM/FM/shortwave radio at left, 1947, **$75**

3915, similar to model *3912,* AM/FM radio and non-automatic phono, **$75**

General Electric

Model 90, large Deco mirror-in-lid pre-war console, 1939, **Rare**

HM-171, 5″ pre-war tabletop with picture only (no sound), 1938, 3-channel push-button tuner below screen, **$3,000**

HM-185, 5″ pre-war console, 1938, 3-channel push-button tuner, **$4,000**

HM-225, 9″ pre-war console, 1938, 5-channel push-button tuner below screen, **$4,000**

HM-226, 12″ pre-war TV with 5-channel push-button tuner, **$4,000**

Hotpoint, painted metal tabletop, mid-1950s, handle on top, **$25**

General Electric HM-171, vision only 5″ tabletop, $3,000.

10C101, 10C102, square-lined wooden console versions of model *10T1,* **$25**

10T1, 10T6, 10″ streamlined Bakelite tabletops, 1949, sloping side, 4 knobs below screen, **$100**

10T4, 10T5, square-lined wooden tabletop versions of model *10T1,* **$35**

12T, 12″ streamlined Bakelite tabletop, similar to model *800,* different grill, **$100**

12T1, 12″ wooden tabletop with screen above 4 knobs, square cabinet, **$20**

14C102, 14C103, console versions of model *14T2,* **$20**

14T2, 14T3, 14″ tabletops, 1950, square corners with simple style, **$25**

15CL100, early color console with 15″ round picture tube, 1954, scarce, **$550**

16K1, 16″ combination with screen behind right door, AM/FM radio and phono behind left door, 1950, **$20**

17T2410, 17T2432, large plastic 17″ portables, 1959, **$10**

21C2460, 21C22550, 21″ wooden consoles with 4 short legs, 1959, **$20**

21T2420, 21T2424, 21″ large plastic portables, 1959, **$10**

24C101, large console, 1951, double doors conceal 24″ screen with knobs at right, **$20**

800, 10″ streamlined Bakelite tabletop, similar to model *10T1,* **$100**

General Electric 800, $100.

801, 10″ console, 1947, small double doors conceal large dial AM radio and screen, **$125**

802, similar to model *801,* full-length doors conceal pull-out phono, AM-FM large dial radio and screen, **$100**

803, 10″ wide wooden tabletop, 1948, unusual design with speaker protruding from top front, **$175**

805, similar to model *800,* different grill, **$100**

806, 807, tall 10″ tabletops, glass screen, slightly rounded top, **$45**

809, console version of model *806,* **$25**

810, 10″ wide wooden tabletop, 1949, screen offset to right front, 4 knobs below, **$65**

814, similar to model *810,* large plastic mask around screen, **$65**

835, 10″ wide tabletop, similar to model *810,* metal mesh grill, **$50**

General Electric 10C101, $25.

General Electric 801, $125.

You're building your future—when you sell—

G-E TELEVISION

**A G-E MODEL FOR EVERY PROSPECT
STOCK ALL FOUR—DEMONSTRATE ALL FOUR**

Popular Priced Table Model 803—Ideal for the prospect who wants the most in performance at a modest budget. Unsurpassed clarity of pictures—big 10-inch direct view tube PLUS AM and FM radio. And a big G-E Dynapower speaker. Handsome modern cabinet.

When you sell a General Electric television receiver, your customer's enthusiasm for G-E television drums up new prospects for you. That's natural. General Electric television receivers are the result of 20 years of pioneering television research. Only General Electric today produces and operates all types of television units—studio equipment, transmitters, micro-wave relays for television networks, and home television receivers. You build solidly for the future when you demonstrate and sell G-E television. For further information on G-E television receivers, see your G-E radio distributor or write *General Electric Company, Receiver Division, Electronics Park, Syracuse, N. Y.*

Complete Home Entertainment In One Cabinet—Model 802—Here in one console you can deliver the finest in television quality, the finest in record reproduction, and the finest in both FM and AM radio. One instrument does it all. Compact and beautiful in its period cabinet of genuine mahogany.

Model 901

De Luxe Console, Big Screen Projection Television—Mammoth screen television 18" x 24", 3 sq. ft. in area. PLUS FM and AM radio—short-wave, and automatic phonograph with the G-E Electronic Reproducer. Beautiful Sheraton-inspired cabinet of genuine mahogany.

Big Screen Projection For Large Homes, Clubs, Cocktail Lounges—Model 910—Customized installation saves precious space. Schmidt Optical System projection television on a screen 18" x 24"—3 sq. ft. in area PLUS AM, FM and short-wave radio.

Only G-E television gives you All these selling features

• NATURAL CLARITY PICTURES—every detail cleanly focused and sharply defined • G-E AUTOMATIC CLARIFIER—safeguards pictures against "noise" and interference • ALL 13 U. S. TELEVISION CHANNELS—each with its own circuit—each factory pre-tuned • AUTOMATIC SYNCHRONIZATION WITH STATION • EXTRA BIG DYNAPOWER SPEAKER • NATURAL TONE—famed feature of the exclusive G-E audio system.

LEADER IN RADIO, TELEVISION AND ELECTRONICS

GENERAL ELECTRIC

PORTABLES • TABLE MODELS • CONSOLES • FARM SETS
AUTOMATIC PHONOGRAPH COMBINATIONS • TELEVISION

General Electric's 1948 televisions.

General Electric 806, $45.

General Electric 810, $65.

General Electric 835, $50.

901, huge projection set with AM-FM radio and phono, 1947, **$200**

910, similar to model *901,* sold without cabinet, **$35**

Globe

Scanning Disc, tabletop mechanical TV receiver in oversized wooden cabinet with rounded top, 1932, **$1,500**

Hallicrafters

T-54, 7″ metal TV, 1948, 13-channel push-button tuner, Raymond Lowey design, **$150**

T-60, rack-mounted projection TV system, no cabinet, **$45**

T-61, 10″ Bakelite TV with push-button tuning beneath rectangular screen, 1949, **$100**

T-64, 10″ custom chassis with push buttons below porthole-look screen, 1949, **$25**

T-67, 10″ wooden version of model *T-61,* **$100**

T-68, large projection console TV, 1949, **$150**

T-69, 15″ custom chassis, 12-channel push-button tuner at right front, no cabinet, **$50**

T-506, 7″ wooden tabletop, 12-channel push-button tuner, 1949, **$150**

505, 7″ wooden tabletop, 1948, 13-channel push-button tuner across front, Raymond Lowey design, **$175**

509, 10″ wooden TV with push-button tuning below porthole-look screen, 1949, **$125**

510, 10″ Bakelite version of model *509,* **$125**

511, 16″ 2-part set, controls and speaker separate, 1950, **$55**

512, 12″ console, very simple styling, 1949, **$35**

514, 7″ portable TV with handle, 1948, lid conceals screen, **$200**

600, 10″ TV with very square lines, 1950, **$50**

715, 12″ Bakelite tabletop, 1950, simple lines, **$75**

760, 761, 16″ wooden console, 1950, **$20**

811, 16″ tabletop, 1950, rotary tuner and 4 knobs below rectangular screen, **$75**

818, 16″ tabletop with porthole-look screen, 1950, similar to model *811,* **$50**

860, 16″ combination with double doors, large TV, 1950, **$50**

1005, 20″ mahogany set on 4 thin legs, 1952, 2 large knobs and small controls under screen, **$15**

Meck *Exclusive*

TELEVISION plus RADIO Combinations
BIG PROFITS FOR DEALERS

Here's the "sell-up" opportunity that really has some "sell" to it. Your customers want this sensible combination of big screen television and AM radio. This Meck "exclusive" can make you some really big money...for it carries the famous Meck big discount for dealers.

If you are getting that "tired feeling" trading dollars on low discount merchandise...give your profits a lift... get on the Meck Profit Line...now, today. Call, write or wire for your confidential price sheet and complete information.

AM RADIO
Television
12½" Tube
$239⁹⁰

If you know your merchandising you know this is it . . . big screen television with that extra sensitivity for clear reception in fringe areas and difficult locations AND AM radio. Beautiful mahogany cabinet...built-in antenna...low price. Model XQR

TV-AM and PHONO COMBINATIONS, too

Lowest retail prices on proven television . . . tops for dealer discounts, these full-size mahogany consoles offer 12½" or 16" television, AM radio in combination with automatic phonograph. Includes built-in antenna. Model XRPS, 12½" TV Combination, retail $299.90.

Model XSPS **$339⁹⁰**
16"TV Combination, retail

For those who want giant screen television in a tabletop model . . . here it is including that big merchandising bonus...AM radio. Features huge 145 sq. inch screen, 16" tube, built-in antenna and rich hand-rubbed mahogany cabinet.
Model XTR
Retail price only............ **$269⁹⁰**

Meck
ISO-RAMIC TELEVISION
JOHN MECK INDUSTRIES, INC.
Plymouth, Indiana

Meck televisions from 1950.

150

1006, blonde version of model *1005,* **$20**

1056, wooden tabletop with 3 knobs below square 21″ screen, 1952, **$20**

1075, brown plastic 21″ tabletop, 1953, 2 large knobs below screen, **$15**

1085, wooden console version of model *1075,* **$15**

Hotpoint (See General Electric)

Jenkins

Model 100, scanning disc mechanical TV, 1932, complete with motor, lamp, and lens, **$1,500**

Radio Visor

Kit, TV kit sold with paper disc and other mechanical parts, 1929, **$1,000**

R-400, mechanical scanning disc TV, lens-projected image onto ground glass screen, peaked-top wooden cabinet, **$2,500**

TV Books, written by Jenkins, circa 1930s, on scanning disc technology, **$35**

JVC

3100D, "Video Capsule," pyramid-shaped TV, 1972, top flips up to expose screen, digital clock radio on front of base, controls at right, **$250**

3100R, similar to model *3100D,* no digital clock, **$250**

3240, "Video Sphere," spherical set, 1972, oval plastic cover in front of screen, chain on top, simple base, **$100;** digital-clock base, **$100**

Meck

XA-701, 7″ portable wooden tabletop, 1948, wooden and cloth front, **$165**

XB-702, 7″ wooden tabletop, similar to model *XA-701,* wooden front, **$165**

XC-703, 7″ leatherette-covered portable with lid and handle, **$175**

XL-750, 10″ wooden tabletop, 1949, screen at front left, **$100**

XN-752, 10″ wooden cabinet TV with rounded top, 1949, **$100**

XQ-776, 12″ version of model *XL-750,* **$65**

XQR, wooden tabletop, 1950, long AM radio dial beside 12″ screen, **$50**

XSPS, 16″ combination with pull-out phono at bottom, long AM radio dial at right of screen, **$25**

XTR, 16″ wooden tabletop version of model *XSPS,* **$35**

Meissner

10-1153, pre-war TV kit, 1939, double chassis and long funnel-shaped 5″ picture tube in black metal frame, **$1,000;** 5″ TV complete with original factory wooden cabinet, **$2,000**

TV-1, 10″ TV kit with custom cabinet, late 1940s, **$75**

Motorola

VF-102, combination 10″ TV with 13-channel tuner behind right door, AM-FM radio and phono behind left door, 1949, **$75**

VF-103, 10″ combination, 1948, 12-channel tuner, **$100**

VK-101, 13-channel 10″ console, 1948, lower area tilts forward to expose AM/FM radio controls and dial, **$125**

VK-106, 10″ console with stepped-up top in center and forward screen, 1948, **$125**

VT-71, 7″ wooden tabletop, 1948, lightweight and inexpensive, the most common 7″ set found today, **$75**

VT-73, leatherette-covered version of model *VT-71,* removable lid and handle on top, **$75**

VT-105, Motorola's first 10″ tabletop, circa 1948, stepped top and forward screen, **$175**

7-TV2, Bakelite version of model *7VT1,* **$65**

7-TV5, leatherette-covered version of model *7VT1,* **$85**

Get the Low-down on
TELEVISION
WITH A *Meissner*
TELEVISION KIT
COMPLETE · · · SAFE
· · · GUARANTEED · · ·
$139⁵⁰ INCLUDING ALL TUBES

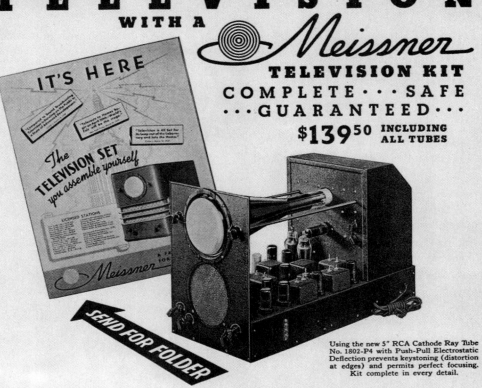

IT'S HERE

The TELEVISION SET *you assemble yourself*

SEND FOR FOLDER

Using the new 5" RCA Cathode Ray Tube No. 1802-P4 with Push-Pull Electrostatic Deflection prevents keystoning (distortion at edges) and permits perfect focusing. Kit complete in every detail.

Meissner has developed this Kit — your OPEN SESAME to the thrilling World of Television — expressly for the Nation's HAMS and experimentors.

The Meissner Television Set has been engineered to the most exacting specifications. It gives you a Video and Audio Receiver, that is highly sensitive, flexible and efficient. You'll not only get superb results but cash in on your technical knowledge and skill by turning out a Set that will be the envy of all who see it — and, of course, at a

great saving over the commercially assembled sets the layman buys.

Get the whole story. Mail coupon for Folder shown above. It tells all about this brilliantly engineered, up-to-the-minute Set . . . explains its many unique features in detail . . . including the SPECIAL SAFETY Devices which *automatically* protect you from all danger of shock from the High Voltage Current.

WRITE FOR OUR NEW 1939-40 CATALOG — OFF THE PRESS JUNE 15TH

YOUR OPPORTUNITY
The early radio experimentors are to-day's leaders in the industry. Television now offers you a similar opportunity to get in on the ground floor. Get started by building the Meissner Television Receiver.

Meissner MT. CARMEL, ILLINOIS

A FAMOUS NAME FOR TWO DECADES

MAIL IN ENVELOPE OR PASTE ON PENNY POSTCARD

MEISSNER MANUFACTURING COMPANY
Mt. Carmel, Illinois, Dept. A-7

☐ Send me the Television Kit Folder
☐ Send me Meissner's complete new 1939-40 Catalog

Name
Address
City   State

Meissner 10-1153, $1,000.

Motorola VK-101, $125.

Motorola VT-71, $75.

7-VT1, similar to model *VT-71,* plastic face-plate with porthole-look screen, **$85**

9VT1, 8″ wooden tabletop 1948, with port-hole-look screen, **$100**

10T2, 10″ tabletop, 1950, gold bezel around screen, rounded top corners, **$75**

10VK10, 10″ console version of model *10VT10,* **$65**

10VT10, similar to model *10T2,* flat top, **$65**

12T, 12VT13, 12″ version of model *10T2,* **$65**

12VK15, 12″ double-door console, 1950, 2 large knobs below screen with gold bezel, **$65**

12VK16, 12VK18, 12″ TVs with painted front glass, **$75**

12VT16, wooden tabletop version of model *12VK18,* **$75**

14K1, 14″ console with square screen surrounded by gold bezel, 1950, **$50**

14P14, square-lined painted metal tabletop, 1959, handle on top, controls on right, **$35**

16VK7, 16″ version of model *12VK15,* **$50**

17K8, 17K11, 17″ consoles with 2 knobs below screen, 1952, **$45**

17P5, painted metal portable with handle on top, controls on right, 1959, **$35**

17T5, 17″ Bakelite tabletop with 2 knobs under screen, 1952, **$35**

17T6, similar to model *17T5,* wooden cabinet, **$35**

19CK2, 19CT1, color TVs with 19″ round tube in modern consoles, 1955, **$300;** with replacement 21″ color picture tube, **$150**

19P1, "Astronaut," suitcase-style early transistor television with removable front lid, unpopular with collectors, **$75**

21C2, wooden 21″ TV on 4 tall spindle legs, 1954, **$425**

Motorola 19P1, $75.

Motorola porthole-look televisions.

4545 AUGUSTA BOULEVARD *Motorola Inc.* CHICAGO 51, ILLINOIS

Motorola's 10" and 12" televisions.

Motorola TV

PRELIMINARY
SERVICE MANUAL

CHASSIS
TS-402 SER
TS-502 SER

MODELS

17K17
Y17K17
17K17B
Y17K17B
17T15A
Y17T15A
17T15AE
Y17T15AE
17T16
Y17T16
17T16B
Y17T16B
21C2
Y21C2
21C2B
Y21C2B
21F5
Y21F5
21F5B
Y21F5B
21K12A
Y21K12A
21K12AB
Y21K12AB
21K12WA
Y21K12WA
21K13
Y21K13
21K13B
Y21K13B
21K14
Y21K14
21K14B
Y21K14B
21K15
Y21K15
21K16
Y21K16
21K16W
Y21K16W
21K17
Y21K17
21T8A
Y21T8A
21T8AE
Y21T8AE
21T11
Y21T11
21T11B
Y21T11B
21T11W
Y21T11W

17K17 SERIES

17T15 SERIES

17T16 SERIES

21C2 SERIES

21F5 SERIES

21K12 SERIES

21K13 SERIES

21K14 SERIES

21K15 SERIES

21K16 SERIES

21K17 SERIES

21T8 SERIES

21T11 SERIES

Motorola 17" and 21" televisions.

156

Motorola 19-inch color
TV set priced at $895.

Motorola 19CK1, $300.

21F5, large combination, 1954, 21″ TV behind right door, radio, storage area and
pull-out phono behind left, **$35**

21K16, unusual console on 4 spindle legs,
1954, sliding board completely covers
front, **$45**

21K98, 21K100, 21″ stereophonic consoles,
1959, **$20**

21P1, 21″ metal tabletop, 1959, flip-up controls on top, **$35**

Motorola 21T10, $25.

21T8, 21T10, large Bakelite tabletops, 1954,
2 knobs under 21″ screen, **$25**

24K1, 24K3, console with 24″ screen and 2
large knobs below, 1954, **$35**

27K2, 27″ version of model *24K1,* **$35**

Muntz

17PD, two-tone version of model *17PS,* **$35**

17PS, simple painted metal portable, 1959,
handle and tuner on top, **$25**

21CP-1, wide 21″ combination, 1959, screen
at right, lift-top radio-phono at left, 4
tubular legs, **$50**

21TB, 21TM, simple wooden tabletops with
21″ tube, 1959, tuner on right side, **$25**

24CB, 24CM, 24″ wooden consoles on 4 tubular legs, 1959, **$50**

Motorola 21K16, $45.

Muntz 21CP-1, $50.

NATIONAL TELEVISION

Presents
ALL-NEW
2 1950 MODELS

YOU'LL BE SOLD ON *Sight*

Place these two new 1950 National Television receivers side by side with any other television receiver. Compare the large (12½") screen — compare the chassis — compare the picture quality — compare the cabinet styling. Because National Television is custom assembled — not mass-produced — there just *is* no comparison! Yet it costs no more.

Model TV-12W
Striking modern mahogany table model with 12½" tube and 2 six-inch oval speakers.
$269.95

● Model TV-10W
Genuine mahogany table model with 10" screen and 2 six-inch oval speakers.
$229.95

● Model TV-7W
Unbeatable TV dollar value. 7" screen with twin speakers. NC enlarging lens available, $16.95.
$129.95

● Model TV-7M
Metal cabinet version of TV-7W. Ideal as "second set" for playroom, den or bedroom.
$119.95

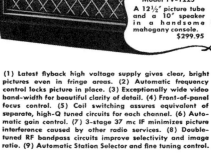

Model TV-1225
A 12½" picture tube and a 10" speaker in a handsome mahogany console.
$299.95

(1) Latest flyback high voltage supply gives clear, bright pictures even in fringe areas. (2) Automatic frequency control locks picture in place. (3) Exceptionally wide video band-width for beautiful clarity of detail. (4) Front-of-panel focus control. (5) Coil switching assures equivalent of separate, high-Q tuned circuits for each channel. (6) Automatic gain control. (7) 3-stage 37 mc IF minimizes picture interference caused by other radio services. (8) Double-tuned RF bandpass circuits improve selectivity and image ratio. (9) Automatic Station Selector and fine tuning control.

Prices Slightly Higher West of the Rockies

NATIONAL COMPANY, Inc.
MALDEN, MASSACHUSETTS
EST. 1914

National televisions made in 1950.

National

TV 7M, 7″ metal version of *TV-7W*, **$225**

TV 7, 7W, 7″ wooden tabletops, 1949, screen in center with 6 knobs below, **$225**

TV-10W, 10″ wooden tabletop, 1949, **$150**

TV-12W, 12″ wooden tabletop with 4 knobs hidden behind drop-down door beneath screen, 1949, **$100**

TV-1201, simply styled 12″ wooden tabletop, 1949, **$75**

TV-1226, 12″ console, 1949, similar to model *TV-1201*, **$50**

TV-1601, 16″ simply styled tabletop, 1949, **$50**

TV-1625, 16″ console, similar to model *TV-1601*, **$50**

Videometer, 7″ metal tabletop, similar to model *TV-7M*, signal meter beside screen, **$325**

Norelco (North American Philips Company)

Protelgram, bare projection system complete with mirrors, tube and electronics, **$15**

Norelco PT 300, $75.

PT 200, console with fixed plastic projection screen, 1948, **$50**

PT 300, similar to model *PT 200*, double doors cover projection screen, **$75**

Olympic

DX 619, double-door console version of model *DX 950*, **$35**

DX 621, large combination set with 16″ screen, double doors painted with Chinese scene, 1950, **$75**

DX 931, 19″ double-door version of model *DX 950*, **$25**

DX 950, wooden tabletop, 1950, 16″ picture tube with 4 knobs below, **$65**

TV-104, TV-106, 10″ wooden tabletops, 1948, **$75**

TV-922, 10″ tabletop, 1948, screen within vertical wooden ribs, 4 knobs at bottom, **$100**

TV-928, 10″ mirror-in-lid TV with radio and pull-out phono behind right door, **$100**

TV-944, TV-945, 12″ wooden TVs, screen at right side of cabinet front, **$75**

TV-947, 16″ console, simply styled TV with double doors, 1950, **$25**

RTU-3, 10″ duplicator, 1949, appears to be a television, actually a remote TV monitor used with a complete set, **$75**

3K119, 3K329, wide consoles, 1962, screen in center of set, TV on 4 spindle legs, **$10**

Olympic TV-922, $100.

Olympic TV-928, $100.

3T100, 3T200, 3T500, 23″ large wooden tabletops, controls to right of screen,
1963, **$10**

9TV12, 9TX11, metal and plastic portables
with 19″ screen, 1962, **$10**

752, 755, 16″ rectangular picture tube tabletop, 1950, **$35**

753, 16″ console version of model *752*, **$20**

Panasonic

TR-005, TR-005C, "Flying Saucer," small
silver sets, 1972, oval-shaped on metal
tripod, **$175**

Philco

Pre-war TV, wide 12″ mirror-in-lid console,
1936, **Rare**

H2010, "Safari," brown portable leather and
plastic TV, 1959, 2″ tube reflected in
magnifier, first transistor TV, complete
with hood, **$125**; black leather and black
plastic hood, **$150**; without plastic
hood, **$75**

Philco H2010, $125.

48-700, heavy 7″ wooden tabletop, 1948, picture tube at right of center, **$175**

48-1000, 10″ tabletop, 1948, unusual styling
with screen a bit above and to the left of
cabinet, popular set, **$300**

48-1001, 10″ tabletop, similar to model *48-
1000*, redesigned with tube within cabinet lines, **$100**

48-1050, unusual 10″ console, 1948, screen in
center of wide cabinet, **$125**

48-2500, huge buffet-style mirror-in-lid set,
1948, common but not popular, **$30**

49-702, 50-702, wooden 7″ tabletops with
screen in center of peaked cabinet, **$175**

Philco 48-700, $175.

Philco 48-1000, $300.

49-1002, 10″ tabletop, 1949, redesign of model *48-1001,* flat top, **$75**

49-1040, 10″ 4-legged consolette, 1949, not popular with collectors, **$45**

49-1076, large 10″ combination with double doors, 1949, **$45**

49-1240, 12″ version of model *49-1040,* door conceals controls, **$35**

TP-5853A

Philco 49-1240, $35.

Philco 51-T1634, $15.

49-1280, large wooden 12″ TV with double doors, 1949, **$50**

49-1475, 14″ wooden console, 1949, double doors, **$35**

50-701, 7″ Bakelite tabletop, shape similar to model *49-702,* **$225**

50-T1600, 50-T1632, 16″ simply styled wooden TV, 1950, screen above 4 knobs, very square lines, **$10**

51-T1601, metal tabletop with rounded top, 1951, screen over 4 knobs, **$15**

51-T1604, wooden tabletop, 1951, 16″ screen above 4 knobs, **$15**

51-T1634, 16″ console version of model *51-T1604,* **$15**

51-T1871, console with 20″ screen over 4 knobs, drop-down phonograph in lower section, **$15**

Predicta

Note: Prices fluctuate widely! Values given here are for clean, complete, not working, unrestored sets. Restored Predictas often sell for twice these prices.

3408, "Debutante," 17″ Predicta TV, 1960, swivel tube above metal body, cloth grill, **$200;** with original metal stand, **$275**

3410, "Princess," 17″ metal Predicta, perforated metal grill, tuner through clear plastic plate at right front, **$200;** with original metal stand, **$275**

3412, "Siesta," 17″ Predicta, similar to model *3410*, clock-timer above tuner, **$225;** with original metal stand, **$275**

4240, marked "Predicta" but conventional 21″ large tabletop with controls on top, **$10**

4242, "Holiday," modern TV with 21″ swivel tube above mahogany tabletop body, 1958, **$200;** blonde finish, **$300**

4641, 4642, traditional-style consoles with 21″ screen, 4 small legs, 1959, **$20**

4654, "Barber-pole," 21″ mahogany console with flat front, rounded back supports swivel screen, 1958, **$350;** blonde finish, **$450**

4660, "Miss America," large swivel console with pop-up controls at top, **$100**

4682, "Riviera," large square TV, 1960, complete set spins on legs, **$65**

4710, "Penthouse," 21″ 2-piece tandem set, 1959, long screen plugs into base modern Danish legs, **$350**

4720, "Tandem," stereophonic 2-piece Predicta, 4 screw-in gold-tone legs, 21″

Philco "Miss America," $100.

screen on long cord, 1960, **$350;** with matching stero phono/amplifier model *1606*, **$500**

4730, "Continental," Danish modern console, 1960, 4 fin-shaped legs and rectangular wooden body support 21″ swivel screen, **$450**

4744, "Townhouse," unusual room-divider TV, 1960, built in swivel screen, **$450**

Philco "Barber-pole," $350.

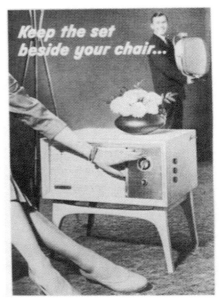

Philco "Tandem," $350.

Pilot TV-952, $125.

Pilot

4090, 9″ pre-war tabletop, 1939, **Rare**

4095, 9″ pre-war console, 1939, screen above radio controls and 5-channel push-button tuner, **Rare**

4125, 12″ pre-war TV with radio set and push-button TV tuner, 1939, **Rare**

TV-37, 3″ low-quality tabletop, 1947, first TV sold for under $100, perforated board cabinet on plywood base, **$150**

Magnifier, marked "Pilot TV," about 4″ plastic lens with tabs to attach to grill, **$100**

"Candid TV," original 3″ model in grey-painted cabinet, **Rare**

TV-950, large projection TV console, 1949, **$75**

TV-952, huge projection set, 1949, center door covers screen, radio behind right door, phono behind left door, **$125**

RCA (Radio Corporation of America)

Bershire Breakfront, 700-lb. breakfront with projection TV and radio-phono, circa 1949, **$350**

Berkshire Regency, 550-lb. projection set, basically bottom half of *Breakfront* model, **$200**

CT-100, large color console (chassis *CTC-2*), 1954, considered first production color set, 15″ round picture tube, **$500**

Dynamic Demonstrator, large breadboard TV with parts labeled, 1949, 10″ picture tube and logo at top, **$250**

RCA TRK-12, $3,000.

GG846, wide color console TV, chassis *CTC-17,* 1959, **$10**

RR-Series, engineer's field test mirror-in-lid pre-war TV, 1937, resembles console radio with mirror under top, rare, **over $6,000**

T-100, similar to model *9T246,* **$25**

T-120, T-121, 12″ versions of model *9T246,* **$20**

TLS-86, projection TV, 1946, tube and controls on top of rolling console, **$150**

TRK-5, pre-war console with 5″ screen, 1939, 5-channel tuner, **$4,500**

TRK-9, 9″ console, 1939, 5-channel tuner, direct view, **$4,000**

TRK-90, 1940 version of model *TRK-9,* **$4,000**

TRK-12, 12″ mirror-in-lid console, 1939, lid lifts to expose radio and 5-channel tuner, most common pre-war, **$3,000;** with 13-channel tuner added in late 1940s, **$2,000**

TRK-120, 1940 version of model *TRK-12,* **$3,000**

TT5, 5″ pre-war tabletop, 1939, 5-channel tuner, vision only (no sound), **$3,500**

RCA CT-100, $500.

4T101, tabletop withh 14″ screen, 1951, **$15**

6T54, 6T64, 6T65, wooden console with 16″ picture tube, 1950, **$35**

6T71, 6T75, similar to model *6T54,* double doors, **$35**

7T112, 7T124, wooden consoles, 1951, 17″ screen, **$20**

8-PT-7010, 8-PT-7011, "Personal portables," small 8″ metal sets, 1956, folding plastic handle on top, **$35**

8-PT-7030, 8-PT-7031, similar to model *8-PT-7010,* metal tripod base, **$55**

8T241, 8T243, redesigns of model *630TS,* 1948, wooden panel around 10″ screen, **$85**

8T270, first 16″ TV tabletop, 1949, **$50**

8TC271, elaborate consolette, 1949, 16″ screen behind double doors, curved legs, **$150**

8TK29, 8TR29, 10″ sets, 1949, 6 knobs below screen, prism reflects logo and radio scale, **$125**

8TS30, wooden tabletop, 1948, redesign of model *630TS,* wooden grills on both sides of 10″ screen, **$85**

8TV321, 8TV323, 1948 redesigns of model *730TV1,* **$75**

9PC41, buffet-style projection set with channel 1 tuner, 1949, **$45**

9T57, 9T79, consoles with 19″ screen, 1951, **$20**

9T246, metal 10″ tabletop, 1949, grill around screen, imitation mahogany finish, **$25**

9T256, similar to model *9T246,* picture magnifier control, **$75**

RCA 7T112, $20.

RCA 9PC41, $45.

TV's top 12½-inch values

The Cumberland. Happy choice for period or contemporary rooms. The perfect choice for viewing pleasure, the budget choice in 12-inch consoles. 2T60.

The Shelby. Compact, maroon-plastic cabinet that's one-fourth smaller than previous 12½-inch sets. Matching Consolette Base at slight extra cost. 2T51.

19-inch pictures
—almost as big as these 2 pages

The York. RCA Victor television's biggest view ... 19-inch screen. Exclusive Million Proof features. Matching Consolette Base is optional, extra. 9T57.

The Hilldale. 19-inch Eye Witness pictures, thrillingly lifelike, in a cabinet of 18th Century elegance. Its performance is equally fine—Million Proof television—Styled to match. 9T77.

The Northampton. Superb—from the pictures on its huge, 19-inch screen to the last detail of its exquisite English Regency cabinet. 9T79.

It's almost unbelievable! Even with our factories smashing record after record, even with the greatest output in our entire history rushed to the field—the cry for more swells louder than ever. RCA Victor Million Proof Television is a sell-out success. Proven in over a million homes. More wanted than ever before. That's why the 18 brand-new TV models, RCA Victor's newest and finest speak for themselves as television's most complete, most profitable line. Million Proof RCA Victor is today's living proof of bigger-than-ever profits for you.

TV-Radio-Phonograph Combinations

The Fairfax. Superb 16-inch Eye Witness television plus AM radio, automatic changers for all-speed records—all in one distinguished cabinet. One of RCA Victor's newest combinations. 6T84.

The Hartford. 16-inch television, luxurious AM-FM radio, RCA Victor "45" and a second changer for 78 and 33⅓ rpm records. Extended tone range, too, for more lifelike music. 6T87.

The Somervell. An invitation to pleasure—at an invitingly low price. Beautifully grained doors conceal 12½-inch Million Proof television, AM radio, automatic record changers for all speeds. 2T81.

The Sedgwick. 19-inch Eye Witness television, AM-FM radio, 2 automatic record changers. Extended tone range makes music more alive, more realistic. 9T89.

The Rutland. Traditional setting for up-to-the-minute entertainment! 16-inch television, AM-FM radio, and changers for all-speed records. Extended tone range adds depth and brilliance to music. 6T86.

RCA VICTOR
DIVISION OF RADIO CORPORATION OF AMERICA

WORLD LEADER IN RADIO ... FIRST IN RECORDED MUSIC ... FIRST IN TELEVISION

RCA's 1950 lineup.

RCA 9T256, $75.

9TC245, 9TC247, 9TC249, 12″ wooden consoles, 1949, veneer panel around screen, **$35**

17-PD-8093, 17-PT-8071, large oval screen portables, 1957, handle on top, controls on side, **$45**

17T211, 17T220, consoles with 17″ screen above 4 knobs, 1953, **$20**

21-CT-55, RCA's second color set, large 21″ round picture tube TV (chassis *CTC-2B*), 1955, **$100**

21-CT-660, 21″ color TV (chassis *CTC-4*), circa 1956, **$15**

21-D-368, 21-D-379, wooden 21″ consoles, 1953, **$20**

21-S-354, 21-S-357, 21″ square-lined wooden sets, 1953, 4 thin legs, **$20**

21-T-313, 21-T-314, 21-T-316, 21″ simply styled wooden consoles, 1953, **$10**

21-T-322, 21-T-323, 21-T-324, similar to model *21-T-313,* double doors, **$20**

24-D-8676, wide wooden console, 1957, screen to left of controls, 4 thin legs, **$15**

621TS, 7″ wooden mahogany tabletop, 1946, Deco-style, RCA's only wooden small screen, scarce and popular, **$400;** blonde finish, **$600**

630TCS, 10″ console, 1946, tube in center, tambour doors, scarce, **$750**

630TS, 10″ wide wooden mahogany tabletop, 1946, screen in center, first mass-produced TV, **$150**

641TV, tall wooden combination, 1947, phono and radio below tambour doors which conceal 10″ screen, **$125**

648PTK, large wooden set, 1947, radio below tambour doors which conceal fixed projection screen, **$100**

648PV, buffet-style projection set with lift-up screen, 1947, **$45**

RCA 621TS, $400.

RCA 17T211, $20.

RCA 630TS, $150.

721TCS, 10″ console version of model *721TS,*
wooden slats below 10″ screen, **$125**

721TS, 10″ tabletop, 1947, redesign of model
621TS, common, **$100**

730TV1, 730TV2, 10″ consoles, 1947, double
doors open to expose screen on left and
radio on right, **$75**

741PCS, tall Deco projection TV, 1947, fixed
screen behind wooden cover, leatherette
trim, **$350**

Raytheon/Belmont

7DX21, wide 7″ tabletop, 1948, screen behind square glass plate at left, large
tuning knob at right, **$125**

7DX22, 7″ portable, 1949, tall case with handle on top, **$100**

10DX21, 10DX22, 10″ consoles, 1948, front
drops down to become desk top, tube
site on desk surface, **$75**

10DX24, 10″ tabletop with porthole-look
screen, 1949, rounded and stepped top,
$100

18DX21, similar to model *7DX21*, **$100**

21A21, 22A21, 22AX21, 7″ tabletops with
13-channel tuner in long window below
small screen, 1947, **$200**

22AX22, 10″ console version of model
21A21, **$200**

C-1105, 12″ console with porthole-look
screen, **$75**

M-1101, 12″ tabletop, 1949, porthole-look
screen, rounded top on cabinet, **$100**

Raytheon 7DX22, $100.

M-1106, M-1107, Bakelite tabletops, 1950,
12″ screen, **$25**

M-1601, 16″ version of model *M-1101,* **$65**

Scott

13-A, unusual 12″ console in large Chippen-
dale cabinet, double doors open to expose 5 knobs plus large rotary tuner and
tuning eye below screen, 1947, rare,
$600

400A, tabletop projection set, pop-up screen
concealed by wooden lid, 1948, complete, **$300**

800BT, huge projection combination, screen
pops-up on right, radio and TV controls
behind doors, 1949, scarce, **$350**

Silvertone (Sears, Roebuck and Company)

101, 12″ tabletop, 1950, very square-lined
cabinet, **$35**

112, 12″ wooden tabletop, 1950, **$35**

125, 10″ wooden tabletop, 1949, rounded
corners on cabinet, **$75**

133, 12″ wooden console with pull-out phono
beneath screen, 1949, **$50**

Raytheon 7DX21, $125.

not just television...
but
SCOTT
PROJECTION TELEVISION

incorporating the highly-preferred

NORELCO  **PROTELGRAM**

Television that is something to behold. Model 800BT three-way combination, with doors swung back and viewscreen in position. Its precisely engineered record-changer will play all three types of standard and long playing records. The pickup is designed to match the full fidelity range of the SCOTT. Cabinet in wide-ribbon mahogany veneers, beautiful beyond description. List price . . . $1975.00 plus nominal installation charge.

Model 400A is shown both open and closed. The viewscreen and reflecting mirror fold quickly and easily into the top of the receiver. The set is only 25 inches wide, 22 inches deep and 14 inches high. List price . . . . $695.00 plus nominal installation charge.

SCOTT TELEVISION ... *The Incomparable*

THREE-WAY COMBINATION
●
TABLE MODEL
●
16" x 12"
192 SQ. IN.
●
FLAT SCREEN

Words fail to express the excellence of SCOTT television.

For those who want the finest. SCOTT enables you to offer the very shrine of perfection in a three-way combination — television, radio and phonograph, merged and blended in one exquisitely designed console, suited to the pretentious home or small apartment and, above all, capable of three-way performance such as SCOTT alone has achieved.

Many will prefer the compactness and portability of the SCOTT table model whose perfection and picture-size are identical to the larger models, yet designed for flexibility in use — by itself, on or near a radio-phonograph, or in another part of the home.

The more your customers know about television the more they will want a SCOTT — the instrument of astounding perfection.

Write for full details.

Here, truly, is big-picture television in a table model. 192 Square inches. The model 400A is shown, with viewscreen raised. The image has no distortion; it is sharp and true right to the corners. No glare. No eye strain. Mahogany, walnut or blond bisque finish.

Shown here on a SCOTT radio-phonograph combination, the model 400A is a completely independent instrument with its own sound system. Or, it may be played through the better types of combinations. Self-contained with TV and sound, it is a boon to the man who needs television only.

SCOTT
RADIO LABORATORIES, INC.
4541 RAVENSWOOD AVENUE
Chicago 40, Illinois

Scott Projection televisions from 1949.

Silvertone 9133, $50.

8130, 7″ wooden tabletop, wide cabinet, 1948, **$135**

8132, 10″ tabletop, 1948, push-button tuner to right of screen, **$75**

8133, 10″ TV-radio version of model *8132,* **$50**

9115, 7″ portable, 1949, leatherette-covered cabinet, handle on top, **$125**

9120, 12″ tabletop, simple styling, 1949, **$35**

9121, 12″ tabletop with double doors, 1949, push-button tuner, **$35**

9122, 12″ mahogany console, similar to model *9121,* **$35**

9128, 12″ blonde console, similar to model *9121,* **$35**

9123, 12″ tabletop, 1949, large square-lined cabinet, **$35**

9125, 10″ Bakelite TV with rounded corners at front and top of set, **$75**

9131, 10″ tabletop similar to RCA model *721TS,* square-lined cabinet with 2 knobs to left and 2 knobs to right of screen, **$100**

9133, 10″ combination, 1950, pull-out phono, **$35**

9134, 12″ combination, similar to model *9133,* **$35**

See All

See All Kit, 1932, mechanical TV kit, complete with mechanical spinning disc, motor, and neon light with socket, **$1,500**

Sentinel

400TV, 7″ portable, 1948, leatherette case with handle on top, metal grill on front with 4 knobs at bottom, **$85**

401TVM, 10″ wooden tabletop with 4 knobs below screen, 1948, **$65**

402, 10″ console, 1948, 4 knobs below screen, **$50**

405, 7″ wooden tabletop, 1948, **$75**

406TVM, 12″ wooden tabletop, 1949, cabinet stepped at top and bottom, **$85**

409TVM, similar to model *401TVM,* 16″ tube, **$50**

411CVM, 12″ typical 1949 console, **$50**

412, 10″ tabletop, 1949, **$55**

415, 12″ console with simple styling and square lines, 1949, **$25**

429-TV, tabletop version of model *431-CV,* **$15**

431-CV, console, double doors conceal screen and 2 knobs, 1951, **$15**

816C, large console color TV with 21″ screen at left, 1956, **$75**

Snaider (See Television Assembly Co.)

Sony

TV 4-203, 4-204, transistor TV with 4″ screen in front center, channel selector at right, oversized handle, 1960, **$35**

TV 5-303W, small metal and plastic transistor TV, 1963, screen to left, controls to right, **$25**

TV-120, transistorized square-lined 12″ portable, 1961, **$20**

TV-500U, small portable with 5″ screen at left, UHF dial and controls at right, 1961, **$20**

411 CVM
The finest in television... gives clear-as-a-bell pictures of 82 square inches.

409 TVM
Full 140 square inch picture... perfectly matched with rich FM sound. Sure-fire sales-maker!

406 TVM
Sells on sight! Crystal clear, undistorted picture—fully 12% larger than the ordinary 12" picture size.

407 TVM
Big 16 inch with 140 square inch screen. Amazingly life-like pictures. Period Style Mahogany Console. Priced right.

401 TVM
More for your TV dollar! A full 60 square inches of picture. In a beautiful hand rubbed mahogany cabinet.

top of the heap

PROFIT WISE,
PERFORMANCE, TOO!

PROFIT-WISE . . . Sentinel is your line. Sensational models that sell . . . that make you money. There's a table model or console and a picture size to please every buyer . . . you make sales and profits when you have Sentinel on the floor.

PERFORMANCE-WISE . . . too, Sentinel is your line. Known for a generation as builders of fine radio. Sentinel now brings you the best in TELEVISION. You can depend on Sentinel performance to sell for you . . . to stay sold.

400 TV
Eye-catching portable! In luggage style leather grain case. 12 channel operation.

Sentinel Radio and Television
EVANSTON, ILLINOIS

Sentinel's 1948 televisions lineup.

170

Sony TV 5-303W, $25.

Sparton 4900TV, $150.

Sony 8-301W, $125.

TV-700U, TV-900U, nearly square portable with handle on top, controls and speaker below screen and on right side, **$20**

8-301W, Sony's first TV, 1960, oval-shaped grey metal TV, 8″ screen above "AC-DC-OFF" push buttons, metal sun visor, **$125**

Sparton

Pre-war 12″ mirror-in-lid TV-radio combination, 1939, rounded Deco lines, **$4,000**

16A211, large wooden color console with 15″ round picture tube, 1955, **$350**

4900 TV, 12″ mirror-in-lid credenza, 1949, very square lines, phono behind right door, AM/FM radio behind right door, TV beneath center lid, **$150**

4916, 4917, 10″ mahogany combination, 1949, large channel selector at lower left corner of screen, **$75**

4918, similar to model **4917,** blonde finish, **$75**

4920, 12″ console with double doors, 1949, **$50**

4931, 10″ console with 5 knobs below screen, 1949, **$75**

4935, 12″ version of model **4931,** **$60**

4951, 10″ mahogany tabletop with screen in center front above large plastic tuning knob, 1949, **$100**

4952, similar to model **4951,** blonde finish, **$100**

4954, tabletop version of model **4931,** **$100**

4960, tabletop version of model **4935,** **$75**

4964, double-door console with 16″ picture tube, 1949, **$50**

Sparton 4952, $100.

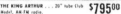

Starette's 1949 televisions.

Sparton 5006, $75.

Starrette "Ambassador," $100.

5002, 5003, square-lined tabletops, 1950, 10″ screen with rounded sides, **$75**

5006, 5007, 10″ tabletops with rounded corners, 1950, **$75**

5010, 10″ wooden tabletop with rounded top corners, **$75**

5011, 12″ version of model *5010,* **$65**

5056, 5057, wooden consoles with 12″ screen, 1950, **$65**

5220, 17″ tabletop with leatherette covering, 1952, **$45**

5225, 5226, wooden versions of model *5220,* **$55**

5262, 5263, 17″ consoles, 1952, 2 large knobs below screen, **$25**

5265, similar to model *5262,* double doors, **$25**

24542, 25544, 26542, consoles with 27″ tube, 1953, **$25**

52412, 56412, similar to model *52413,* Duncan Phyfe legs, **$75**

52413, 56413, square-lined 24″ TVs with bent iron legs, 1953, **$50**

Starrette

Ambassador, 16″ tabletop, 1949, stepped-up top, **$100**

Adams, simple 12″ combination with double doors, buffet-look, **$35**

Chinese Hancock, similar to *John Hancock* model, Chinese detailing to cabinet, **$95**

Cleveland, square-lined 16″ combination, double doors open to expose AM/FM radio and phono, **$45**

Cosmopolitan, similar to *Gotham* model, huge breakfront over set, **$125**

Gotham, large 16″ combination, 1949, similar to *Adams* model, **$25**

Henry Hudson, 16″ tabletop, 1949, wooden mask around screen, **$45**

Henry Parks, 16″ simple console, 1949, 4 knobs across center, **$35**

Jackson, 16″ console, tube to left, AM/FM and TV controls to right, modern-style cabinet, **$100**

Jefferson, 12″ console with double doors, inlaid panels on front, 4 legs, **$100**

John Hancock, wide 16″ combination with modern legs and double doors, 1949, **$45**

King Arthur, 20″ tavern model, speaker to left of screen, knobs hidden below, **$75**

Lincoln, similar to *Cleveland* model, **$45**

Nathan Hale, 12″ tabletop with speaker to right of screen, 1949, **$65**

Stewart-Warner

AVC-1, AVC-2, small mirror-in-lid consoles, 1948, 10″ screen, **$100**

AVT-1, small consolette with direct vision 10″ screen, 1949, **$45**

Stewart-Warner T-711, $75.

T-711, T-712, consoles, 1948, right door opens to expose 10″ screen and 13-channel tuner, large dial radio behind left door, **$75**

21T-9300H, tabletop with 21″ screen and 2 knobs below, 1953, leatherette, **$15**

27C-9212, wooden console TV with 27″ screen, 1953, very square lines, **$10**

9121, combination version of model *9126,* TV behind right door, phono and AM/FM radio behind left door, **$15**

9126, 17″ wooden tabletop, 1951, 2 large knobs below screen, **$15**

9127, console version of model *9126,* **$15**

Stromberg-Carlson

112, pre-war 12″ large console TV with 5-channel push-button tuner, 1939, lid reflects TV image on right side, radio on left side, **Rare**

K-1, large wooden 15″ color TV, 1955, **$350**

TC-10, 10″ TV with porthole-look screen, 1949, perforated front, picture expander in large tuner control at right, **$125**

TC-19-LM, large 19″ console with double doors, 1949, **$45**

TC-125-HM, 12″ wooden tabletop with porthole-look screen, 4 knobs in vertical row at right, wooden cover on top, **$125**

TC-125-LA, console with porthole-look screen, 1949, similar to model *TC-10,* large controls at bottom left and right of 12″ screen, **$85**

TS-16-PM, 16″ combination, 1949, double doors open to expose large screen in center, phono at left and AM/FM radio at right, **$75**

TS-125-LM, square-lined tabletop with 12″ screen at left, continuous AM/FM/TV tuner at right, 1949, **$65**

TV-10-L, scarce TV with 7-channel push-button tuner and 10″ tube, 1947, **$250**

TV-10-P, large 10″ combination version of model *TV-10-L,* left door conceals screen, right door conceals radio and phono, **$250**

TV-12-H2, 12″ tabletop, stepped top, screen above 5 knobs, continuous tuner and FM radio dial at right, **$100**

TV-12-LM, 12″ double-door console version of model *TV-12-H2,* **$65**

TV-12-M5M, 12″ combination, 1947, 13-channel continuous tuner, Chinese motif on double doors, **$85**

$565

Stromberg-Carlson TS-125-LM, $65.

TV-12-PGM, 12″ combination, 1947, contemporary cabinet, screen and speaker behind left doors, radio and phono behind right doors, **$35**

TV-125-LM, 12″ console with screen on left, vertical TV and AM/FM dial at right, **$65**

317-RPM, large console with 17″ screen over double doors concealing AM radio and phono, 1951, **$35**

421-CDM, similar to model *421-CM,* double doors, **$20**

421-CM, console version of model *421-TX,* **$20**

421-TX, mahogany tabletop, 1952, 21″ tube with curved screen, **$15**

Sylvania

14P101, "Holiday," metal TV, 1957, simple design with controls on side, **$25**

14P201, "Fiesta," two-tone version of model *14P101,* handle, **$35**

21C405, 21C607, 21″ Halolight console with light flush around screen, **$100**

Sylvania 21T208, $100.

Sylvania 245, $35.

21C529, "Sylouette," Halolight with plastic-covered light in front of screen, 1959, **$200**

21C534, "Sylouette," colonial-style wooden base version of model *21C529,* **$125**

21T110, 21T208, 21″ Halolight tabletops, 1957, with or without stand, **$100**

21T121, large painted metal portable with 21″ screen, 1959, controls on top, **$20**

24C603, 24″ version of model *21C534,* **$100**

24T101, 24T301, 24″ Halolight tabletops, 1957, **$100**

172K, 172M, large corner consoles with Halolight, 21″ TV with bookcases on each side, 1952, **$125**

245, 12″ console with simple styling, 1950, 4 knobs below screen, **$35**

247, 16″ console version of model *245,* **$25**

Tele-King

C-816, 16″ console version of model *T-616,* **$35**

KC-42, 24″ console, 1953, **$10**

KD-42, KD-43, similar to model *KC-42,* double doors, **$10**

KD-71X, 17″ combination with right door concealing TV screen and left door concealing radio and pull-out phono, 1952, **$20**

T-510, 10″ tabletop, 1949, square-lined front screen over 4 knobs, **$75**

T-616, 16″ tabletop with screen above 4 knobs, 1949, **$50**

T-712, 12″ tabletop version of model *T-510*, **$65**

210, wide wooden tabletop, 1948, 10″ screen surrounded by wooden ribs, **$100**

310, 10″ console with screen and wooden mask over 4 knobs, 1948, **$65**

410, 10″ tabletop with 4 knobs below screen, 1949, **$75**

512, 12″ wooden TV with screen above 4 knobs, 1949, **$65**

612, console version of model *512*, **$50**

710, console version of model *410*, **$65**

Tele-Tone

TV-149, 7″ wide wooden tabletop, 1948, screen over 2 center knobs, grill on right and left panels over 2 additional knobs, **$75**

TV-208, 7″ portable with porthole-look screen, 1948, handle on top, **$75**

TV-209, 10″ tabletop with porthole-look screen, 1949, similar to model *TV-249*, **$150**

TV-220, 7″ TV, 1949, vertically styled set with porthole-look screen, handle and lid, **$100**

TV-249, 10″ tabletop with screen above 2 left and 2 right knobs, 1949, **$75**

TV-250, -255, 10″ Bakelite tabletops, 1949, rounded corners on cabinet, **$75**

TV-279, 10″ console version of model *TV-249*, **$100**

TV-282, 10″ 4-legged console, 1948, double doors open to expose screen and controls, similar to model *TV-249*, **$75**

TV-285, 16″ wooden tabletop, 1959, very square lines, **$35**

TV-286, 16″ square-lined console, 1950, **$55**

TV-287, 12″ wooden tabletop, simple, square-lined styling, **$55**

TV-300, 10″ black Bakelite tabletop, 1950, similar to model *TV-250*, **$100**

Tele-Tone TV-208, $75.

TV-301, brown Bakelite version of model *TV-300*, **$100**

TV-305, 12″ tabletop, screen to left of front, surrounded by large mesh grill, **$65**

TV-306, wooden tabletop with square lines, 1950, large glass mask in front of 16″ screen, **$35**

TV-307, 16″ wooden console, 1950, square lines, **$35**

TV-308, 19″ console, 1950, **$10**

Tele-Tone TV-301, $100.

TV-315, 12″ wooden tabletop, 1950, **$35**

TV-318, wooden tabletop, 1950, 14″ rectangular picture tube, **$25**

TV-322, TV-323, black or brown Bakelite version of model *TV-301,* **$35**

TV-324, TV-337, 16″ rectangular-tube wooden tabletops, 1950, **$15**

Television Assembly Co. (Snaider)

Auditorium, large 1949 projection set with fixed screen at top of 6-foot-high set, **$75**

Champion, 12″ tabletop, 1949, continuous tuner and 4 knobs below screen, **$75**

Sports-View, 15″ TV with screen at left, controls concealed behind small door under grill at right, 1949, **$75**

P-520, projection set, 1948, supplied in cabinet without front panel, for custom installations, **$45**

Transvision

7″ kit

    Assembled 3-channel TV complete with front plate, 1947, **$225**

    3-channel TV in original factory-built cabinet, **$300**

7BL, 7″ set with 5-channel tuner, cabinet with built-in magnifier, **$375**

7CL, 7″ consolette, tabletop on speaker table, **$250**

Transvision 10BL, $200.

7FL, 7″ set with 13-channel tuner, complete with cabinet, **$250**

10A, complete TV kit with 10″ picture tube and cabinet, 1948, **$150**

10BL, 10CL, 10″ set complete with built-in magnifier, **$200**

12A, 12″ complete TV kit with tube and cabinet, 1948, **$125**

12BL, 12″ version of model *10BL,* **$200**

15″ and larger completed kits from the 1950s, **$25**

UST (United States Television)

KRV-12831, 12″ combination with double doors concealing tube over 5 knobs on left and radio over slide-out phono on right, 1948, **$45**

KRV-15831, 15″ version of model *KRV-12831,* **$35**

P-520, 5′-high projection set, 1949, rack-mounted system with no cabinet, **$25**

T-502, double-door combination set 10″ screen, 1948, **$45**

T-507, projection TV with pop-up screen, radio and phono, 1948, **$125**

T-508, unusual large leatherette projection set, 1948, includes phono, **$200**

T-525, T-530, wooden projection TVs, 1949, **$125**

T-10823, 10″-wide tabletop with screen in center and 4 controls at right, 1948, **$75**

T-15823, 15″ tabletop, 1948, screen a bit above cabinet, knobs form inverted V below screen, **$125**

621, projection TV with swing-up screen, **$125**

Videodyne

10FM, 10″ tabletop, 1948, continuous tuner at right of screen, rounded left top edge and right side, **$175**

10TV, 10″ wooden tabletop, 1948, 13-channel tuner at right of screen, rounded left top edge, **$175**

UST televisions from 1948.

Center Dial — Channel selector switch and fine tuning.

Videodyne 10TV, $175.

12FM, 12″ tabletop version of model *10FM,* **$150**

12TV, 12″ version of model *10TV,* **$150**

Viewtone

VP-100, "Futura," 7″ tabletop, poor quality construction, 1947, cabinet similar to radio-phono, scarce, **$400**

VP-101, "Adventurer," 7″ console, 1947, very primitive construction with radio and TV, scarce, **$400**

7″ combination, 1947, large poorly constructed square-lined wooden TV/radio/phono, with area to store records, scarce, **$400**

Western Television (Empire State)

Visionette, box-shaped wooden scanning disc TV, 1933, **$2,000**

Empire State, over 4′-high wooden cabinet with radio and TV controls, scanning disc projects onto screen top, **$3,500**

Westinghouse

H-181, 10″ double-door highboy, 1948, doors open to expose 10″ screen and controls, 4 tall legs, **$125**

H-196, wooden tabletop, 1949, 10″ screen over 5 knobs, rounded cabinet top, **$85**

H-207, 10″ wooden combination, 1947, TV behind left door, similar to model *H-196,* **$65**

H-196

Westinghouse H-196, $85.

H-217, 12″ combination with doors, similar to model *H-207,* **$50**

H-216, large 16″ console, 1949, lid on top at left lifts up and tube pulls up, controls behind right front door, **$175**

H-223, wooden tabletop, similar to model *H-196,* flat top, **$75**

H-225, -226, consoles, 1948, double doors conceal screen and 5 knobs, **$50**

H-242, -251, 12″ tabletops, 1948, mechanically moved masks at top and bottom of porthole-look screen, 5 knobs, **$75**

H-601, H-602, wooden consoles, 1948, screen behind doors with 4 knobs at right, **$50**

H-603, H-608, wide consoles, 1948, similar to model *H-601,* **$50**

H-610, 10″ tabletop, 1948, 4 knobs to right of masked screen, **$65**

H-216, A

Westinghouse H-216, $175.

H-610T12,

Westinghouse H-610, $65.

H-655K17

Westinghouse H-655, $35.

H-611C12, large console with 12″ screen behind double doors, 1948, **$55**

H-626, 16″ tabletop, 1950, square-lined cabinet, large tuner at lower right corner, **$45**

H-627, H-628, H-629, tall consoles, 1950, screen similar to model *H-626,* **$35**

H-655, H-657, 17″ consoles, 1951, large tuner at lower right corner near screen, **$35**

H-738, H-739, very square-lined tabletops with 17″ screen, 1951, tuner at lower right, **$25**

H-760, H-761, tabletops, similar to model *H-738,* 21″ screen, **$15**

H-760T21

Westinghouse H-760, $15.

H-840CK15, large early color TV, double doors conceal 15″ screen, released in April 1954 (actually preceded RCA *CT-100*), **$450**

WRT-700, pre-war 5″ tabletop, 1939, 5-channel push-button tuner, vision only (no sound), rare, **$3,500**

WRT-701, pre-war 5″ console version of model *WRT-700,* radio chassis above TV chassis, rare, **$4,500**

WRT-702, pre-war 9″ direct-view console with radio and 5-channel tuner, 1939, rare, **$4,000**

WRT-703, pre-war 12″ mirror-in-lid console, 1939, lid lifts to expose screen with 5-channel tuner at right, 3-band push-button radio at left, rare, **$2,500**

17T247, 17″ painted metal portable, 1959, handle on top, **$25**

H-611C12,
H-615C12

Westinghouse H-611C12, $55.

NOW—A COMPLETE LINE!
ZENITH TELEVISION
WITH
GIANT CIRCLE SCREEN *and* BULLS EYE AUTOMATIC TUNING

From the ultra-magnificent combinations to the beautifully streamlined table models, every Zenith† Television set hits the "bulls eye" for sales appeal. Every one has the sensational Zenith advancements found in *no* other television set... the Giant Circle Screen for a bigger, brighter, clearer picture... and Bulls Eye Automatic Tuning—one knob, one twist, there's your station, your giant picture, your sound... automatically pre-tuned to perfection!

Yes, Zenith has what it takes to assure the ultimate in customer satisfaction and bring you the most beautiful profit picture in television.

SEE YOUR ZENITH DISTRIBUTOR

ZENITH RADIO CORPORATION
6001 Dickens Ave., Chicago 39, Ill.

THE ZENITH GOTHAM. Zenith Television with "Big B" Giant Circle Screen; "Twin Cobra"† Tone Arms; Genuine Zenith-Armstrong FM and Zenith long distance AM radio; all superbly combined in a console of breath-taking beauty in imported mahogany veneers. **$695***
(plus Federal excise tax.)

THE ZENITH WALDORF. Modern television console of imported Afara veneers in blonde finish. With "Big B" screen. **$489⁹⁵***

WILSHIRE model with "Super A" screen, $449.95.* Both models also available in mahogany finish.

THE ZENITH MAYFLOWER. Period table set in mahogany-finished veneers of imported Afara. Has "Super A" television screen. **$389⁹⁵***

Matching table, 26 inches high, available at $29.95.* Receiver and table also in blonde finish.

THE ZENITH MARLBOROUGH. Super deluxe! Zenith Television with "Giant C" Giant Circle Screen. Plus "Twin Cobra" Record Player; FM-AM and Short Wave Radio. In an authentic Regency console of hand glazed Honduras mahogany veneers, a masterpiece of the furniture craftsman's art. . . . *(plus Federal excise tax.)* **$1150***

ZENITH HAS THE GREAT VALUES
†®

TELEVISION *and long distance* **RADIO**

Suggested retail price.
West Coast prices slightly higher.
Prices subject to change without notice.

Zenith 12" porthole televisions from 1949.

181

ZENITH FIRST!

to Keep You FIRST in TV Sales!

ZENITH'S NEW 1950 "PRESIDENTIAL" LINE OF
Black Magic Television

With the Great, New "Super-Range" Chassis!

The most terrific selling story in TV history—that's Zenith's new 1950 line! With both Black Magic Television and the years-ahead, super-powered "Super-Range" chassis, Zenith brings clearer, sharper television to areas where many other sets can't even hold an acceptable picture.

Now you can back up your claims of Zenith superiority with stronger-than-ever, customer-convincing *proof*—proof that stamps Zenith as the far-and-away greatest buy ever offered by any dealer, anywhere. This year, it's Zenith for popular prices . . . better performance . . . bigger profits!

The Jackson. Model G2437R. Beautiful new console in genuine Mahogany veneers. "Giant C" Giant Circle Screen plus all Zenith's great chassis features. **$429.95***

The Fillmore. Model G2437E. Stunning new style in lustrous blonde-finished cabinet. "Giant C" Giant Circle Screen—165 sq. inches of picture area. **$439.95***

The Monroe. Model G2439R. New Zenith Console with Glare-Ban "Black" Picture Tube—165 sq. inches of picture area. Gorgeous cabinet of genuine Mahogany veneers. **$399.95***

The Lincoln. Model G2438R. Zenith's new "Super-Range" chassis with Glare-Ban "Black" Picture Tube in handsome new cabinet of genuine Mahogany or Walnut veneers. 165 sq. inches of picture area. **$359.95***

The Harrison. Model G2356R. New console brings the utmost in picture quality in a "Big B" Giant Circle Screen. 18th Century cabinet of genuine Mahogany veneers. **$309.95***

The Tyler. Model G2355E. Greater distance, greater clarity in this striking console with 105 sq. inches of picture area. In handsome blonde finish. **$289.95***

The Adams. Model G2350R. Choice of genuine Walnut or Mahogany veneers in new Zenith Console. "Big B" Giant Circle Screen. With Blaxide "Black" Picture Tube. **$269.95***

The Garfield. Model G2327. Popular Table Model in smart, long-wearing Walnut Brown Pyroxylin. "Big B" Giant Circle Screen plus new "Super-Range" chassis. **$219.95***

* Plus Federal Excise Tax. Prices subject to change without notice. West Coast and Far South prices slightly higher.

Look to Zenith to be FIRST with the Finest in Television!

Zenith 16" porthole televisions from 1950.

182

21K224, 21K226, tall wooden consoles, 1959, controls at top front, **$20**

17C28, wide console, 1959, lift-up door on left opens to expose phono, **$25**

17T247, painted metal portable, 1959, **$25**

21K226, 21K275, 21″ consoles, 1959, large screen above speaker grill, **$10**

21T206, 21T218, large tabletops with controls above 21″ screen, 1959, **$10**

660C17, console with 17″ screen behind left door, AM/FM radio and pull-out phono behind right door, 1951, **$25**

Zenith

C-1715, C-1720, painted metal portables with handle on top, 1959, 17″ screen with controls above, **$35**

C-2225, C-2330, 21″ metal portables, 1959, tuner at upper right, **$10**

C-3011, C-3013, large wide 21″ consoles, 1959, **$20**

C-4007, 24″ console with "Space Command" remote control, 1959, **$25**

G2322, brown Bakelite tabletop, 1950, 12″ screen, **$65**

G2340, G2442, 12″ consoles with porthole-look screen (chassis *24G22*), 1950, **$125**

G2957, G2958, 12″ large double-door combinations with porthole-look screen (chassis *23G23*), **$75**

H2029, H2030, 17″ rectangular screen TVs (chassis *20H20*), 1951, **$35**

H2226, H2227, 12″ wooden TVs with porthole-look screen (chassis *22H200*), 1951, **$100**

H2229, H2253, H2330, 17″ rectangular screen wooden TVs (chassis *22H21* or *22H22*), 1951, **$35**

H2437, H3469, 16″ TVs with porthole-look screen (chassis *24H20*), 1951, **$75**

K1812, K1815, 17″ rectangular TVs (chassis *19K20*), 1953, **$35**

K2230, 21″ rectangular screen TV (chassis *21K20*), 1953, **$25**

L2894H, "Stratosphere," unusually styled wide 27″ TV with radio and phono in compartment over cabinet, **$100**

T1814, T1816, 17″ painted metal tabletops, 1955, protrusions on both sides to carry set (chassis *16T20*), **$45**

T2250, T2360, wooden consoles (chassis *19R21*), 1955, 21″ rectangular screen, **$25**

T2294, 27″ huge combination (chassis *22T21*), circa 1955, **$25**

24G20, 12″ tabletop (chassis *G2420*), 1950, button below screen to change from porthole-look to rectangular image, **$150**

24G21, console version of model *24G20* (chassis *G2454*), **$125**

27T96, 28T92

10″ or 12″ wooden tabletops with porthole-look screen (chassis *27F20* or *28F22*), 1948, **$150**

10″ or 12″ console versions with or without double doors, **$125**

Large 10″ or 12″ combinations with TV, radio and phono, **$75**

28T96, similar to model *28T92*, 16″ porthole-look screen, **$75**

37T99, 42T99, 16″ combinations with porthole-look screen, 1948, **$75**

Appendix

There are many clubs and organizations of radio and television collectors across the United States. By joining the local clubs, a hobbyist can often receive a newsletter several times a year which accepts advertising and which offers information on the hobby and local activities. Most newsletters are sent free of charge to club members, but often a group will send a sample newsletter and accept a single advertisement from a non-member.

Most clubs sponsor local meetings and swap meets, a specialized type of flea market where anything pertaining to radio/television electronics is available. In general, anyone can attend the club swap meets and they give the novice, as well as the advanced collector, a chance to interact with members and an opportunity to buy or sell radio/television related items.

The following list gives the address of the club and states whether or not ads are accepted from non-members (this is helpful if you wish to sell or find a single item but are not a collector) and if meetings and swap meets are held. Please consider joining one or more of the radio/television clubs in your area.

Arizona

Arizona Antique Radio Club (AARC), 8311 Via de Sereno, Scottsdale, AZ 85258. The AARC publishes a quarterly newsletter and allows non-members to advertise. This club sponsors two swap meets yearly.

Alabama

Southern Vintage Wireless Association (SVWA), 3049 Box Canyon Rd., Huntsville, AL 35803. This club has a quarterly newsletter which accepts non-member advertising. The SVWA has three swap meets yearly.

Alabama Historical Radio Society (AHRA), 4721 Overwood Circle, Birmingham, AL 35222. This club issues a monthly newsletter and accepts non-member advertisements. They sponsor a large swap meet during the month of May, plus they also have several smaller meets.

California

California Historical Radio Society (CHRS), P.O. Box 31659, San Francisco, CA 94131. Publishes a journal twice yearly and accepts ads from non-members. The CHRS has monthly meetings. Phone: (415) 978-9100.

North Valley Chapter-California Historical Radio Society (NVC-CHRS), P.O. Box 99-2443, Redding, CA 96099. This northern California club publishes a newsletter six times a year. No advertising is accepted. They have an annual show and meet.

Colorado

Colorado Radio Collector (CRC), 1249 Solstice Lane, Fort Collins, CO 80525. The

CRC publishes a newsletter six times a year and accepts ads from non-members. The club also sponsors seven swap meets yearly, with a major meet and auction each September.

Florida

Florida Antique Wireless Group (FAWG), Box 738, Chuluota, FL 32766. FAWG publishes a quarterly newsletter and allows non-members to advertise. They hold three large and numerous small swap meets yearly.

Illinois

Antique Radio Club of Illinois (ARCI), RR3, 200 Langham, Morton, IL 61550. This club publishes a journal and accepts advertisements from non-members. The ARCI has several swap meets and auctions yearly. They hold a major three day swap meet in Elgin, each summer or fall.

Indiana

Indiana Historical Radio Society (IHRS), 245 No. Oakland, Ave., Indianapolis, IN 46201. Publishes a newsletter and accepts non-member ads. They have swap meets and meetings.

Kansas

Mid-America Antique Radio Club (MAARC), 10201 West 52nd Terrace, Shawnee Mission, KS 66203. Publishes a quarterly newsletter, but does not accept non-member ads. This club has two auctions and several meets each year.

Michigan

Michigan Antique Radio Club (MARC), 2590 Needmore Highway, Charlotte, MI 48813. Publishes a quarterly newsletter, but does not accept advertisements from non-members. They have quarterly swap meets, plus one large meet each year.

Minnesota

Northland Antique Radio Club (NARC), Box 18362, Minneapolis, MN 55418. Publishes a newsletter six times a year, but you must be a member to advertise. NARC has swap meets and meetings throughout the year.

Mississippi

Mississippi Historical Radio and Broadcasting Society (MHRBS), 2412 C St., Meridian, MS 39301. This club issues a monthly newsletter and accepts non-member ads. They have monthly meetings with swap meets and a large annual meet.

Nebraska

Nebraska Antique Radio Collectors Club (NARCC), 905 West First, North Platte, NE 69101. This club publishes a monthly newsletter which accepts ads from non-members. It holds monthly meetings with swap meets.

New Hampshire

New England Antique Radio Club (NEARC), RR1, Box 36, Bradford, NH 03221. This club's bulletin is sent out four times a year and they sponsor four swap meets each year.

New Jersey

New Jersey Antique Radio Club (NJARC), 92 Joysan Terrace, Freehold, NJ 07728. This club meets monthly and has quarterly swap meets in central New Jersey. It publishes a quarterly newsletter which accepts non-member ads.

New York

Niagara Frontier Wireless Association (NFWA), c/o Art Albion, 440 69th St., Niagara Falls, NY 14302. This club publishes their *Chronicle* quarterly, but they do not accept non-member ads. The NFWA has four meetings a year.

Ohio

Society for Preservation of Antique Radio Knowledge (SPARK), 2673 So. Dixie Dr., Dayton, OH 45409. This group publishes two newletters but only allows members to advertise. They have four swap meets a year.

Antique Radio Club of Ohio (ARCO), 2929 Hazelwood Ave., Dayton, OH 45419. ARCO publishes a quarterly newsletter and allows non-members to advertise. Holds several meetings and swap meets each year.

Oklahoma

Oklahoma Vintage Radio Collectors (OKVRC), P.O. Box 721197, Oklahoma City, OK 73172. The club has a newsletter which accepts non-member advertisements. They sponsor monthly meetings plus swap meets.

Oregon

Northwest Vintage Radio Society (NVRS), Box 82379, Portland, OR 97282. The NVRS publishes a monthly newsletter and sponsors two swap meets and three buy/sell auctions.

Pennsylvania

Delaware Valley Historic Radio Club (DVHRC), P.O. Box 624, Lansdale, PA 19446. The DVHRC is a new club and does not yet publish a newsletter. Periodic meetings with swap meets and auctions are held.

Virginia

Mid-Atlantic Antique Radio Club (MAARC), 1312 Deep Run Lane, Reston, VA 22090. Publishes a monthly bulletin and non-members may advertise. Monthly swap-meets and auctions are held.

Index

Page references in italic type indicate advertisements.